RECOVERING NINETEENTH-CENTURY
WOMEN INTERPRETERS OF THE BIBLE

Society of Biblical Literature

Symposium Series

Christopher R. Matthews,
Series Editor

Number 38

RECOVERING NINETEENTH-CENTURY
WOMEN INTERPRETERS OF THE BIBLE

RECOVERING NINETEENTH-CENTURY WOMEN INTERPRETERS OF THE BIBLE

Edited by

Christiana de Groot

and

Marion Ann Taylor

Society of Biblical Literature
Atlanta

RECOVERING NINETEENTH-CENTURY WOMEN INTERPRETERS OF THE BIBLE

2/09

Library of Congress Cataloging-in-Publication Data

Recovering nineteenth-century women interpreters of the Bible / edited by Christiana de Groot and Marion Ann Taylor.
      p. cm. — (Society of Biblical Literature symposium series ; no. 38)
    Includes bibliographical references and indexes.
    ISBN: 978-1-58983-220-6 (paper binding)
    1. Bible—Feminist criticism—History—19th century. I. de Groot, Christiana. II. Taylor, Marion Ann.
    BS511.3.R44 2007
    220.6082—dc22   2007015209

Contents

Acknowledgments

The editors wish to acknowledge some of the many hands that brought this volume to fruition. In addition to applauding the contributors, we want to recognize Miriam Diephouse, who aided in the editing process and compiled the indices. We are grateful to the Calvin Center for Christian Scholarship for its support in preparing the manuscript for publication. Further, these essays would not have seen the light of day were it not for the commitment of Christopher R. Matthews, the SBL Symposium Series editor, to grant these forgotten voices a much-deserved hearing in the academy. We also want to state our appreciation to the Canadian Society for Biblical Studies, which has included a session on women interpreters of the Bible at its annual meeting for the past five years. We especially thank David Jobling, who at the end of that first session, having listened to six presentations, commented on how significant this work was and encouraged us to consider publishing the essays. His vision was instrumental in initiating this volume. Finally, we are indebted to these remarkable women interpreters of the nineteenth-century whose work continues to engage and inspire us.

Abbreviations

BAR	*Biblical Archaeology Review*
ER	*The Encyclopedia of Religion.* Edited by Mircea Eliade. 16 vols. New York: Macmillan, 1987.
JEH	*Journal of Ecclesiastical History*
OBT	Overtures to Biblical Theology
OTL	Old Testament Library
SBLDS	Society of Biblical Literature Dissertation Series
WBC	Word Biblical Commentary
WC	Westminster Commentaries

Recovering Women's Voices in the History of Biblical Interpretation

Christiana de Groot and Marion Ann Taylor

Since 2003, the Annual Meeting of the Canadian Society for Biblical Studies has devoted a session to women interpreters of Scripture. Each of the chapters in this volume was first delivered as a paper at one of these sessions. The contributors and attendees were entranced by the biographies of these remarkable women and their inspiring work, and this warm reception encouraged us to polish and distribute these contributions to a wider audience. The publication of these compositions in the Society of Biblical Literature Symposium Series brings to fruition a process that began not only several years ago, but almost two centuries ago, with the initial publication of these women's writings. At that time, their interpretive work did not become part of the canon of biblical scholarship and as a result was not passed on to subsequent generations of interpreters. Contemporary publication of essays on women interpreters is especially gratifying because it indicates the openness of the academy to women's contributions. We trust that this volume, and others like it, will continue to bring to light the writings of women who were significant interpreters of Scripture in their own time, yet whose work was forgotten.

The reasons that women's contributions were not valued and included in the received tradition are many and multifaceted. Gerda Lerner's analysis is seminal in presenting factors that contributed to their neglect. She begins by demonstrating that women have been reading, reflecting, and writing on the Bible for a millennium at least.[1] In fact, for the few women who were educated and literate, the Bible was often the only book they read and were instructed about. Because it was sacred Scripture and because its teachings were crucial to authorizing the patriarchal traditions of the West, men taught it to women. Lerner quickly surveys the

---

1. Gerda Lerner's classic essay, "One Thousand Years of Feminist Biblical Criticism," in idem, *The Creation of Feminist Consciousness from the Middle Ages to Eighteen-Seventy* (New York: Oxford University Press, 1993), 138–66, documents the misogyny of the Western Christian tradition and the repeated efforts of women to combat the arguments claiming that they were morally and intellectually inferior to men.

messages about gender, based on Scripture, that women learned from theologians such as Tertullian, Augustine, and Aquinas. Women learned that alone they were not the image of God but only when they were one with a man, that they were the cause for the suffering and evil in the world, that they seduced and tempted men, that motherhood was their greatest glory, and that they must submit to their husbands, be silent in worship, and have their heads covered. Given this constant stream of negative and restricting messages, it is remarkable that a few women dared to express their thoughts on Scripture.

When women wrote, they often expended much effort refuting the misogynistic and androcentric claims of the biblical interpretation they had inherited. Each generation of women interpreters covered the same ground in order to overcome the same hurdles on the road. Each wrestled with the classic set of texts that had silenced them: the opening chapters of Genesis; the words of Paul to the church in Corinth; and the instructions to Timothy. Lerner demonstrates that again and again women interact with these biblical texts without the benefit of the writing of those who have gone before. Even those women who were remarkable speakers and writers in their lifetime were quickly forgotten and their legacy lost.[2] For example, a work as significant and recent as Elizabeth Cady Stanton's *Woman's Bible Commentary* languished until second-wave feminism.[3] Only in the 1970s was it reprinted and again made available.[4] The history of this work is typical. Lerner demonstrates that because women's theological study did not receive institutional support, either from the church or the academy, their writing was ephemeral, and the memory of them was lost. With the publication of this volume and others like it, this pattern of discontinuity will end. We hope that in the future the work of women interpreters will exist alongside the work of men and that the student of the Bible can stand on both their shoulders and see further.

This volume picks up where Lerner stopped. Although she surveyed some women from the nineteenth century, her selection was quite limited. She included only women from the United States who were key voices in the suffragist movement.[5] This volume will not duplicate her studies or the studies of any other survey. For this reason, certain key voices, such as Elizabeth Cady Stanton or

---

2. Marla Selvidge's *Notorious Voices: Feminist Interpretation, 1500–1920* (New York: Continuum, 1996) studies many forgotten male and female biblical interpreters.

3. Published in two parts in 1895 and 1898 in New York by the European Publishing Company.

4. Reprinted with an introduction by Barbara Welter and the new title *The Original Feminist Attack on the Bible* (New York: Arno, 1974).

5. Lerner included the Grimké sisters, Matilda Gage, and Elizabeth Cady Stanton. See her "One Thousand Years of Feminist Biblical Criticism," 159–66.

Anna Julia Cooper, are not included.[6] Rather, this volume includes only women whose work as biblical interpreters has not been examined before. [7]

NINETEENTH-CENTURY SOCIAL CONTEXT

In addition, this volume limits itself to nineteenth-century, English-speaking women interpreters of the Bible. Each of these descriptors requires elucidation. We will focus on the nineteenth-century context first of all. This century saw very significant changes in the social, political, and economic arenas that dramatically affected the lives of women. The developments in Great Britain and the United States are not completely parallel but are similar enough to be studied together. In addition, many women traveled across the Atlantic, resulting in cross-pollination of ideas, writings, and strategies for reform.[8] On both sides of the Atlantic, the shift from preindustrial to modern industry and from a largely rural to an increasingly urban population resulted in changes in men's and women's roles and the relationship between the public and private.[9] Whereas the home had previously been the site of economic production, child rearing, and domestic activity, with both father and mother involved in overlapping ways, this now changed. The advent of factory work and trades practiced away from home resulted in men being more and more absent from the day-to-day affairs of the household; economic activity was no longer integrated into home life. Men's daily routine involved a time away from home that was devoted to work, whereas their time at home was devoted to leisure. While at work, men's activity was tailored to the needs of production, efficiency, rationality, standardization, and competition—needs that were contrasted with those of home life. For men, home was to be an oasis, a sanctuary from the alienation experienced in the working world, and it was the task of the wife and/or mother to ensure that this happened. She was entrusted with caring for her husband and children, completing household duties, and instructing their children. She was not to produce income but to spend it wisely, ensuring the comfort of her family. She was

---

6. They are included in vol. 1 of *Searching the Scriptures: A Feminist Introduction* (ed. E. Schüssler Fiorenza; 2 vols.; New York: Crossroad, 1997).

7. The newly published *Let Her Speak for Herself: Nineteenth-Century Women Writing on Women in Genesis* (ed. M. Taylor and H. Weir; Waco, Tex.: Baylor University Press, 2006), introduces the writings of fifty women. Excerpts from primary sources of many of the women studied in this volume are included.

8. A number of women who are studied in this volume had books published on both sides of the Atlantic and read each other's work. For example, Annie Besant's work was published in London and Chicago, and Elizabeth Cady Stanton writes of hearing Besant speak when she visited England.

9. See Nancy Cott, *The Bonds of Womanhood: "Woman's Sphere" in New England, 1780–1835* (New Haven: Yale University Press, 1977), especially her chapter entitled "Work" (19–62).

economically dependent on her husband and limited to the home for her work-place. It was during this time of transition that the saying "A woman's work is never done" was coined by Martha Moore Ballard in 1795.[10] On the foundation of these wide-ranging economic and social changes, the ideology of separate spheres crystallized.

As various scholars have demonstrated, the ideology of separate spheres was especially prized by the middle class.[11] It was not attainable for the lower class, because it presumed that wives and mothers stayed at home with their children and did not contribute to the family income. Lower-class women, in the nine-teenth century as today, did not have the choice to stay home—their earnings were needed to feed, clothe, and house the family. Nor were these divisions of labor particularly apt for the upper class. Upper-class families were very rooted to place and functioned as part of an extended family. Women were not isolated in the nuclear family, nor was there a strict separation between public and pri-vate work. It was the rising middle class in the new urban society that especially aspired to the ideal of separate spheres. It was a sign of status if women were maintained at home, busy with the work of educating their children and supervis-ing the domestic help, free from daily chores. For middle-class women, the image of being delicate, of not being able to handle difficult decisions, and of having an inferior intellect was cultivated. There was no such luxury for lower-class women. They did much of the heavy work in factories, in the mines, and in the fields, and according to Joan Perkin, they comprised three-quarters of nineteenth-century women in England.[12]

Hand-in-hand with the ideology of separate spheres went the cult of domes-ticity, also called the cult of true womanhood.[13] Yet these ideals involved two contrasting forces. On the one hand, women's sphere became more limited: they

---

10. Quoted in Cott, *Bonds of Womanhood*, 19.

11. Lillian Lewis Shiman, "The Two Spheres," in *Women and Leadership in Nineteenth-Century England* (New York: St. Martin's, 1992) describes how class figured into the two spheres ideal in England. The article by Linda K. Keeber, "Separate Spheres, Female Worlds, Women's Place: The Rhetoric of Women's History," *Journal of American History* 75 (1988): 9–39, traces its functions in the United States. She cautions that this language described an ideal and not the actual situation of most women in the nineteenth century. That reality was much more complex than this neat dualistic system would suggest.

12. See Joan Perkin's graphic account of girls' and women's labor in "Cheap Labour: The Lives of Unmarried Working-Class Women," in idem, *Women and Marriage in Nineteenth-Century England* (New York: New York University Press, 1993), 169–85. She also describes the disconnect between the ideal of wives and mothers who stayed at home, supported by the wages of their husbands, and the necessity of women's work to provide for the family in "Obliged to Be Breadwinners: The Lives of Married Women Workers," 186–201.

13. Barbara Welter, "The Cult of True Womanhood: 1820–1860," *American Quarterly* 18 (1966): 151–74, describes the four cardinal virtues of women as presented in the literature of nineteenth-century America: piety, purity, submission, and domesticity.

operated in the home that was no longer an economically productive unit. Once married, they were dependent on their husband's production of wealth. At the beginning of the century, they did not have independent legal standing, could not vote, keep their earnings, or inherit property. Women did not directly affect public events but only administered the affairs of the family. The goal of their life was to serve others—not in the way that the man served his wife and children as an independent provider who could initiate and have a direct involvement in public affairs but in a dependent, subordinate role.[14] Yet this more limited role became more and more glorified in the popular literature of the time. As the home became the haven in a heartless world, so wives and mothers became the "angel of the house" on whom the family depended for their happiness, tranquility, and spiritual guidance.[15] The vocation of motherhood was applauded as crucial for the maintenance of proper society. By raising morally upright children, women secured a smoothly functioning democracy and a Christian society.

The elevated role of mothers was new. Prior to the late eighteenth and nineteenth centuries, women were entrusted with looking after the physical needs of children, while men were entrusted with shaping their character and providing moral and religious guidance.[16] Women's new responsibility for the education and moral formation of the young in matters of faith is one of the reasons for the many books written by women on Scripture in the nineteenth century. Mothers became the parent who read and instructed children in the Bible and who taught lessons on virtues and proper morals to young people. Much of the biblical interpretation explored in this volume was written by women carrying out their new-found vocation of instructing the young and, by extension, the poor and unlearned.

Furthermore, the ideology of separate spheres created the seedbed for the rise of feminism.[17] Women were defined now by their gender, not their class.[18] There was solidarity between women. They had common tasks and were addressed as members of one group. The notion of sisterhood developed, and organizations

---

14. Cott, *Bonds of Womanhood*, 20–23. Elizabeth Rundle Charles's poem on ministry reflects this view of women's roles: "Since service is the highest lot, / And angels know no higher bliss, / Then with what good her cup is fraught / Who was created but for this" (cited by Marion Taylor in "Elizabeth Rundle Charles: Translating the Letter of Scripture Into Life," 161 n. 58 below).

15. The poem "Angel of the House," on the joys of wedded bliss, was written by Coventry Patmore. Published in two parts, in 1854 and 1856, it can be found in its entirety online at http://www.victorianweb.org/authors/patmore/angel (cited 3 October 2006).

16. Cott, *Bonds of Womanhood*, 84–87.

17. The term *feminism,* meaning advocating for women, was not extant for most of the nineteenth century. The *Oxford English Dictionary* lists its first use as descriptive of an ideology or movement in 1894, in the *Daily News* of 12 October.

18. Cott, *Bonds of Womanhood*, 98–100.

formed that enabled them to carry out their roles as moral guardians. Movements such as the temperance movement in both the United States and England were almost entirely women's movements. In these organizations, they learned the skills of organizing, administering events, writing proposals and pamphlets, and public speaking.[19]

The evangelical movement also contributed to the strengthening of women's voices. The revivals of the eighteenth and nineteenth centuries, with their emphasis on the gifts of the Spirit, resulted in women becoming involved in the work of teaching and preaching. Many women taught Sunday school, a responsibility that was considered a continuation of their domestic duty. In this role, women needed to be careful readers of Scripture and thus employed study aids so that they could illuminate the text for others. This new role created opportunities for women to study, teach, and produce guides for teachers.[20] In addition to teaching, some women felt called to preach. Methodists and Quakers in England and the United States had to deal with women who claimed to be inspired and aspired to the pulpit.[21] Although there was opposition to women in the pulpit, some were allowed to preach and engaged in the writing of sermons. This volume studies the work of several women who preached with their pens. Etty Woosnam, Mary Cornwallis, and Harriet Beecher Stowe all employ the rhetoric of a preacher in their writings.

Whether in the church or in the meeting hall, women worked together outside the home in arenas that were understood to be extensions of the domestic realm. These involvements resulted in some women becoming critical of the ideology of separate spheres. In an ironic way, the ideology itself had created the context that made visible the inherent inequities of their situation. The two spheres were separate and unequal. Some women became aware that the glorified language of women's high calling masked the limitations imposed on them. Both Cott, writing with regard to the United States, and Shiman, writing concerning England, trace the pattern of feminism growing out of and responding to the injustices of separate spheres.[22] Ultimately, the feminist sensitivities honed

---

19. Lillian Lewis Shiman describes the movement of women to repeal the Contagious Diseases Acts as the nursery school of the British women's movement and the temperance movement as their primary school in *Women and Leadership*, 150.

20. The work of Sarah Trimmer, studied in this volume by Heather Weir, is a clear example of this agenda. She wrote *A Help to the Unlearned in the Study of the Holy Scriptures: Being an Attempt to Explain the Bible in a Familiar Way, Adapted to the Common Apprehensions, and according to the Opinions of Approved Commentators* (London: Rivington, 1805).

21. See both Nancy Hardesty's *Women Called to Witness: Evangelical Feminism in the Nineteenth-Century* (Nashville: Abingdon, 1984) and Shiman's "The Call to Preach," in *Women and Leadership*, 20–33.

22. See Cott's concluding chapter, "On 'Woman's Sphere' and Feminism," in *Bonds of Womanhood*, 197–206; and Shiman's final section, "1875–1900: The Great Shout," in *Women and*

through women's involvement in the temperance and abolitionist movements came to fruition in movements for women's rights: the right of married women to own property and keep their earnings, to initiate divorce, to receive an education, and to vote.

ADVANCES IN BIBLICAL SCHOLARSHIP IN THE NINETEENTH CENTURY

In addition to the wide-ranging changes in women's roles, the nineteenth century witnessed profound changes in the field of biblical studies as the methods and conclusions of German critical scholarship gradually spread to the English-speaking world. The response to this new scholarship was varied. John Rogerson concludes that critical ideas and methods were sometimes applied and more often refuted in England from 1800 to 1857. He also argues that they became much more widely known through a number of highly publicized and controversial critical works by English scholars and church leaders from 1858 to 1879 and virtually "triumphed in England, albeit in a form adapted to Evangelical and Catholic versions of progressive revelation," by the close of the nineteenth century.[23] German critical scholarship spread more gradually, however, in North America. Jerry Wayne Brown argues for two waves of criticism in America. The first wave, he suggests, collapsed by 1870 due to the Civil War and the death of the first generation of critically informed American scholars.[24] The second wave of criticism, which began in the 1880s, established criticism securely in the intellectual world of America and provoked great controversy in the academy and the church over such issues as the nature of Scripture and the relationship between faith and criticism.[25]

Leadership, 121–204. Both scholars see the movements of the nineteenth century culminating in the success of women's suffrage in the twentieth century.

23. John Rogerson, *Old Testament Criticism in the Nineteenth Century* (London: SPCK, 1984), 273–88. Rogerson shows, for example, how the controversial publications such as Samuel Davidson's *The Text of the Old Testament* (1859), *Essays and Reviews* (1860), Colenso's multi-volume work on the Pentateuch and Joshua (1862–79), and the ensuing debates did much to promote critical scholarship. See also W. B. Glover, *Evangelical Nonconformists and Higher Criticism in the Nineteenth Century* (London: Independent Press, 1954).

24. Jerry W. Brown, *The Rise of Biblical Criticism in America 1800–1870: The New England Scholars* (Middletown, Conn.: Wesleyan University Press, 1969), 8, 180. See also Ira Brown, "Higher Criticism Comes to America, 1880–1900," *Journal of the Presbyterian Historical Society* 38 (1960): 193–212.

25. The work of William Henry Green of Princeton Seminary challenges Brown's two-wave theory. Green stepped into the public eye as a reviewer of the works of German scholars as early as 1850 and continued to engage German critical scholarship in the classroom and in print throughout his long career. However, even the renowned Green admitted that the naysayers had failed to keep the latest forms of German infidelity from the shores of America by 1900. See

Developments in science also affected biblical interpretation. Geological evidence and theories called into question the historicity of the seven-day creation account in Gen 1 and Bishop James Ussher's (1581–56) dating system, which placed creation at 4004 B.C.E. The tension between scientific evidence and the opening chapters of Genesis led to increased reflection on the literary genre of this passage. Charles, for example, asked her readers to consider whether the creation story was to be read as "fact, or poem? parable, or history?"[26] Elsewhere Charles suggests that the theory of evolution and the Genesis account are compatible. She wonders whether "indwelling life, continuous communication of life, countless variations and adaptations of life, from need to need, from stage to stage,"[27] are not implied in the statement, "The Spirit of God moved on the face of the waters" (Gen 1:2). Darwin's theory of evolution also provided a new model for thinking about development in the biblical history. Many interpreters found the developmental paradigm helpful for explaining troubling moral behavior of biblical characters. Harriet Beecher Stowe, for example, explained some of the actions of Abraham and Sarah using the evolutionary model.

The nineteenth century also witnessed an explosion of new data about the ancient Near East. Archaeologists described, and in some cases imported, spectacular finds that visitors to the British Museum and readers of books with drawings and photographs of archaeological remains viewed with great interest. Moreover, travel to the Holy Land became more accessible and affordable, and many travelers shared their experiences of life in the biblical world—its smells, tastes, and sights—with wide readerships. Charles's travels, for example, transformed the way she read and interpreted Scripture. Such new data helped to shift the focus of many readers to the literal-historical sense of the text that scholars such as Benjamin Jowett (1817–93) were advocating. Jowett argued, for example, that the traditional layered interpretation of Scripture should be set aside and only the original meaning considered.[28]

The developments in the academy, science, travel, and archaeology, however, did not obliterate the traditional noncritical approach to the Bible, which as Gerald Bray suggests, "remained influential in the churches, and at the popular level generally."[29] Indeed, a noncritical approach to the Bible flourished in Britain and America. Most of the books on the Bible written by nineteenth-century

---

Marion Ann Taylor, *The Old Testament in the Old Princeton School (1812–1929)* (San Francisco: Mellen Research University Press, 1992), 167–251.

26. See Marion Taylor's fuller discussion and citation in this volume in "Elizabeth Rundle Charles," 157–58 below.

27. Ibid., 156.

28. Benjamin Jowett, "On the Interpretation of Scripture," in idem, *Essays and Reviews* (London: Parker & Son, 1860), 419.

29. Gerald Bray, *Biblical Interpretation: Past and Present* (Downers Grove, Ill.: InterVarsity Press, 1996), 306.

women are part of this *vox populi*.[30] Most of these women practiced noncritical exegesis, which retained the distinction between the literal and spiritual senses of the text.[31] They used modern insights from science, history, and geography to aid their reading but were not willing to dispense with a spiritual and theological understanding of the text. They continued to use traditional methods of discerning God's voice in the book that they continued to regard as much more than "any other book."[32]

WOMEN AS INTERPRETERS OF SCRIPTURE

Finally, this volume includes the writing of women interpreters. The decision to publish women's writing challenges several assumptions. For example, the genre of biblical interpretation requires careful consideration. If this volume included only those women who wrote academic commentaries on the Bible, the result would be a very slim book. For example, Donald McKim's *Historical Handbook on Major Biblical Interpreters*, published in 1998, includes only two women interpreters: Phyllis Trible and Elisabeth Schüssler Fiorenza.[33] Not surprisingly, they are twentieth-century women who have been highly educated, teach in well-known universities, and write monographs and commentaries that are recognized by the academy. Other books surveying the history of interpretation in the nineteenth century also omit the contributions of women. For example, Roy A. Harrisville and Walter Sundberg's *The Bible in Modern Culture: Baruch Spinoza to Brevard Childs* includes no women interpreters as subjects worthy of study.[34] The closest Harrisville and Sundberg's volume comes to recognizing women's contributions is the footnote that indicates that the translator of David Friedrich Straus's *The Life of Jesus Critically Examined* into English was Mary Ann Cross, née Evans (1819–80),[35] otherwise known as George Eliot. The titles of these two works both suggest to the reader that the whole breadth of biblical interpretation will be surveyed; that is certainly not the case. Both of these volumes overlook the significant contributions of women and thus perpetuate the impression that only men wrote important books in the area of biblical interpretation. Indeed, one of

---

30. Most of their exegetical writings were practical and popular in nature and grew out of ministry-based projects. For example, Sarah Hall's *Conversations on the Bible* is addressed to young people and intends to keep them on the straight and narrow way. See the chapter on her written by Bernon Lee in this volume.

31. Bray, *Biblical Interpretation*, 306.

32. This was Jowett's dictum, advocated in "On the Interpretation of Scripture," 377.

33. Donald McKim, *Historical Handbook on Major Biblical Interpreters* (Downers Grove, Ill.: InterVarsity Press, 1998).

34. Roy A. Harrisville and Walter Sundberg, *The Bible in Modern Culture: Baruch Spinoza to Brevard Childs* (2nd ed.; Grand Rapids: Eerdmans, 2002).

35. Ibid., 91 n. 18.

the purposes of this volume is to critique the dominant picture of the history of interpretation by exposing the writing of women who have not been included.

Although women interpreted Scripture, they did not usually write the commentaries or monographs that were typical of their male peers. A key reason is that the halls of higher learning did not open their doors to women. For most of the nineteenth century, women were not allowed to attend or teach in the university.[36] They did not have the opportunity to engage as equals in learned conversations about biblical studies. With a few exceptions, scholars were neither their dialogue partners nor their targeted readership. Hence, the scholarly essay, monograph, and commentary were not their preferred literary genres.

For these reasons, when we seek to recover women's contributions, we must cast the net of what constitutes interpretive work more widely. When we look beyond the academic commentary on the Bible and include catechetical and devotional writing, moral instruction, poetry, hymns, tracts, and commentaries written for the unlearned, then we discover a treasury of women's writings. This variety of genres corresponds to the variety of audiences addressed by women writers. Out of acceptable female roles such as mother and teacher of children, Sarah Trimmer wrote a commentary entitled *A Help to the Unlearned in the Study of the Holy Scripture* (1805), and Sarah Ewing Hall wrote *Conversations on the Bible* (1818), a commentary on the Bible in the form of conversation between a mother and her two young children. Christina Rossetti composed devotional prose on the commandments, *Letter and Spirit* (1883). With rare exceptions, women interpreters are not addressing the academy. Their readers include children, young adults, young women, the laity, those who are unlearned, and the general public, and as a result, the genres they employed vary widely.

The fact that most women were not addressing the academy does not mean that they were not following the developments in the fields of theology and biblical studies. Not all of the authors surveyed here were well educated, but several, such as Florence Nightingale, Harriet Beecher Stowe, and Elizabeth Wordsworth, were very learned. Although their formal education was minimal, their learning was self-directed and/or under the tutelage of a family member.[37] In each case, the women were born into a family that was highly educated and had a father and sometimes other family members who were actively engaged in scholarship and who valued the efforts of their daughter or wife. Both Stowe and Wordsworth participated in family projects that centered on interpreting Scripture. Stowe worked with her husband, Calvin Stowe, and Wordsworth with her father,

---

36. The University of London was the first to admit women to degree programs in 1878. In the United States, Oberlin College was the first to grant women the bachelor of arts degree in 1841.

37. Stowe was an exception. At the age of thirteen she attended Hartford Female Seminary, a school newly established by her sister, Catherine Beecher.

Christopher Wordsworth. Nightingale was tutored by her father and received the equivalent of a Cambridge education, and she became a dialogue partner of Benjamin Jowett, the Regius Professor of Greek at Oxford. Nightingale and Wordsworth read Hebrew and Greek, and all three were conversant with biblical scholarship. Because they integrated these new ideas into their work of interpretation, they functioned as a conduit, passing on the developments of biblical scholarship to the laity. For example, Nightingale's revision of the Bible to make it accessible for children included a heading at Isa 40 that indicated that the following section of the book derived from the Babylonian exile. By popularizing the results of biblical scholarship, women interpreters played an important role in shaping the faith of those in the pews, and for this work they need to be recognized.

Of those women who followed the emerging critical study of the Bible, there were those such as Nightingale who embraced this new scholarship and those who perceived it as threatening. For example, Mary Anne SchimmelPenninck was aware of recent scholarship, yet she chose to reject it. Her work on the psalms remains largely precritical. Between the extremes of SchimmelPenninck and Nightingale are others, such as Stowe and Wordsworth, who adopted some but not all of the advances, as well as those women who were not conversant with biblical scholarship. The authors included here reflect the variety of responses to the rise of the historical-critical method in the nineteenth century.

The spectrum of responses to the new developments in biblical scholarship is linked to the differing assessments of the nature and authority of Scripture. Most of the women included in this volume are Christians and hold the view that the Bible is the inspired word of God. For this reason, they are not willing to explicitly criticize the contents of Scripture; yet some notice the questionable morality and diversity of views within Scripture. They utilize a variety of hermeneutical strategies to respond to these challenges. Some, such as Wordsworth, Stowe, and Nightingale, adopt a developmental approach to the theology and ethics presented in Scripture. They posit that there is movement in Scripture from a more primitive to a more enlightened faith and therefore can conclude that the ethics and religion of the New Testament are superior to the Old Testament. This approach allows them also to advocate that Scripture is not the last word on what God intends for humanity. The trajectory is to be followed. In various ways, women integrated their views on God's will for women with their reading of Scripture from the vantage point of faith.

Not all the women studied here are Protestant Christians or believers. Catherine McAuley's dialogues illuminate the accusations that Protestants made concerning the faith of Catholics and allow us to hear a Catholic defense of their beliefs and practices—a defense that claims to revere the Bible as much as any Protestant. McAuley's use of Scripture in the daily rituals of convent life put into practice her stated views on the authority of Scripture. Annie Besant is the only voice included in this volume who repudiated the status of Scripture as God's word. At one time the wife of an Anglican clergyman, she later concluded that not only had Christianity shackled women by its primitive teaching, but that this teaching was based in Scripture. When she wrote her two pamphlets, *Woman's Position according to the Bible* (1885) and *God's Views on Marriage* (1890), she mocked believers. For her, the Old and New Testaments have no special status— they are purely human books whose contents are oppressive to women and should be disregarded.

In addition to the variety in the evaluation of historical criticism and the status and authority of Scripture found among the women's works included in this volume, there is also a wide spectrum of views on proper women's roles, the status of women, what it means to be a woman, and what women's interpretive work entails. This diversity of views is due in part to the differing social locations of the women represented here. Nightingale and Sarah Ewing Hall belonged to the highest echelons of society. Both had inherited wealth and did not need to earn a living. Another group of interpreters are middle class. Women such as Mary Cornwallis, Stowe, and Wordsworth are members of families headed by clergymen or scholars. Some women through changed circumstances began as middle class, then came precariously close to losing their support. Besant's separation from her husband resulted in her needing to write and speak to be self-supporting. McAuley worked as a maid when she was a young woman, giving her first-hand experience of the needs of the poor, especially impoverished young women.

The family situations of the women presented here vary as well. Most are married women with children and sometimes grandchildren. A few are single, and one is separated from her husband. Many write explicitly out of their roles as grandmothers, mothers, wives, or single women. In the case of Christina Rossetti, she built on her status as a single woman to authorize her writing. She claimed that she was not subservient to any man because she was not married. She was under God's authority alone and hence spoke with the voice of a prophet.

Although this volume intentionally includes women from several social classes, there is not a predictable way that social location affects their interpretation of Scripture. For example, most of the women studied here show no awareness of the class implications of the ideal of separate spheres. In their writing, few women reflect explicitly on class or show awareness of the very different realities experienced by upper-middle- and lower-class women. Besant and Josephine Butler are exceptions. In her tracts, Besant writes of the inequities in the marriage laws in England that established the economic and legal dependence of women on their husbands. Butler was an advocate for the repeal of the Contagious Diseases Acts that discriminated against female prostitutes.[38]

---

38. Shiman discusses the inequities of the Contagious Diseases Acts, initially passed in 1864, and the role of women to repeal them in 1886 in "This Revolt of the Women," in *Women and Leadership*, 138–50.

A few women begin to reflect on the system and the inherent tensions within it. For example, Hall applauds women's high calling as teachers of their children and is aware that this vocation is not supported. She calls for men to be more involved with their families and decries the sad state of education for girls. Stowe, who endorses the cult of domesticity, is also very critical of men's limitations in their work in the church. In her novel *The Minister's Wooing*, she describes the pastoral care given by the slave Candace as much more effective than that of the pastor, Dr. Hopkins. Some, such as SchimmelPenninck and Wordsworth, are simply silent about their social and political context. Others, such as Etty Woosnam, promote the ideal of woman as the angel of the house, the one entrusted with moral guidance. She extols the ability women have to influence their husbands and, using Eve as an example, admonishes women to use their power to good ends. Although all women were affected by their social context, some reflected on it openly in their writing and others did not. Some were reformers, and others supported the status quo.

The interpretive works studied in this volume also reveal a diversity in self-awareness as women. Authors such as Stowe and Woosnam write as women on women in the Bible. Here we find the most explicit discussion of women's roles, women's virtues, and women's realities. However, many women show no explicit self-reflection on their identity as women. In writing on the psalms, SchimmelPenninck does not engage in feminine exegesis. When Wordsworth concerns herself with variations in the manuscript traditions, she does not engage the ancient languages as a woman per se but as a student of ancient languages. These women demonstrate that a person's gendered identity is dynamic—sometimes explicitly engaged and sometimes not. Some, such as Nightingale, seem to have a weak sense of female identity. In her Annotated Bible, she nowhere comments on or identifies with the female characters in the text. The only character she does identify with is Joseph. However, when we consider that her work as an independent woman, active in the affairs of state and in running a hospital in a war situation, has no parallel in Scripture, we can understand this. She creatively responds by redefining the meaning of mother to include the care for all in need. While identifying with Joseph, she revises the epitaph from "a father to Pharaoh" to "a mother to many."[39]

This variety of self-reflection on women's roles and identities reveals the breadth of interests that female as well as male interpreters have. Not only were men concerned with how evolutionary theory affected biblical interpretation, so also were women. An interest in science is not beyond the purview of women; neither is an interest in history or archaeology or ancient languages. In including this variety of women's works, we wished to demonstrate that women interpreters of Scripture are interested in women's issues as well as the many other issues that

---

39. See the discussion in Christiana de Groot's essay on Nightingale, 117 n. 1 below.

are addressed by the careful reader of Scripture. This decision sets this volume off from the *Women's Bible Commentary*, which instructed its contributors to write self-consciously as women.[40] Such limitation results in a volume that does not consider the full range of exegetical issues usually addressed by commentaries.[41]

As the foregoing indicates, there is no unified woman's voice to be found among the nineteenth-century women interpreter's included here. This diversity reflects an intentional decision of the editors. This volume positions itself differently from other works on women's interpretation. For example, unlike Lerner's essay[42] or Schüssler Fiorenza's edited volume *Searching the Scriptures: A Feminist Introduction*, this book does not restrict itself to women who are feminist interpreters of the Bible. Rather, it reflects the diversity of views held by women in the nineteenth-century English-speaking world.

In making this decision, we are honoring the many different experiences that women have. We align ourselves with third-wave feminism that recognizes the multiplicity of women's experience and the various intersections of race, class, sexual orientation, and religion. We distance ourselves from the tendency of second-wave feminism to describe women's experience in universal terms—as if all women have a singular experience.[43] For example, Stanton's *The Woman's Bible* reflects a classic second-wave feminist conviction that all women's reality is the same. Since then, women of color and women from the two-thirds world have shown that this is not the case. Rather, Stanton's universal woman's experience is an educated, white, middle-class woman's experience.[44] The inclusion of women who express a variety of viewpoints on women's experience reflects this new awareness of the plurality of women's realities.[45]

The limitation that we have put on the women included in this volume is one of time and place: the nineteenth-century, English-speaking world. Their histori-

---

40. Carol A. Newsom and Sharon H. Ringe, eds., *Women's Bible Commentary: Expanded Edition, with Apocrypha* (Louisville: Westminster John Knox, 1998).

41. Newsom and Ringe (*Women's Bible Commentary*, "Introduction to the First Edition," xix–xxv) indicate the parameters of this commentary.

42. Lerner, "One Thousand Years of Feminist Biblical Criticism," 138–66.

43. See Jo Reger, "Introduction," in *Different Wavelengths: Studies of the Contemporary Women's Movement* (ed. J. Reger; New York: Routledge, 2005), xv–xxx, for an insightful discussion of the overlapping yet distinct themes of first-, second-, and third-wave feminism.

44. Ursula King, "Introduction," in *Feminist Theology from the Third World* (ed. U. King; London: SPCK, 1994), is a clear example of the need to contextualize women's voices and of the variety of women's experiences.

45. The volume includes papers that were presented at Annual Meetings of the Canadian Society for Biblical Scholarship; hence it does not reflect the fullest variety of voices that could have been included. For example, there are no Jewish women represented in this volume, although some, such as Grace Aguilar, were very significant. For a more complete list of nineteenth-century women interpreters, see the volume of primary sources collected by Taylor and Weir in *Let Her Speak for Herself*.

cal context binds them together. This restriction makes this volume comparable to *Reading the Bible as Women: Perspectives from African, Asia and Latin America*,[46] although that volume is unlike this one in limiting the focus to women's issues and its method to postcolonial criticism. In contrast, the goal of this volume is akin to that of an archaeologist faithfully to record and reconstruct the past. As such, the criteria for inclusion is that a woman interpreter made a significant contribution to her time. Each one of the authors studied here had a loyal following: they all had a marked affect on their community. From our vantage point as readers in the twenty-first century, some writers have value as cultural artifacts: their writings endorsed roles that are now considered outdated. Others have value as reformers: they were instrumental in bringing about changes that still affect us today, and their views can still sound radical after more than a hundred years. Others have value as spiritual mentors: they are inspiring models for women of today. All connect women and men to their past by recovering the voices and experiences of their foremothers and rectifying their absence from history.

We have arranged the essays in chronological order according to the author's birth date. This arrangement will highlight the slowly expanding opportunities that women had as interpreters. From being limited to the roles of mothers writing for children or teachers writing for the laity, they become heads of women's colleges at Oxford University and wrote for students. In the intervening years, education became more and more available to women, and as a result, women became more and more conversant with biblical scholarship and in dialogue with biblical scholars. This trajectory continues past the parameters of this volume. In the twentieth century, women in Great Britain, the United States, and Canada had full access to the academy. For example, Sara Anna Emerson studied biblical languages and was the first woman to be granted a doctor of philosophy degree from Yale University in 1903. Her dissertation was entitled "The Historic Nucleus of the Stories of Abraham Contained in the Book of Genesis." Another example is Elizabeth Mary MacDonald, who was awarded a doctor of philosophy degree in the department of Near Eastern Studies at the University of Toronto in 1928. She was the first woman to receive this degree, and her dissertation was published as *The Position of Women as Reflected in Semitic Codes of Law* in the newly established Oriental series of the University of Toronto Press in 1931.[47] The halls of higher learning had opened their doors to women, and women entered.

---

46. Phyllis Bird, ed., *Reading the Bible as Women: Perspectives from Africa, Asia, and Latin America*, Semeia 78 (1997). The women included in this volume could very fruitfully be analyzed according to their awareness of imperialism. Some, such as Nightingale, were intensely involved with issues of empire, and many operated with notions of the superiority of occidental over oriental cultures.

47. See Rebecca Idestrom, "Elizabeth Mary MacDonald: An Early Canadian Contribution to the Study of Women in the Ancient Near East," paper presented at the Annual Meeting of the Canadian Society for Biblical Studies, Halifax, 2003.

Finally, a word about the contributors to this volume. Unlike similar volumes that include only women contributors, we have included a man as a contributor. This, too, reflects a conscious decision on the part of the editors. It reveals our hope that not only women but also men will find the work of past women interpreters valuable. Their insights are beneficial and accessible not only to women but also to men. Although women's experience is unique to women, men can empathize with that experience. As women have been reading and understanding literature written by men for centuries and through reading this literature have come to understand men's values, viewpoints, and realities, we assume that men can understand and learn from women as well. We intend that Bernon Lee's inclusion here is not tokenism but that he is the first of many men who will choose to engage in this new area of study.

There are many more valuable writings of women interpreting Scripture that have not been included here due to pragmatic considerations of time and space—the harvest is great. This volume is but a beginning that we hope will encourage and inspire fellow scholars to retrieve still other forgotten voices of women interpreters. The voices that are included here, we trust, will enlighten the reader on the richness and depth of women's biblical interpretation in the nineteenth century and enhance our understanding of the multiplicity of meanings of the biblical text.

Bibliography

Bird, Phyllis, ed. *Reading the Bible as Women: Perspectives from Africa, Asia and Latin America. Semeia* 78 (1997).

Bray, Gerald. *Biblical Interpretation: Past and Present.* Downers Grove, Ill.: InterVarsity Press, 1966.

Brown, Ira, "Higher Criticism Comes to America, 1880–1900." *Journal of the Presbyterian Historical Society* 38 (1960): 193–212.

Brown, Jerry W. *The Rise of Biblical Scholarship in America 1800–1870: The New England Scholars.* Middletown, Conn.: Wesleyan University Press, 1969.

Cott, Nancy F. *The Bonds of Womanhood: "Woman's Sphere" in New England, 1780–1835.* New Haven: Yale University Press, 1977.

Glover, W. B. *Evangelical Nonconformists and Higher Criticism in the Nineteenth Century.* London: Independent Press, 1954.

Hardesty, Nancy. *Women Called to Witness: Evangelical Feminism in the Nineteenth Century.* Nashville: Abingdon, 1984.

Harrisville, Roy A., and Walter Sundberg. *The Bible in Modern Culture: Baruch Spinoza to Brevard Childs.* 2nd ed. Grand Rapids: Eerdmans, 2002.

Jowett, Benjamin, "On the Interpretation of Scripture." Pages 330–433 in idem, *Essays and Reviews.* London: Parker & Son, 1860.

Keeber, Linda K. "Separate Spheres, Female Worlds, Women's Place: The Rhetoric of Women's History." *Journal of American History* 75 (1988): 9–39.

King, Ursula, "Introduction." Pages 1–22 in *Feminist Theology from the Third World.* Edited by Ursula King. London: SPCK, 1994.

Lerner, Gerda. "One Thousand Years of Feminist Biblical Criticism." Pages 138–66 in idem, *The Creation of Feminist Consciousness from the Middle Ages to Eighteen-Seventy.* New York: Oxford University Press, 1993.

McKim, Donald, ed. *Historical Handbook on Major Biblical Interpreters.* Downers Grove, Ill.: InterVarsity Press, 1998.

Newsom, Carol A., and Sharon H. Ringe, eds. *Women's Bible Commentary: Expanded Edition, with Apocrypha.* Louisville: Westminster John Knox, 1998.

Patmore, Coventry. "The Angel of the House." No pages. Cited 3 October 2006. Online: http://www.victorianweb.org/authors/patmore/angel.

Perkin, Joan. *Women and Marriage in Nineteenth-Century England.* New York: New York University Press, 1993.

Reger, Jo. "Introduction." Pages xv–xxx in *Different Wavelengths: Studies of the Contemporary Women's Movement.* Edited by Jo Reger. New York: Routledge, 2005.

Rogerson, John. *Old Testament Criticism in the Nineteenth Century.* London: SPCK, 1984.

Schüssler Fiorenza, Elisabeth, ed. *Searching the Scriptures: A Feminist Introduction.* 2 vols. New York: Crossroad, 1997.

Selvidge, Marla J. *Notorious Voices: Feminist Biblical Interpretation, 1500–1920.* New York: Continuum, 1996.

Shiman, Lillian Lewis. *Women and Leadership in Nineteenth-Century England.* New York: St. Martin's, 1992.

Stanton, Elizabeth Cady, et al. *The Woman's Bible,* parts 1 and 2. 1895, 1898. Repr. as *The Original Feminist Attack on the Bible.* New York: Arno, 1974.

Taylor, Marion A. *The Old Testament in the Old Princeton School (1812–1929).* San Francisco: Mellen Research University Press, 1992.

Taylor, Marion A., and Heather Weir, eds. *Let Her Speak for Herself: Nineteenth-Century Women Writing on the Women of Genesis.* Waco, Tex.: Baylor University Press, 2006.

Welter, Barbara. "The Cult of True Womanhood: 1820–1860." *American Quarterly* 18 (1966): 151–74.

HELPING THE UNLEARNED:
SARAH TRIMMER'S COMMENTARY ON THE BIBLE*

Heather E. Weir

In her seminal work *The Creation of the Feminist Consciousness*, Gerda Lerner surveyed the work of women interpreters of the Bible.[1] Along with the feminist and protofeminist writers she dealt with, she noted that there was a "continuing tradition of women's religious writing."[2] Lerner chose not to consider the female religious writers of the eighteenth and nineteenth centuries, "since they do little or nothing to challenge the patriarchal tradition."[3] Sarah Trimmer's monumental biblical commentary, *A Help to the Unlearned in the Study of Holy Scriptures: Being an Attempt to Explain the Bible in a Familiar Way*, published in 1805, is one of the works Lerner ignored in her analysis. Trimmer's traditionalist work, grounded in the liturgy of the Church of England, does, however, subvert the patriarchal tradition in surprising ways. Understood in its context, Trimmer's work challenges an oversimple division of women's writings into feminist and traditionalist categories.

Sarah Trimmer was born Sarah Kirby in 1741 in Ipswich, Suffolk, England.[4] She was educated in the Christian faith by her father, Joshua Kirby (1716–74), who was well read in theology and the only lay member of a local clerical club. His knowledge of divinity and appreciation of the established Church of England

---

* This chapter was initially a paper presented at the Canadian Society of Biblical Studies Annual Meeting, London, Ontario, May 2005. The insightful questions and comments of members on the presentation have shaped the revision printed here. Christine Dearden and Maureen Louth also read early versions and helped clarify my ideas.

1. Gerda Lerner, *The Creation of Feminist Consciousness: From the Middle Ages to Eighteen-Seventy* (New York: Oxford University Press, 1993), 138–66.

2. Ibid., 139.

3. Ibid.

4. Biographical information on Trimmer is taken from the memoir that introduces volume 1 of Trimmer's letters and journals: *Some Account of the Life and Writings of Mrs. Trimmer, with Original Letters, and Meditations and Prayers, Selected from Her Journal* (2 vols.; London: Rivington, 1814).

were passed on to his daughter. Trimmer wrote of her education in the faith: "I am happy to say, for my own part that I do not remember the time when I did not believe in the Father, Son, and Holy Ghost; in the *immortality of the Soul;* and in a *future state of Rewards and Punishments*."[5] While Trimmer's education in faith occurred in the context of her family, she also went to school, where she studied English literature and learned to read French. After the Kirby family moved to London when she was fourteen, Trimmer's education continued at home, where her reading was directed by her father.[6]

Trimmer was influenced by her father's faith and also by his work as an author and artist. Joshua Kirby was a published author, as was his father, John Kirby (ca. 1690–1753);[7] later in her life, Trimmer may have been more comfortable with the idea of being a published author because of her family members' experiences. Joshua Kirby was appointed as tutor in perspective drawing to the Prince of Wales, later George III, in 1756. Trimmer met a variety of people through her father's court appointment, including Samuel Johnson, whose published prayers and journals later encouraged her to keep her own spiritual journal.[8] Kirby also taught his daughter to appreciate art; Trimmer later used pictures to teach young children about the Bible.

About 1759, Joshua Kirby moved his family to Kew on his appointment as Clerk of the Works at Kew and Richmond. There Sarah Kirby met James Trimmer, and they were married in 1762. The Trimmers lived in Brentford, across the Thames from the royal residence at Kew. James and Sarah Trimmer had twelve children; the eleven who survived infancy were all educated at home by their mother, although her sons were sent out to learn classics from a local clergyman. Trimmer took the education of her children quite seriously and read many books on the theory and practice of education.[9] The publication of Anna Barbauld's *Lessons for Children* in 1779 prompted Trimmer's friends to persuade her to write about education from her experience and study. Between 1780 and

---

5. Sarah Trimmer, *An Essay on Christian Education* (London: Rivington, 1812), 204.

6. Her later writing suggests that she read widely. One work she read and studied was Milton's *Paradise Lost*. See Trimmer, *Some Account*, 1:8–9.

7. John Kirby published a geographical survey of Suffolk: *The Suffolk Traveller* (Ipswich, U.K.: 1735). Joshua Kirby published two works on perspective drawing and architecture: *Dr. Brook Taylor's Method of Perspective Made Easy* (London: n.p., 1754); and *Perspective of Architecture Deduced from the Principles of Dr. Brook Taylor* (London: n.p., 1761).

8. For a list of some of the people Trimmer met in London and Johnson's influence on Trimmer's journal writing, see *Some Account*, 1:8, 66

9. The memoir of Trimmer's life that introduces her journals and letters records this interest in education. "She [Trimmer] would say, that as soon as she became a mother, her thoughts were turned so entirely to the subject of education, that she scarcely read a book upon any other topic, and believed she almost wearied her friends by making it so frequently the subject of conversation" (*Some Account*, 1:14).

her death in 1810, Trimmer published extensively, commonly producing at least one work in a year.[10] Most of her works were written to assist parents and teachers in giving children a Christian education. She wrote out of her experience of teaching her own children and from her involvement in Sunday and charity schools.[11]

The Bible was the key to Christian education for Trimmer, so it is not surprising that she published several books on teaching the Bible. Even her first published work, *An Easy Introduction to the Knowledge of Nature and Reading the Holy Scriptures* (1780), which focuses on teaching children about the created world, ends with a section on reading the Bible. Trimmer's major work on the Bible was *Sacred History Selected from the Scriptures* (1782–84). This six-volume work was intended for children who could read for themselves. In these books Trimmer combined excerpts from Scripture with her own notes and reflections.

A Help to the Unlearned, first published in 1805, was Trimmer's final work on the Bible. It was written for adults and was based on a lifetime of hearing, reading, teaching, and writing about the Bible. The purpose of *A Help to the Unlearned* is stated in the first paragraph of the introduction, which reads:

> The following book was composed with the hope of rendering the study of the Bible easy and profitable to those who have but little leisure, or who may not be able to understand expositions of Scripture in which more learning is displayed. The endeavour of the compiler has been to explain what is difficult, as far as is necessary for Christians in general to understand it; and to direct the attention of the Bible student to such passages and texts as require particular consideration, in order to produce a rational faith and right practice, founded immediately upon the word of God.[12]

---

10. Different counts of Trimmer's works abound; Pauline Heath puts the total number of her works at forty-four (see Pauline M. Heath, "Mrs. Trimmer's Plan of Appropriate Instruction: A Revisionist View of Her Textbooks," *History of Education* 32 [2003]: 385). Heath does note the difficulty of counting Trimmer's works in her 1995 dissertation by comparing counts of her works published in different sources: the numbers given were nineteen, twenty-one, thirty, and thirty-one. See Pauline M. Heath, "The Works of Mrs. Trimmer (1741–1810)" (Ph.D. diss., University of London, 1996), 7. *Some Account*, the edition of Trimmer's journals and letters edited by her children, lists twenty-nine books by Trimmer.

11. Sunday schools and charity schools were popular ways of educating poor children. Sunday schools were held on Sundays and focused on teaching reading and moral behavior. Charity schools were held on weekdays and often included marketable skills in the curriculum. Trimmer and her family were involved in both kinds of schools in Brentford beginning in 1786.

12. Sarah Trimmer, *A Help to the Unlearned in the Study of the Holy Scriptures: Being an Attempt to Explain the Bible in a Familiar Way, Adapted to Common Apprehensions, and according to the Opinions of Approved Commentators* (London: Rivington, 1805), i. Subsequent references to *Help to the Unlearned* will be provided within the text.

The rest of this essay will unpack this stated purpose as it was realized in the body of the work. It will then suggest ways that Trimmer, although conservative in her stated views, pushed the boundaries of her ordered female world.

Trimmer identified her audience as those who had little leisure or who may not have understood more scholarly commentaries on Scripture. In the applications of Scripture passages to life, Trimmer addressed both Christian men and women. Often she included herself in the applications by speaking of what we learn from a particular verse or chapter. For example, in her comments on Deut 8:10–20, she wrote, "From these verses we should learn to *bless the* Lord in time of prosperity, and we should remember that every blessing we enjoy is the gift of his bounty, taking particular care never to ascribe our success to our own power, wisdom or industry; but always remembering who bestowed upon us the power, the wisdom, and the strength" (108). At times Trimmer addressed a particular group in an application. For example, her remarks on Gen 21, when Hagar and Ishmael were sent away from Abraham's household, were addressed to young people who may have to move away from home to earn a living:

> But the Lord showed that he had not forsaken Ishmael though he had sent him away from his father's house: let us from this learn never to despair. Young people, in particular, who are obliged to leave their parents in order to get a livelihood, may take comfort from this part of Ishmael's history, as it proves that they may be under the protection and care of their heavenly Father in every place, and that God is ever ready to hear the prayer of those who call upon him in their time of their distress, and to help in their necessities. (25)

Trimmer also addressed other specific groups of people, including parents, servants, young men and women, soldiers, those who were poor, those of middle rank, and employers. Her work was written primarily for adults, perhaps especially those adults whom she had taught as children in Sunday school. They were not, however, the only ones she was attempting to educate; Trimmer intended her work to be helpful to as many people as possible in their understanding of the Bible.

Trimmer was convinced that reading and understanding the Bible were extremely important. Her introduction calls on her readers to learn from the translators of the Bible in considering the Bible an inestimable treasure. Neglecting the Bible is to be considered a great sin: "We should also consider how great must be the sin of those, who being possessed of this 'inestimable treasure,' seldom look into the Bible, but spend the time that should be employed in studying the Scriptures, in reading books which corrupt the mind, and lead to the practice of wickedness" (ii). Trimmer saw the Bible as a guide to lead Christians to heaven, as the pillar of cloud led the children of Israel through the desert to the Promised Land. Her remarks on Num 9 read: "Consider what a great advantage it was to the Israelites to have a *token of the* Lord's PRESENCE continually before them in the cloudy pillar, to guide them in all their movements, and that

Christians have in respect to their spiritual enemies instead of this token, the *holy scriptures*, which God has graciously caused to be written as a guide to direct them to HEAVEN" (87).

A *Help to the Unlearned* was intended as a guide to the Bible student. It was to be read alongside the Bible. Trimmer instructed her readers first to read the scripture passage covered in one section of the book, then read what she had written on the passage. Because Trimmer's intent was to "explain what is difficult as far as is necessary for Christians in general to understand it" (i), she did not comment on each verse. Her remarks are grouped by chapter, with some chapters broken into smaller sections for more detailed remarks. For example, Judg 5, the Song of Deborah, is described in a single short paragraph, and Judg 6, Gideon's call and defeat of the Midianites, is divided into four sections for more detailed remarks. At times, several chapters are combined together for some very brief remarks. For example, the "shocking and dreadful things" related in the final three chapters of Judges are covered in only one paragraph (147). Trimmer did not directly address the moral difficulties of these chapters; rather, she told her readers not to meditate on them.

Trimmer clarified difficulties readers might have with the language of the Bible. Her experience as a Sunday school teacher led her to conclude "that it is the business of the teacher to explain the figurative language as soon as possible,"[13] so she carefully elucidated metaphorical language used in the psalms, prophets, and parables. The comments on Ps 24 note that "by *lifting up the heads of the gates, ver. 7 and 9*, is only meant their being opened" (300). Even figurative language explained in the biblical text is clarified; for example, readers are told what the grapes in the song of the vineyard in Isa 5:2–4 symbolize: "By *the grapes* he [the Lord] expected, were meant obedience to God's holy laws and ordinances; the *wild grapes* signified wicked practices, directly contrary to his precepts and commandments" (390–91). The prophet's explanation of the metaphor is found in verse 7: "For the vineyard of the Lord of Hosts is the house of Israel, and the men of Judah his pleasant plant: and he looked for judgment, but behold oppression; for righteousness, but behold a cry" (KJV). Trimmer thus assisted her readers' understanding by clarifying language she thought might be difficult.

Trimmer's concern to "direct the attention of the Bible student to such passages and texts, as require particular consideration" required that some passages receive detailed comments and others receive little attention. For example, the first three chapters of Genesis are explained in some detail. *Help to the Unlearned* contains eight pages on those three chapters but only a single sentence on the Song of Songs: "This book is understood to relate to Christ and his church, but being all figurative language it is not easy to explain it; you may therefore pass it over, without puzzling yourself to understand it, as all which it is designed to

---

13. *Some Account*, 1:144.

teach us is taught in plainer words in the other parts of Scripture" (387). Trimmer's stated reason for passing over the Song of Songs was the difficulty of the figurative language; her desire to explain figurative language in other places may indicate that other considerations came into her decision to avoid comment on this book. Trimmer also avoided other passages with sexual content, including the rape of Dinah in Gen 34 and the story of Tamar and Judah in Gen 38 (35, 38). Trimmer was probably influenced by a cultural tendency to avoid discussing sexuality openly; the late eighteenth century and early nineteenth century were marked by a shift in what was considered polite conversation.[14]

Trimmer did not explain how she decided which passages and texts required "particular consideration." She may have been influenced by the "Table of Lessons" found in the *Book of Common Prayer*, although this could not have been her only consideration. Trimmer treated the Song of Songs and the book of Ezekiel quite differently, although both were left out of the Anglican lectionary. Trimmer passed over Song of Songs in one sentence but included at least a paragraph on every chapter in Ezekiel.[15] Further, she did not comment on some passages that were included in the lectionary; for example, Lev 18 and 20 were dismissed by Trimmer as relating "entirely to the Israelites" (80). Trimmer was certainly influenced by the lectionary and the liturgy of the *Book of Common Prayer*, but it was not the only criteria she used to decide whether or not to comment in detail on a particular chapter of the Bible.

The Bible student's study was to "produce a rational faith and a right practice, founded immediately upon the word of God" (i). This statement could be adhered to by all Protestants. What distinguished Trimmer's Bible study was her understanding of Scripture, which was rooted in the practices and liturgy of the Church of England. Trimmer heard Scripture read publicly week after week, surrounded by the liturgy of the *Book of Common Prayer*. The liturgy was the context in which she learned, understood, and taught the meaning of the Bible. In Trimmer's mind, the Church of England embodied rational faith and right practice, and she read Scripture in the light of that faith and practice.

The importance of liturgy for Trimmer's understanding of Scripture is evident from her introduction. For example, Trimmer included a collect or prayer from the liturgy in the introduction for the use of her readers.

---

14. For a discussion of this shift in sensibility, see Noel Perrin, *Dr. Bowdler's Legacy: A History of Expurgated Books in England and America* (New York: Atheneum, 1969).

15. The table of lessons found in the *Book of Common Prayer* was revised in 1871. For the 1662 version of this table, which Trimmer was familiar with, see F. E. Brightman, *The English Rite: Being a Synopsis of the Sources and Revisions of the Book of Common Prayer* (London: Rivington, 1915). Morning and evening prayer services using readings from the table of lessons were commonly held in many homes; the Trimmers probably held daily services for their household.

The way to profit by the Bible is so admirably pointed out in one of the Collects of our excellent Liturgy, that we will add it here for instruction and use, as it fully explains what every one ought to do, and at the same time it furnishes words, which, when accompanied by the sincere wishes of the heart, cannot fail of being approved by the Divine Author of the Sacred Volume.

Collect for the second Sunday in Advent. Blessed Lord who hast caused all Holy Scripture to be written for our learning, grant that we may in such wise hear them, read, mark, learn, an inwardly digest them, that by patience and comfort of thy holy word, we may embrace and ever hold fast, the blessed hope of everlasting life, which thou hast given us in our Saviour Jesus Christ. (iv)

Further evidence of the importance of the liturgy to Trimmer is found in her remarks on Exod 30:31–33, in which the oil and perfume used in the service of the tabernacle are banned from other uses:

The strict charge not to employ the holy oil and perfume to any other uses than those prescribed in the law, tended to inspire men with great reverence for religion and things set apart for divine service. The like reverence ought to be observed by Christians for holy things, particularly for the Books of Scripture, and the Common Prayer Book, which should never be thrown carelessly about, dirtied, dog's-eared, or scribbled in. (72)

Trimmer set the *Book of Common Prayer* next to Scripture as a holy object.

Trimmer often referred to Church of England services in her comments on the Pentateuch; these references show concern that her readers understand the proper purposes of the services included in the Anglican liturgy. She clearly saw support and precedent for the services and prayers in the regulations around worship in the Pentateuch; she read the Old Testament in light of the New Testament, seeing the church's liturgy and ceremonies in Israel's worship.[16]

The *Book of Common Prayer* divided the Psalter so that it could be read through each month in daily morning and evening prayer services; Trimmer included that division of the Psalms in her commentary. The practice of the morning and evening sacrifices described in Exod 29:38–42 was analogous to the daily services of morning and evening prayer, during which prayers (instead of sacrifices) were offered to God. Communion, or the sacrament of the Lord's Supper, was an important part of Trimmer's life as a member of the Church of England. Trimmer applied the significance and care for detail in the purification ceremonies described in Num 19 to her readers as follows:

---

16. In her comments on Exod 24:1–9, Trimmer told her readers that they would "understand these things better" after they read St. Paul's epistles; clearly the cultic ceremonies of the Old Testament were to be understood in light of the New Testament (*Help to the Unlearned*, 68).

those Christians who neglect the means of cleansing their souls from the defilement of sin, must be totally unfit to hold any communion with God; of course it is very dangerous to neglect receiving the sacrament of the Lord's Supper, which was ordained by Christ for this purpose. Yet it is a general practice for people of all ranks to turn their backs upon the holy table, the altar of the Lord, as if there were no use in going to it. (93)[17]

Trimmer also used passages from the Pentateuch to instruct her readers to have respect for properly ordained ministers of the church. Trimmer's comments from Num 16, which describes Korah's rebellion and the resulting plague, warn her readers

not to presume to take upon themselves to act as the *ministers of* God without being properly ordained to the holy office: and the faith of those who followed Korah, Dathan, and Abiram, when they set themselves up against Moses and Aaron, should serve as a warning to thoughtless people who suffer themselves to be enticed by strange teachers who are not in holy orders, to *forsake* and even to *despise* their proper pastors, the regular ministers of the church. (92)[18]

Trimmer's remarks on Lev 27 and Num 18 remind her readers that tithes were to be given for the support of those in ordained ministry. She read both of these texts in light of the Gospels and Epistles and was concerned that ministers be supported in a "comfortable and decent manner" (93). Her remarks clearly indicate that tithes were an obligation on all members of the church: "To refuse to pay tithes is despising the commandments of God" (83).

The ministers that Trimmer instructed her readers to respect and support were always male. Trimmer did not dispute the traditional subordination of women to men within the church. Her comments on 1 Cor 14 show that she thought ordained ministers should be men (719). This seems consistent with Trimmer's acceptance of a hierarchical structure in society. As a woman from the middle ranks, she accepted both an ordered society and a conservative social outlook. In her comments on 1 Pet 2:13–18, she argued from verse 16 that liberty

---

17. Note that Trimmer enjoyed frequent communion and encouraged others to participate in the sacrament as often as possible. It appears from her journal that she participated on average once a month. In a correspondence with a young man who had just lost his wife (see *Some Account*, 2:94–105), Trimmer indicated that most people who attended church did not participate in communion; she described herself as one of the few who participated. Her correspondent admitted that he had not taken the sacrament at his wife's funeral and was interested in Trimmer's view that he should become a frequent communicant. It seems that a high regard for the sacrament may have meant people avoided taking it because they felt it was only for the most devout. See Doreen Rosman, *The Evolution of the English Churches 1500–2000* (Cambridge: Cambridge University Press, 2003), 245–46.

18. Trimmer may have had Methodist itinerant lay preachers in mind when she mentioned these "strange teachers." See Rosman, *Evolution of the English Churches*, 159–60.

was not a reason to overthrow the king and government. She then stated, "God has not put all mankind upon a footing of equality" (795).[19] Despite these overtly stated conservative views, Trimmer subverted tradition in this commentary in at least three ways. First, she used her writing as an opportunity to preach. Second, she wrote her own liturgy. Third, despite her traditionally stated views of women's place, she did not take opportunities to emphasize the subordinate place of women and used gender-inclusive terms in surprising places.[20]

Within the Church of England, it was expected that sermons would be preached by ordained clergy. Trimmer warned her readers against running out to hear lay preachers, possibly Methodist itinerants, instead of their properly ordained ministers. Despite these warnings, Trimmer herself preached in her writing.[21] One example of Trimmer's tendency to preach is found in her remarks on Gen 47:13–27. This passage describes the people of Egypt who came to Joseph for grain during the seven years of famine. Trimmer linked this passage to bread riots in England, of which there were several in the second half of the eighteenth century.[22] The content of her sermon sounds quite conservative to twenty-first-century ears; however, the form is radical—a woman preaching to her contemporaries:

> Observe with what prudence and equity Joseph divided the land of Egypt among the people, giving them back four fifths of the land when their distresses had occasioned them to give all into the King's hands; and what an advantage it was to the people themselves that they submitted their concerns to his management, instead of wasting the corn, as they most probably would have done in the years of plenty, and been clamorous for a supply in the years of scarcity. It is certainly a great trial to poor people when bread is scarce and dear, but they never mend their condition by impatience; whereas when they behave with respect to their superior, and submit quietly to their governors, they are sure to meet with friends to help them in the time of necessity. What a sad state thousands would have

---

19. Here Trimmer probably wrote with the French Revolution in mind.

20. Often canonical texts and their commentaries are seen as texts used to wield power and maintain the status quo. However, Aaron Hughes suggests that canonical texts and their commentaries can also be used to subvert power structures, as commentaries reinterpret the canon's record of the past for the present. See Aaron Hughes, "Presenting the Past: The Genre of Commentary in Theological Perspective," *Method and Theory in the Study of Religion* 15 (2003): 153.

21. Others have also characterized Trimmer as a preacher. For example, see Christine L. Krueger, *The Reader's Repentance: Women Preachers, Women Writers, and Nineteenth-Century Social Discourse* (Chicago: University of Chicago Press, 1992), 82.

22. Bread riots commonly occurred when prices rose after a poor harvest. See E. N. Williams, *The Ancien Régime in Europe* (London: Penguin, 1970), 531. In her journal, Trimmer commented on the bountiful harvest in August and September 1795. She prayed that both rich and poor would be thankful for this harvest, the best in years (*Some Account*, 2:232, 239).

been in if the Egyptians had gone and burnt the granaries in which the corn was laid up, instead of complying with Joseph's good rules and regulations. (44)

Respecting authority in times of trouble seems to be a favorite subject for Trimmer. This theme is revisited in her comments on Deut 20: "It is no uncommon thing in times of scarcity for poor people, who are ill-advised by evil-minded men, to destroy corn, and other fruits of the earth, by burning barns and stacks &c.; which is only increasing the distress of the country, and depriving some of God's creatures of the food provided for their sustenance" (114). Although Trimmer supported the status quo in her explicit statements here, she was subverting it by exercising her voice. She was a woman, yet she spoke with authority, applying biblical texts to the present situation of her audience. She preached.

As we have seen, Trimmer elevated the *Book of Common Prayer* and regarded it as a secondary canon. She consistently read the Pentateuch in light of Anglican liturgy and practice, finding parallels between the cultic ceremonies described in the text and the practices of the Church of England. In one case she found no suitable parallel in contemporary practice, so she suggested a form of prayer that her readers could use. Her comments on Deut 26, on tithes and firstfruits, remind her readers to set aside part of what God gave them for the relief of the poor and needy. As they did this, she suggests that her readers could pray: "Lord, when mankind were sinners and slaves to Satan, thou of thy grace and goodness didst mercifully deliver them, and sentest a Redeemer to bring us salvation and conduct us to the Heavenly Canaan; blessed be thy name, O Lord!" (115). Then after they had given their tithes and helped the poor, her readers could pray, "I have done, O Lord, as thou commandest; look down, I beseech thee, from thy holy habitation, and bestow thy blessing upon me!" (115–16). Trimmer's reverence for the Church of England liturgy did not prevent her from suggesting her own additional prayers and services to her readers.

Finally, her discussions of women and their roles in home and society were ambiguous in surprising ways. In the eighteenth and early nineteenth centuries, the Church of England defined the place of women in the social order and in the home by using a theology of subordination: women were subordinate to their husbands in the home and to men in general in the wider social order.[23] Trimmer's comments on 1 Cor 14:34–35 recognize, but do not emphasize, the silence of women in churches; they focus on the orderly nature of church services and the orderly nature of liturgical worship (719–20).[24] Trimmer, as we have seen, preached using her pen. Somehow she must have thought her written sermons to both men and women were not forbidden in the injunction against women

---

23. For more on the "theology of subordination," see Sean Gill, *Women and the Church of England: From the Eighteenth Century to the Present* (London: SPCK, 1994), 11–38.

24. Trimmer commented on the role of women specifically only in one sentence: "Observe, ver. 34, 35, what the Apostle says about *women setting up for preachers in the churches*" (719).

speaking in the church. Further, her comments on 1 Tim 2:11–15 sound very traditional, but they emphasize that it was their husbands that women were not to have authority over, not men in general (765). Male commentators such as Mathew Henry placed great emphasis on the submission of women in interpreting these two passages; Trimmer did not use the word *submission* in her remarks.[25]

Trimmer also used gender-neutral language in unexpected places. In Prov 7, Dame Folly lures a foolish man to her house. Trimmer recognizes that the warning in this chapter seems to be directed to men but then degenders the language in the rest of her comments on this passage:

> The frequent warnings of the wise man [the author of Proverbs], from the beginning of the book, to guard men against impurity and adultery show that these sins are highly offensive in the sight of God, and ruinous to those that practice them; such being the case, those who are truly wise avoid the snares of the wanton. We find, in this chapter, that the impure and unclean are fond of pleasures and finery. Solomon [the assumed author of Proverbs] shows that we cannot too studiously avoid persons of this character. (363)

Notice the shift in Trimmer's language from her use of the term "men" (possibly including all humankind) to speaking to the more explicitly inclusive "those" and "we." Similarly, her discussion of Prov 9, in which Lady Wisdom builds a house and invites men who would be wise to eat, acknowledges the female personification of wisdom but does not emphasize it: "In these verses wisdom is described under the similitude of a person who has provided a feast, of which she earnestly entreats all mankind to partake" (364). Trimmer's commentary does not directly question the assumed place of women in family, church, and society, but her emphases and use of language display ambiguity in her thinking on gender roles.

To conclude, we have seen that Trimmer interpreted Scripture in the context of the liturgy of the Church of England. The liturgy was not just a lens through which Trimmer read the biblical text but a structure in which the text was embedded; the liturgy surrounded the text and brought meaning to the text. This reminds us of the importance of understanding an interpreter's context in order to understand her or his interpretation of Scripture.

Although Trimmer's stated views were conservative and upheld distinctions between ranks and the prevailing social order, the very fact that she wrote

---

25. See the sections on 1 Cor 14:34–35 and 1 Tim 2:9–15 in vol. 6 of Matthew Henry, *Matthew Henry's Commentary on the Whole Bible* (London: Revell, n.d.). Trimmer acknowledged the "great assistance" she found in Henry's commentary in Sarah Trimmer, *Sacred History: Selected from the Scriptures with Annotations and Reflections* (6 vols.; London: Dodsley, Longman & Robinson, and Johnson, 1782), 1:382.

this book was a radical act. She taught everyone who read it, regardless of social standing, to better understand the Bible. In it she preached and wrote liturgy. While Trimmer cannot easily be labeled an early feminist like her contemporary Mary Wollstonecraft,[26] Trimmer displays some ambiguity about the traditional roles of women in society. Trimmer reminds us of the difficulty of using the labels "feminist" or "conservative" in our description of others' work—any thorough interpretation of the Bible is complex and cannot be neatly labeled.

Bibliography

Brightman, F. E. *The English Rite: Being a Synopsis of the Sources and Revisions of the Book of Common Prayer*. London: Rivington, 1915.

Caine, Barbara. *English Feminism 1780–1980*. Oxford: Oxford University Press, 1997.

Gill, Sean. *Women and the Church of England: From the Eighteenth Century to the Present*. London: SPCK, 1994.

Heath, Pauline M. "Mrs. Trimmer's Plan of Appropriate Instruction: A Revisionist View of Her Textbooks." *History of Education* 32 (2003): 385–400.

———. "The Works of Mrs. Trimmer (1741–1810)." Ph.D. diss. University of London, 1996.

Henry, Matthew. *Matthew Henry's Commentary on the Whole Bible*. Vol. 6. London: Revell, n.d.

Hughes, Aaron. "Presenting the Past: The Genre of Commentary in Theological Perspective." *Method and Theory in the Study of Religion* 15 (2003): 148–68.

Krueger, Christine L. *The Reader's Repentance: Women Preachers, Women Writers, and Nineteenth-Century Social Discourse*. Chicago: University of Chicago Press, 1992.

Lerner, Gerda. *The Creation of Feminist Consciousness: From the Middle Ages to Eighteen-Seventy*. New York: Oxford University Press, 1993.

Perrin, Noel. *Dr. Bowdler's Legacy: A History of Expurgated Books in England and America*. New York: Atheneum, 1969.

Rosman, Doreen. *The Evolution of the English Churches 1500–2000*. Cambridge: Cambridge University Press, 2003.

Some Account of the Life and Writings of Mrs. Trimmer, with Original Letters, and Meditations and Prayers, Selected from Her Journal. 2 vols. London: Rivington, 1814.

Trimmer, Sarah. *An Essay on Christian Education*. London: Rivington, 1812.

———. *A Help to the Unlearned in the Study of the Holy Scriptures: Being an Attempt to Explain the Bible in a Familiar Way, Adapted to Common Apprehensions, and according to the Opinions of Approved Commentators*. London: Rivington, 1805.

———. *Sacred History: Selected from the Scriptures with Annotations and Reflections*. Vol. 1. London: Dodsley, Longman & Robinson, and Johnson, 1782.

Williams, E. N. *The Ancien Régime in Europe*. London: Penguin, 1970.

---

26. Mary Wollstonecraft is considered the founder of modern feminism. See Barbara Caine, *English Feminism 1780–1980* (Oxford: Oxford University Press, 1997), 23–56. Wollstonecraft used Scripture in her argument for women's rights in her 1792 work, *A Vindication of the Rights of Women* (New York: Matsell, 1833). To my knowledge, no one has examined Wollstonecraft's use of Scripture in this work.

Mary Cornwallis: Voice of a Mother[*]

Marion Ann Taylor

In 1817, Mary Cornwallis, the wife of the Rev. William Cornwallis, Anglican rector of the parish of Elham and Wittersham, Kent, England, published her four-volume *Observations, Critical, Explanatory, and Practical, on the Canonical Scriptures.* A second edition of this substantial work of about two thousand pages was published in 1820.[1] This essay will recover the forgotten voice of Mary Cornwallis and her work as an interpreter of Scripture. It will also explore her relationship with her daughter Caroline Cornwallis, who became a scholar in her own right.

Little is known about the life of Mary (née Harris) Cornwallis (1758–1836) before her marriage to William Cornwallis (1751–1827), who served his parish in Kent for over fifty years.[2] The Cornwallises had two daughters. The first married James Trimmer, the son of the renowned author and educator, Sarah Trimmer (1741–1810), and died in 1803 shortly after giving birth to a son, James Cornwallis Trimmer. The Cornwallises' second daughter, Caroline Frances Cornwallis (1786–1858), reacted to her sister's death by forsaking "all the follies of [her] age" and committing herself to a life of scholarship.[3] The many languages Caroline Cornwallis learned (including Latin, Greek, Hebrew, German, Anglo-Saxon, and Egyptian) and her studies of theology, philosophy, science, history, law, and politics enabled her to help her mother with her publishing projects and prepared her for her later career as an author, scholar, feminist, and social advocate.[4]

---

[*] I am grateful for the ATS Lilly Research Expense Grant in the fall of 2004 that allowed me to have access to Cornwallis's commentaries, which are unfortunately difficult to find.

1. Mary Cornwallis, *Observations, Critical, Explanatory, and Practical, on the Canonical Scriptures* (2nd ed.; 4 vols.; London: Baldwin, Cradock & Joy, 1820).

2. William Cornwallis was ordained 9 March 1778.

3. Caroline Francis Cornwallis, *Selections from the Letters of Caroline Frances Cornwallis: Also Some Unpublished Poems; and an Appendix, Containing "Philosophical Theories and Philosophical Experience"* (ed. M. C. Power; London: Trübner, 1864), 267–68.

4. Kathryn Gleadle, "Cornwallis, Caroline Frances (1786–1858)," *Oxford Dictionary of National Biography* (ed. H. C. G. Matthew and B. Harrison; 60 vols.; Oxford: Oxford University Press, 2004), 13:472–73.

Mary Cornwallis was an exceptional woman. She was an evangelical Anglican and devoted herself to the study of Scripture. Using what she regarded as "the most approved commentaries," she systematically studied the Scriptures, making careful notes on her reading.[5] She shared her work with her children and found it sparked discussion and debate. The death-bed request of her daughter a month after the birth of her son, that her mother "watch over my son for good," spurred Cornwallis on to rework her manuscript for her grandson, James Cornwallis Trimmer (1:v). She worked incessantly on her project, even when she was in poor health. She hoped that her grandson would one day approve of the "sound doctrine and heartfelt sentiments, which flow from a heart deeply concerned for [his] interests, both temporal and eternal" (1:vi). James Trimmer's untimely death at the age of twelve[6] inspired Cornwallis to publish her life's project as the means of endowing a free primary school for children in her husband's parish in memory of her grandson.[7] Cornwallis dreaded the publicity that the publication of her commentary would bring and feared that she would discredit "the high subjects which had occupied her pen." She knew that women rarely published commentaries on Scripture. Nevertheless, the higher goal of helping others through her work won the day (1:vi).

Mary Cornwallis's educational background is unknown. However, she read widely and knew French, Hebrew, and probably Greek and Latin. She was interested in theology, history, travel, and issues debated in contemporary society, including accessibility to education. Her daughter Caroline's published letters suggest that the Cornwallis women shared many interests, including the reading of academic books and journals. Caroline Cornwallis wrote to a friend that she and her mother were "looking over" and "quarrelling with Warburton's *Divine Legation*,"[8] a book Caroline Cornwallis judged as learned "but of little purpose."

---

5. Cornwallis, *Observations*, 1:v. Subsequent references to *Observations* will be provided within the text.

6. Elizabeth Trimmer, the sister of James Trimmer, was the primary caregiver of her nephew James following his mother's death. Both Elizabeth and James Cornwallis Trimmer suffered from ill health and died within days of each other in April 1816. See Doris M. Yarde, *The Life and Works of Sarah Trimmer: A Lady of Brentford* (Hounslow, U.K.: Hounslow & District Historical Society, 1972), 25–26.

7. The school was called the Reverend Cornwallis's Church of England Primary School and was built in Wittersham, Kent. The advertisement to the second edition of *Observations* reads: "The free school for boys is endowed in perpetuity; where all resident in the parish will be entitled to five years instruction in religious knowledge, reading, writing, and arithmetic, and have the benefit of four years more gratuitous instruction at a night school, twice a week, during the winter months, after they have been dismissed from day school. Should the work continue in demand, as there is some reason to hope, a girls' free school is the next object of the profits" (*Observations*, n.p.).

8. William Warburton (1698–1779) was an English critic, Anglican priest, and later bishop. *Divine Legation of Moses Demonstrated on the Principles of a Religious Deist from the*

She also alluded to the "little fidgety domestic concerns" that took the Cornwallis women away from the academic studies they loved:

> It is provoking to have one's heart in a Greek Lexicon while the rest of the body is superintending the making of a pudding or roasting a fowl; and, unfortunately, on the faith of Anne's acting the part of housekeeper, we took a younger and more inexperienced cook than we should otherwise have thought of, and now the business of teaching this young thing falls heavily on me.[9]

Despite such household chores, the Cornwallis women had the time and the means to buy any books they wanted to read. For example, during a prolonged illness, Caroline Cornwallis ordered a copy of Bishop Samuel Horsley's translation and notes on the book of Hosea for her "amusement."[10] This book became foundational to her mother's study of Hosea. Like the notorious group of women writers of the eighteenth century known as the Bluestockings, the Cornwallis women kept up to date with contemporary scholarship through reading and conversation.[11]

Mary Cornwallis and her daughter worked together preparing *Observations* for publication. In a letter to her friend, Caroline Cornwallis suggests that the idea of endowing a school was hers and that she encouraged her mother in her dream to raise money to endow the school:

> My chief employ now is the looking over my mother's MS., which is nearly completed, and which she begins to think of publishing. If people would be tempted to read it, I think it might do good by compressing into one view all that the wisest and the best have thought upon Scripture subjects up to the present time. This is her scheme to amuse herself, and I have started another, which serves to amuse us all, but which is also a secret at present. No less than the endowment

---

Omission of the Doctrine of a Future State of Reward and Punishment in the Jewish Dispensation (2 vols.; London: n.p., 1737–41) provoked interest and controversy well into the nineteenth century.

9. Cornwallis, *Selections from the Letters*, 21.

10. Samuel Horsley, *Hosea: Translated from the Hebrew, with Notes Explanatory and Critical* (London: Robson, 1801). In a letter dated 7 January 1815, Caroline Cornwallis wrote: "On the strength of Dr. W.'s medicines I have sent for Horsley's *Hosea* to amuse me 'when graver thoughts have chafed my mind' " (*Selections from the Letters*, 16).

11. Susan Staves calls attention to the relationships between women writers and clergy/scholars. She cites Hannah More's letter to Frances Boscawen in which More notes that she was reading Bishop Robert Lowth's new translation of Isaiah and recommended his *De sacra poesi*: it "has taught me to consider the Divine Book it illustrates under many new and striking points of view; it teaches to appreciate the distinct and characteristic excellence of the sacred poetry and historians, in a manner wonderfully entertaining and instructive" (Susan Staves, "Church of England Clergy and Women Writers," in *Reconsidering the Bluestockings* [ed. N. Pohl and B. A. Schellenberg; San Marino: Huntington Library, 2003], 82).

of a school in this parish. My mother flatters herself that her publication may contribute something towards the object, and this leads her to think of publishing. I flatter myself that my death will contribute still more towards it.... This is the very prettiest of all my multifarious schemes in my own opinion, and I very earnestly wish and pray that nothing may prevent its being carried into execution in due time.[12]

The success of Mary Cornwallis's first publishing venture encouraged her to publish *A Preparation for the Lord's Supper, with Companion to the Altar, Intended for the Use of Ladies* (1826) and doubtless influenced her daughter's later publishing efforts.

Cornwallis's four-volume work looks very much like a standard multivolume biblical commentary that addresses textual, interpretive, and practical issues arising from a careful study of the Bible. Cornwallis, however, did not have a formal theological education and relied on the resources of the academy and church as well as her own experiences as mother, wife, and clergy spouse to guide her reading of Scripture. The extensive notes Cornwallis took to aid her own understanding of Scripture became the foundation for her commentary, which contains more long quotations and summaries of the views of scholars and theologians than is normally the case. The resources that Cornwallis utilized to write her book are remarkably wide-ranging and include classic and contemporary commentaries on the entire Bible,[13] commentaries on individual books,[14] collections of sermons,[15] and essays on a wide variety of subjects, including travel, oriental customs, mythology, and theology.[16] While she preferred the writings of "eminent Anglican divines," she included the works of non-Anglicans if she thought their

---

12. *Selections from the Letters,* 19–20.

13. These included Humphrey Prideaux, *Connection of the History of the Old and New Testament* (1716); Robert Gray, *A Key to the Old Testament and Apocrypha* (1790); and George D'Oyly and Richard Mant, *The Holy Bible according to the Authorized Version: With Notes, Explanatory, and Practical Arranged by under the Direction of the Society for Promoting Christian Knowledge* (1881). Spurgeon judged this latter work as "a compilation most appreciated among Episcopalians" (Charles H. Spurgeon, *Commenting and Commentaries* [1876; repr., Grand Rapids: Baker, 1981], 38).

14. These included Isaac Newton, *Observations upon the Prophecies of Daniel and the Apocalypse of St. John* (1733); Benjamin Blayney, *Jeremiah and Lamentations* (1784); and Robert Lowth, *Isaiah: A New Translation* (1791).

15. She cited Bishop Horne's sermons. See, e.g., *Christ and the Holy Ghost the Supporters of the Spiritual Life, and Repentance the Forerunner of Faith: Two Sermons [on Prov. xx. 27; and Isaiah xl. 3–5] Preached before the University of Oxford* (1755).

16. Of note are Sir William Jones, "An Essay on Eastern Poetry," in *The History of the Life of Nader Shah: King of Persia: Extracted from an Eastern Manuscript* (1773); Samuel Burder's *Oriental Customs* (1802); Sir John Chardin, *Sir John Chardin's Travels in Persia* (1720); Robert Lowth, *Lectures on Hebrew Poetry* (1753); Jacob Bryant, *A New System; Or, An Analysis of Ancient Mythology* (1776).

exegesis was helpful. She was particularly impressed by the translation and commentary on Song of Songs by Thomas Williams, "a dissenter from the doctrine of the established church."[17] Cornwallis also cited a few female writers, including her daughter's mother-in-law, Sarah Trimmer. Cornwallis's summaries and citations of the views of scholars on various texts allow us to determine which interpretive issues she considered important. They also provide an important window into the intellectual world of a well-educated evangelical Anglican woman of the late eighteenth and early nineteenth centuries. Cornwallis's interest in questions about the dating and interpretation of prophetic books such as Daniel reflect changing attitudes to Old Testament history and prophecy during this period.[18]

As important as the comments derived from traditional and contemporary authorities are, Cornwallis's own voice of a woman who read and interpreted Scripture is more interesting and consequential. She often includes her own opinions and homilies, and these often reflect her particular social location. In what follows, I highlight four distinctive perspectives embedded in Cornwallis's observations on the biblical texts. The first perspective is that of a mother of two daughters. Cornwallis is interested in what Scripture says relating to women, and her voice as a mother giving advice to young women surfaces frequently. The second perspective is that of a grandmother. Cornwallis often includes words of counsel to young men, which were written with her grandson in mind.[19] The third perspective is that of "mother of the parish," the rector's wife who is a wise woman, pastor, preacher, exhorter, and teacher. The fourth perspective is that of an Anglican lay theologian and apologist. This angle occurs when Cornwallis enters into theological debates with free thinkers, atheists, Moravians, and Catholics.

CORNWALLIS AS MOTHER

Like most women of her period, Cornwallis regarded her vocation as mother very highly. She supervised her children's education from a very early age, encouraging

---

17. Thomas Williams, *The Song of Songs, Which Is by Solomon: A New Translation, with a Commentary and Notes* (London: Williams, 1801).

18. Cornwallis writes: "Modern Jews deny Daniel to have been a prophet; and infidel Christians have asserted that his predictions, relative to the kings of Syria and Egypt, were written after the times of Antiochus Epiphanes, consequently after the events had taken place, which he affects to foretell" (*Observations*, 3:358).

19. For example, Cornwallis wrote: "The interesting object so solemnly confided to my maternal love, being of that sex which is most exposed to temptation; most ardent and enterprising; least protected in the course of education, and with little leisure for reflection; it became a constant subject of consideration, how all the dangers might be obviated to which you would be exposed, and I could devise no method so effectual as to invite your attention to the Scriptures, and to make them the medium through which my own sentiments might be conveyed to you" (*Observations*, 1:vi).

them to read English and French, to write, and to draw. She developed an educational plan that suited the specific needs of each of her children. She encouraged the imagination of her youngest child, Caroline, for example, who had a temper that was "irritable to the highest degree," and yet "affectionate and generous as it is warm."[20] Cornwallis also watched over her daughters' spiritual lives. Her own studies of Scripture became the focus of her teaching. Comments interspersed throughout *Observations* reflect Cornwallis's interests in texts that contained directives and information that a mother would want all women, especially her daughters, to know. The motherly voice of Cornwallis resounds in her observations on texts that focus on issues relating to women.

Cornwallis's comments on Prov 31 illustrate her motherly approach to textual and interpretive issues. Cornwallis sets out differences in the opinions of scholars in respect to the identity of King Lemuel, the stated author of Prov 31. Following the traditional identification of Lemuel as Solomon, she reads the chapter in light of the family history of David and Bathsheba.[21] She identifies with the "tender sympathies" of Bathsheba, including her motherly approach "to incite her son to the virtues of sobriety" by reminding him of the needs of "the afflicted, the oppressed, [and] the needy" (3:48). Cornwallis then reads verses 10–31 as a eulogy to that "unfortunate and much-injured Bathsheba, who herself, refined in the furnace of affliction, had shown such anxiety to preserve her son from the snares which had entangled his father in sin" (3:48).

Cornwallis moves from describing what the text meant in its original context to what it means for those called to be wives and mothers. She is uncomfortable with reading the entire text prescriptively and draws attention to the differences between the culture of ancient Israel and that of modern England. She directs young women to look beyond historical particularities to such enduring principles as loyalty, hard work, planning, education, and oversight:

> Difference of customs in different nations and climes, will necessarily produce diversity in the proper occupations* of women, as well as in their duties; but fidelity, economy, active industry, prudent foresight, improving and intelligent conversation, careful education of children, and a constant concern for the tem-

---

20. In her journal Mary Cornwallis described at length her daughter Caroline's personality and even included extracts of her daughter's prose and poetry (*Selections from the Letters*, 444–45).

21. Simon Patrick, a commentator whose work Cornwallis used, writes: "It is generally taken for granted, both by Hebrew and Christian writers, that King Lemuel, whose mother gave him the precepts contained in this chapter, was Solomon; whom Bath-sheba took early care to instruct in his duty, being, as some of no small name fancy, divinely inspired with the gift of prophecy. But as all this depends merely upon conjecture, and that without the least ground, so there is not good reason assigned why Solomon should here be called Lemuel" (Simon Patrick et al., *A Critical Commentary and Paraphrase on the Old and New Testament and the Apocrypha* [ed. R. Pitman; new ed.; 6 vols.; London: Priestly, 1822], 3:349).

poral and eternal interests of all with whom she is connected, will ever render a woman dear to her husband, "whose heart doth safely trust in her," and cause her to be blessed by her children, honoured by her servants, and respected by all who know her. (3:48–49)

Citing Burder's *Oriental Customs* as her source, Cornwallis adds a footnote (marked with an *) to her comment on women's proper occupations, noting that distinguished women of the past spent their time spinning and embroidering, an elegant art that women continue to practice.[22] Cornwallis then used historical information and her own experiences as a woman in England to help her determine how the text continued to speak to women in light of the problem of the cultural distance between the world of the text and the world of the reader.

Cornwallis offers further advice on sex and marriage when she comments on texts such as 1 Cor 6:11. Her motherly voice rings out when she warns against marrying a "libertine who, restless and uneasy in himself, is incapable of tasting the tranquil pleasures of domestic life" (4:297). With vehemence she declares, "woe be to the thoughtless and unprincipled female who embraces the fatal maxim that a reformed rake makes the best husband!" (4:297). Similarly, in her commentary on 1 Pet 3:1–7, Cornwallis counsels a woman to examine the "principles and temper" of the man she might marry because he will become "her master." (4:438). Cornwallis's use of the term "master" reflects the political and social reality in England in the early nineteenth century that a woman gave up her legal rights when she got married, since she was considered one with her husband in law.[23] Land, possessions, children, and even a wife's body were considered the property of the husband.[24] Like many women who found ways to maneuver within the restrictions imposed by marriage, Cornwallis offers "hints" about how submission in marriage can work to a woman's advantage:

---

22. See Samuel Burder, *Oriental Customs: An Illustration of the Sacred Scriptures, by an Explanatory Application of the Customs and Manners of the Eastern Nations, and Especially the Jews, Therein Alluded To* (London: Whittingham, 1802).

23. In his *Commentaries on the Laws of England* (1765–69), Sir William Blackstone wrote: "By marriage the husband and wife are one person in law: that is, the very being or legal existence of the woman is suspended during the marriage, or at least incorporated or consolidated into that of her husband, under whose wing, protection, and *cover*, she performs everything" (cited in Philip Mallett, "Women and Marriage in Victorian England," in *Marriage and Property* [ed. E. M. Craik; Aberdeen: Aberdeen University Press, 1984], 162; see also Joan Perkin, *Women and Marriage in Nineteenth-Century England* [London: Routledge, 1988]).

24. Mallet writes: "As with her children, so too with her own person: in theory at least a married woman's body belonged to her husband. If she left his house, he could enforce this right by a writ of *habeas corpus;* he could claim damages against his wife's alleged lover for 'trespass ... in his marital property'; and until 1891 the Courts would hold his right to keep his wife as a prisoner in his house" ("Woman and Marriage in Victorian England," 162–63).

> This is a hint to every wise women, how to make her obedience subservient to her own comfort, and the eternal interests of the man to whom she is united; by force she could effect nothing, because her strength is inferior; by disputes and clamours she would be as little successful, because the ardent nature of man inclines him to resist opposition; by low cunning, or mean acts, she would only incur his contempt. All that then remains is, that, after having exerted prudence in the choice of a husband, she should secure his confidence by upright conduct, and his affection by kind compliance; that he, finding her always actuated by right motives, may listen to her counsels in matters of importance. (4:438)

As a mother who desired her daughter(s) to marry well and thrive within marriage, Cornwallis uses Scripture and her own experiences as the basis for teaching about marriage. There is a dialogue between Scripture and experience.

Cornwallis as Grandmother and Spiritual Guardian of Young Men

Another perspective that threads itself through the commentary is that of the concerned grandmother and spiritual guardian of James Cornwallis Trimmer. In her commentary on Proverbs, a book directed particularly to young men (e.g., Prov 1:8–33), Cornwallis takes every opportunity to apply the message of the text to her grandson and, by extension, all young men.[25] Commenting on the series of warnings against the infamous "strange woman" in Prov 5:1–14, Cornwallis advises that young men seek shelter within their families:

> The youth who, with the desire to preserve his innocence, seeks shelter in the bosom of his own family; who cherishes a taste for useful study and occupation, and the society of the wise and good; shall escape from the snares of the wicked, and enjoy the peace which springs from an approving conscience. (3:9)

In another sermon for James based on Prov 7, Cornwallis expresses her deepest desire that James keep his mind pure. Using the rhetoric of the pulpit, she writes:

> May those who still possess an uncorrupt mind watch over and guard it with diligence as their best treasure; for, when once lost, it can never be restored. Sweet and peaceful will be the evening of their days, who pass the morning of their youth in innocence: like the setting sun in fine weather, it will cast a luster on all around them, and become the source of comfort both to themselves and others. (3:11)

As to choosing a life partner (Prov 12:4–8), Cornwallis advises that a young man "prefer worth to beauty; good sense to superficial accomplishments; and religion,

---

25. Cornwallis's grandmotherly perspective also chimes in the book of Daniel as she regards Daniel and his friends as good role models for young men. See *Observations*, 3:358–94.

to wit or free thinking" (3:18). Then, having married a "virtuous woman," a husband should treat his wife with "confidence and kindness; with consideration and respect; and not, like too many, despise the treasure because it is his own" (3:19).

Unlike many male commentators, Cornwallis does not blame the woman in Proverbs who tries to seduce young men. Rather, she blames men for seducing and corrupting "the unhappy woman" in the first place. Taking on the mantle of a preacher, she strongly exhorts men to treat women properly:

> Would men for a moment consider the extent of the mischief done to themselves by undermining and subverting the good principles of women, they would, upon motives of self-interest, pursue a different course. Where are they to find domestic comfort but in the integrity of those who constitute their families as wives, sisters, daughters, or servants? What madness therefore is it in them to enter as it were into a conspiracy against their own happiness, by sowing the seeds of vanity in the female mind, by unsettling its religious principles, by breaking down the fence of natural modesty, by encouraging those Christian graces which render women useful members of society, and a blessing in the domestic circle! (3:5)

Unlike many nineteenth-century women who placed the responsibility for virtuous living squarely on the shoulders of women, Cornwallis recognizes that men's attitudes toward women and sexuality shape society's values. She recognizes the double standards in English society regarding women and sexuality that the reformer Josephine Butler (1828–1906) later brought into public view in her protests against the Contagious Diseases Acts of 1864, 1866, and 1869.

Cornwallis as Mother of the Parish

Cornwallis's third perspective is that of the mother of the parish. Cornwallis took her role as a clergy spouse seriously and was actively involved in the life of the parish. She was particularly interested in religious education. Her book *A Preparation for the Lord's Supper, with Companion to the Altar, Intended for the Use of Ladies* demonstrates her interest in both practical and academic issues related to the ongoing life of the church.[26] Her desire to teach others extended to the readers of *Observations* whom she desired might be able to study Scripture "with the same perseverance that she has done, and experience the same blessed results— joy and peace in believing" (1:vi). As shown above, her commentary went beyond teaching about the content of Scripture; it also preached its message.

Although Cornwallis supported many traditional views on women's roles, her commentary on 1 Tim 3, which sets out the qualifications for bishops and

---

26. Gleadle suggests that the views expressed in this work are similar to Cornwallis's contemporary, Hannah More (1745–1833) ("Cornwallis, Caroline Frances," 13:472).

deacons, not only reveals her own sense of vocation as a clergy wife but also points toward her embryonic feminism. Cornwallis wonders why the apostle neglected to set out the characteristics of a bishop's wife, since he notes in verse 11 that deacons' wives are to be "grave, not slanderers, sober, faithful in all things" (KJV). Cornwallis explains the apostle's omission and in so doing reveals her own understanding of a clergy wife's powerful role as mother of the parish:

> We may conclude the omission to arise from the idea, that if the latter (deacons' wives) were so responsible, the former (clergy wives) could not fail to consider themselves as much or more so. Every good woman will gladly conform to the character given, ver. 11; she will take pleasure in assisting her husband in the lesser duties of his ministry. While he acts as the father, she will a prove a mother to the parish; and we know that a tender mother delights to instruct, to guide, to comfort, to protect, the children of her love, and if compelled to reprove, she will do it with gentleness. (4:386)

Cornwallis identifies herself as the mother of the parish of Elham and Kent, and her commentary shows her fulfilling that role; she instructs, guides, comforts, protects, and reproves.

Cornwallis also elucidates the potentially problematic directive in 1 Tim 3:11 that wives be "grave" (4:386). She suggests that this directive does not mean that wives are to be gloomy or morose but rather free "from all levity in dress or manner: for without a certain dignity of character, all attempts to reform others would be fruitless and ridiculous" (4:387).[27] Cornwallis elevates clergy wives, setting them apart in dress, character, and calling. They are "more responsible than other women, even in things apparently trifling," and for their hard work and faithfulness in this life, Cornwallis offers "recompense in the world to come" (4:387). For Cornwallis and her contemporaries, dress was a marker of rank. Sarah Trimmer, for example, advises: "children certainly should wear clothes suited to the condition of their parents, that the distinction of ranks may be kept up in the community, though they should not be made proud of them."[28] For Christian women of all classes, dress also reflected character. To avoid "the contagion of the love of dress which at the present day rages like a mania among all ranks of females," Trimmer advises Christian mothers to cultivate humility and modesty in their daughters so that they will be "cornerstones polished after the

---

27. Cornwallis fleshes out her views on dress in her comments on 1 Pet 3:5, where she writes: "Every prudent woman will, in her attire, consider her age and station, as well as her husband's taste and circumstances, and seek to be distinguished more for neatness and simplicity than for show and expense" (*Observations*, 4:438–39).

28. Sarah Trimmer, *An Essay on Christian Education* (London: Rivington, 1812), 80. I am indebted to Heather Weir for directing me to Trimmer's comments on fashion.

similitude of a palace" (Ps 144:12).[29] Thus, Cornwallis's views about the distinctives of clergy wives reflect assumptions about the relationship of faith, fashion, and class common in her day.

Cornwallis's comments on the advice about widows in 1 Tim 5 similarly show her high view of the importance and power of women. She underscores the importance of the advice given to Timothy about respecting "women of all ages and conditions," given that "not only the present, but the future welfare of thousands, is involved in the opinions and conduct of the female sex" (4:389). Cornwallis then strays from the subject of Timothy's letter with a diatribe against "men, who, instead of behaving to young women 'with all purity,' as 'sisters,' seek to corrupt their minds by flattery, or to poison them by insinuating libertine principles, [and by doing so] lay the foundation of their own miseries, and sooner or later discern their error" (4:389). Cornwallis places the responsibility for the just and equitable treatment of women squarely on the shoulders of men, who have the power to shape women's lives. With great eloquence and passion, Cornwallis, the mother of the parish, admonishes men, arguing for women's education:

> Did they consider women as individuals on whom all their dearest interests hang, as capable, if their minds were rightly formed, of being rendered interesting companions, kind counselors, faithful friends, prudent managers, careful mothers, they would pursue a very different plan; they would employ the advantages of their own superior powers and education to inculcate right principles and right ideas; to communicate knowledge and to discourage every thing frivolous or unworthy in them. This might be done without laying aside those agreeable manners, which form the charm of mixed societies. (4:389)

Cornwallis then draws her comments back to the subject of widows and raises the contemporary problem of older women in English society. She laments that her contemporaries make "pitiful attempts" to hide "the advance of age" instead of basking in the position of "honour and respect" that they deserve (4:389). Cornwallis concludes her exposition on 1 Tim 5 with a priestlike exhortation to widows:

> Let not, then, the widow's heart be overwhelmed with sorrow! Let her heart not be dismayed at her seemingly forlorn and desolate condition; for God is her friend, her mighty defense and succour; and if she place her trust in him, he will assuredly turn her sorrow into joy. (4:389)

Cornwallis's comments on women in her exposition of 1 Timothy show her nascent feminism. She clearly believes in the power and influence of women. Indeed, commenting on Prov 14:1, Cornwallis defines woman as "the architect,

---

29. Ibid., 79.

who upon a sure and solid foundation, erects a fair edifice, which for its order, symmetry, and agreeable aspect, both within and without, invites the approbation of all who behold it, or who are so happy as to dwell under its roof" (3:21). Cornwallis is not asking for full equality with men, but she avers that if women have to be subject to men, men have to be worthy of women's respect. Cornwallis believes that a good marriage is based on mutual honor and respect. She demands improved education for women. She places the responsibility for change on men, whose lives in turn depend on women. Her daughter Caroline developed her mother's views and became an outspoken feminist in her later years.[30]

Cornwallis as an Anglican Lay Theologian and Apologist

Cornwallis felt called to speak to issues that affected individuals, the church community, and society. She had firm convictions about matters of theology and ecclesiology and voiced them often in *Observations*. One of the many places where Cornwallis's theological views surface is her commentary on Song of Songs. Unlike Sarah Trimmer, who encourages her readers to "pass over" the Song of Songs, arguing that it was "all in figurative language" and that its theology was "taught in plainer words in other parts of Scripture,"[31] Cornwallis takes on its interpretive challenges. She follows a traditional typological-allegorical reading of the Song as depicting the love between Christ and the church and argues against reading it as a song describing the love between Christ and the individual believer. She thought this reading encouraged the type of religious enthusiasm practiced by the Moravians and other sects.[32] To prove her point, she cites the respectful and reverent responses of Thomas and Mary Magdalene to meeting the risen Christ, "the one exclaiming, 'My Lord, and my God'; the other simply Master" (3:67). Cornwallis also worries that an individualized reading of the Song blurs the lines of distinction between divine and human. Accordingly, she sets out her doctrine of God: "Let us remember that all familiarity between God and his creatures is entirely unbecoming; and that he who came in our nature to die for us, will come again to be our judge" (3:67).

Finally, Cornwallis takes on those who challenge the Christian faith. In her concluding remarks on the Minor Prophets, she reveals that her experiences of reading the prophets have been so delightful and uplifting, "the language ... so

---

30. Caroline Cornwallis wrote two highly influential articles on the inequities of married women's legal status published at the height of the Parliamentary debates over proposed changes to married women's rights in 1856 and 57 (Gleadle, "Cornwallis, Caroline Frances," 473).

31. Sarah Trimmer, *A Help to the Unlearned in the Study of the Holy Scriptures: Being an Attempt to Explain the Bible in a Familiar Way* (London: Rivington, 1805), 387.

32. Although Cornwallis advocated a typological reading of Song of Songs, she was not prudish. Her commentary on the sexually graphic prophetic texts Ezek 16 and 23 demonstrates that she has no trouble discussing offensive sexual imagery (*Observations*, 3:317–19, 325–27).

sublime—the matter so wonderful," that she wonders if infidels and deists have ever read them "with common attention, if at all" (3:490). Cornwallis's faith was unfaltering. The years she spent preparing her study notes and manuscript for publication grounded her faith and gave her confidence to staunchly defend it.

Conclusions

Mary Cornwallis was a unique interpreter of Scripture. The sheer volume of her interpretive work makes her stand out as a voice that needs to be heard. The quality of her commentary is also impressive. To be sure, the sections of her work where she quotes or summarizes the opinions of great Anglican divines are not as interesting as her own comments on the text. Still, these sections reveal much about what Cornwallis viewed to be important in the text and about the resources she drew upon to interpret the Bible. It is in her own comments, however, that we find the voice of a well-educated woman who rather unintentionally enters into the male world of commentary writing. She follows the traditional format of a commentary and uses all the resources available to her.

Cornwallis also reads Scripture as a woman: she reads as a mother of two daughters, a grandmother, the mother of the parish, and an informed Anglican aware of the theological and moral issues of her day. Her writing opens a window and allows us to see into Cornwallis's world. To the question, "Does Cornwallis read the Scriptures differently because she is a woman?" the answer is yes and no. She closely follows a traditional male genre of interpretation, but she also allows her own female interpretive lens to ask questions of the text that allow her to apply the text to her own life and the lives of her readers.

Finally, Caroline Cornwallis's role in preparing her mother's massive life's work reminds us that books are not written in a vacuum. Caroline provided her mother with encouragement, academic expertise, and editing skills as she read and edited thousands of pages of her mother's manuscript. This experience was formative for Caroline Cornwallis. She followed her mother's example, and Caroline's writings, which are broader in focus and greater in number than her mother's, had an even greater impact on her generation than her mother's did. Still, Mary Cornwallis's *Observations* is a remarkable work of scholarship, devotion, and love. Both the author and her work deserve a place in the history of the interpretation of the Bible.

Bibliography

Burder, Samuel. *Oriental Customs; Or, An Illustration of the Sacred Scriptures, by an Explanatory Application of the Customs and Manners of the Eastern Nations and Especially the Jews, Therein Alluded To.* London: Whittingham, 1802.

Cornwallis, Caroline Francis. *Selections from the Letters of Caroline Frances Cornwallis: Also Some Unpublished Poems; and an Appendix, Containing "Philosophical Theories and Philosophical Experience."* Edited by M. C. Power. London: Trübner, 1864.

Cornwallis, Mary. *Observations, Critical, Explanatory, and Practical, on the Canonical Scriptures.* 2nd ed. 4 vols. London: Baldwin, Cradock & Joy. 1817, 1820.

Horsley, Samuel. *Hosea: Translated from the Hebrew, with Notes Explanatory and Critical.* London: Robinson, 1801.

Gleadle, Kathryn. "Cornwallis, Caroline Frances (1786–1858)." Pages 472–73 in vol. 13 of *Oxford Dictionary of National Biography.* Edited by Henry C. G. Matthew and Brian Harrison. Oxford: Oxford University Press, 2004.

Mallett, Philip. "Women and Marriage in Victorian England." Pages 159–89 in *Marriage and Property.* Edited by Elizabeth M. Craik. Aberdeen: Aberdeen University Press, 1984.

Patrick, Simon, et al. *A Critical Commentary and Paraphrase on the Old and New Testament and the Apocrypha.* Edited by Rev. R. Pitman. New ed. 6 vols. London: Priestly, 1822.

Perkin, Joan. *Women and Marriage in Nineteenth-Century England.* London: Routledge, 1988.

Spurgeon, Charles H. *Commenting and Commentaries.* 1876. Repr., Grand Rapids: Baker, 1981.

Staves, Susan. "Church of England Clergy and Women Writers." Pages 81–103 in *Reconsidering the Bluestockings.* Edited by Nichole Pohl and Betty A. Schellenberg. San Marino: Huntington Library, 2003.

Trimmer, Sarah. *An Essay on Christian Education.* London: Rivington, 1812.

———. *A Help to the Unlearned in the Study of the Holy Scriptures: Being an Attempt to Explain the Bible in a Familiar Way.* London: Rivington, 1805.

Williams, Thomas. *The Song of Songs, Which Is by Solomon: A New Translation, with a Commentary and Notes.* London: Williams, 1801.

Yarde, Doris M. *The Life and Works of Sarah Trimmer: A Lady of Brentford.* Hounslow, U.K.: Hounslow & District Historical Society, 1972.

CONVERSATIONS ON THE BIBLE
WITH A LADY OF PHILADELPHIA*

Bernon P. Lee

Sarah (Ewing) Hall's voice comes from the margins of the enterprise of biblical interpretation. Recovering her voice will enrich the tapestry that is the history of biblical interpretation. Highlighting a lesser-known voice may provide a complement or correction to the traditions of biblical interpretation as they currently exist. In pursuit of this goal, this essay seeks to describe the method and the content of Sarah (Ewing) Hall's interpretation of the Hebrew Bible in her book, *Conversations on the Bible*. In particular, the chapter attends to the manner in which Hall contributes to the transformation of the genre of catechistic literature through the adaptation of its formal features in the promotion of her literary agenda.

Hall's book is a paraphrase of the Hebrew Bible.[1] The author presents the summary as a discourse of instruction initiated by a mother with her young children (Fanny, Catherine, and Charles). Her work is a unique contribution to the genre of catechistic literature in Western Europe and America in the nineteenth century. The popularity of her book is indicated in the series of editions produced within ten years of publication. Here I reference the fourth edition, issued in 1827.[2] Hall's changes and additions to the book among the various editions (1818, 1821, and 1827) were designed to render the book more appealing to young readers.

A secondary focus is Hall's engagement with the social conditions of her time, in particular the roles of women in family and society. Therefore, this essay will

* An earlier draft of this chapter was read as a paper at the Grace College Religious Studies Symposium, 17 February 2005. I am grateful for the fruitful discussion that has arisen from that meeting.

1. Sarah (Ewing) Hall, *Conversations on the Bible* (4th ed.; Philadelphia: Harrison Hall, 1827).

2. The first and second editions of the book were published in 1818 and 1821, respectively, in Philadelphia. A third edition was published in London without the permission of the author.

also engage two essays from a selection of Hall's shorter pieces compiled by her son Harrison Hall.[3] In these two works Hall displays a movement toward an egalitarian perspective in discussing the relationship between the sexes, even as she upholds a predominantly domestic role for women.

Sarah (Ewing) Hall: A Brief Biography

Sarah Ewing was born in Philadelphia on 30 October 1761.[4] Her father, the Rev. John Ewing, was provost of the University of Pennsylvania and pastor of the First Presbyterian Church in Philadelphia. In line with customary practice of the day, Sarah Hall received little formal education, having been inducted by her mother into the incessant cycles of household duties at a young age. The Rev. Ewing possessed a passion for intellectual inquiry and the ability to communicate the most complex matters in simple terms. In conversation with the steady stream of learned personages who frequented the Ewing home, Rev. Ewing allowed his daughter access to some of the most cultured conversation in Philadelphia. During the few hours of reading stolen away from domestic chores, Sarah Hall acquired an interest in astronomy and its principles of inquiry. Beyond the sciences, Hall cultivated an interest in history and literature. From the recitation of Greek and Latin literary texts by her brothers, she became familiar with classical works and the grammar of the classical languages. Later Hall would pursue learning Hebrew to enhance her understanding of biblical texts.

Sarah Ewing married John Hall, the son of a wealthy plantation owner in Maryland, in 1782. The newlyweds lived in Maryland for the next eight years. Having obtained a position as secretary of the land office in the district of Pennsylvania, John Hall moved his family to Philadelphia in 1790. The family later moved

---

3. Harrison Hall, ed., *Selections from the Writings of Mrs. Sarah Hall, Author of Conversations on the Bible* (Philadelphia: Harrison Hall, 1833). This collection deals with a variety of issues ranging from the currents of biblical interpretation to the function of education for women. The two chapters "On the Extent of Female Influence, and the Importance of Exerting It in Favour of Christianity" (1–16) and "On Female Education" (17–24) are of interest for this study because they focus on Hall's views on the relationship between the sexes.

4. The bulk of the information in this section is derived from Harrison Hall's memoir on the life of the author, which stands at the beginning of his volume of selected articles by Sarah Hall ("Memoir of the Life of Mrs. Sarah Hall," in Hall, *Selections from the Writings*, ix–xxxiv). Hall's memoir is supplemented by various dictionary entries on the author: Sarah Josepha Hale, *Woman's Record; or, Sketches of Distinguished Women from the Creation to A.D. 1854: Arranged in Four Eras with Selections from Female Writers of Every Age* (2nd ed.; New York: Harper & Brothers, 1855), 877–78; James Grant Wilson and John Fiske, eds., *Appleton's Cyclopaedia of American Biography* (7 vols.; New York: Appleton, 1888), 3:44–45; Stanley Jasspon Kunitz and Howard Haycraft, *American Authors 1600–1900: A Biographical Dictionary of American Literature* (New York: Wilson, 1938), 328; Nancy Hardesty, "Sarah Ewing Hall," in *American Women Writers* (ed. L. Mainiero; 4 vols.; New York: Ungar, 1980), 2:224–25.

to Lamberton, New Jersey, in 1801. John Ewing's ill health and financial difficulty led the family to return to his paternal estate in Maryland in 1805. In 1811, the family returned to Philadelphia, where John Ewing passed away from gout in 1826. Sarah Hall died on 8 April 1830 at the age of sixty-nine. Of the eleven children born to her, two died before attaining adulthood. A third child, Thomas M. Hall, entered the naval service of a South American state and was never heard from again. The eldest, John E. Hall, preceded Sarah Hall in death (1829).

While resident in Philadelphia, Sarah Hall became acquainted with the city's leading literary figures. When Joseph Dennie founded *The Port Folio* in 1800, a literary periodical of prominence in the city, Hall became a frequent contributor in regular correspondence with the editor.[5] In addition to several works of poetry, Hall wrote essays on a variety of matters of concern for the social conscience of America at that time. The breadth of her interest is evident through a survey of some of the titles in the anthology of Hall's writings compiled by her son: "On Female Education," "On Duelling," "Biblical Criticism," "The Garden of Wedlock."[6] In all areas of interest, Hall brought a vibrant interpretation of the Christian faith to bear upon her views.

CATECHISM: THE CONTOURS OF A GENRE

Sarah (Ewing) Hall's book may be considered to be an example of catechistic literature. As the appellation suggests, catechistic literature is didactic in purpose. It typically functions in a religious community in the process of cultivating the neophyte, usually a child, into a system of values essential to the practice of the religion. Patricia Demers identifies three main features that define the genre: (1) the prominence of the element of volition in accepting responsibility for correct behavior and thought; (2) the use of dialogue as a tool for pedagogy; and (3) consistent allusion to biblical models and principles.[7]

The concerns of religious pedagogy produce the formal features of the genre. Behind the emphasis on volition is the Christian conviction of the depravity of humankind. The exhortation to shun evil and choose good presupposes an innate

---

5. Harrison Hall ("Memoir of the Life," xv–xvii) describes Dennie as an individual of "gentlemanly character" and "companionable qualities" who lacked the tenacity and industry to become an author. However, he possessed the talents of an editor and, in his taste for literature, "a delicate perception of the beautiful, in sentiment and style." Contributors to *The Port Folio*, as noted by Hall, include individuals who later came to hold the highest positions in the federal government. Hall considered it a great honor for his mother (Sarah Hall) to be a favored correspondent of Dennie. *The Port Folio* was a journal combining works of literary flavor and sociopolitical commentary.

6. Hall, *Selections from the Writings*.

7. Patricia Demers, *Heaven upon Earth: The Form of Moral and Religious Children's Literature, to 1850* (Knoxville: University of Tennessee Press, 1993), 61–62.

proclivity on the part of humans for transgressing the boundaries set by the divine. That the goal of catechistic literature is to teach correct behavior to youth inclined toward the opposite is evident in the dedicatory epistle to Nathanael Vincent's catechism, *The Principles of the Doctrine of Christ*. Vincent exhorts youth to find value in the saving knowledge and grace of Jesus Christ and to avoid corruption and ignorance that leads to God's departure from the people.[8] The thinking of Puritan writers on the depravity of the human condition motivates their emphatic portrayal of grim consequences for the unrepentant in literature designed for children.[9] Puritan writers of children's stories depict death engulfing individuals at a premature and unexpected point in time, depriving the unregenerate of the opportunity for repentance. Ruth MacDonald illustrates this theme in the writings of, among others, James Janeway, Cotton Mather, and Thomas White.[10] While the possibility of premature death for children was ever-present in seventeenth-century England, the prospect of facing death and the fires of hell without the saving grace of God was presented as the ultimate horror. These biographical accounts of children's lives portray a stark contrast between the pious and the unregenerate. The authors lose no opportunity to emphasize the reassurance of God's love for the pious, as well as the inconsolable grief, pain, and regret of those outside the fold. The purpose of these descriptions, as MacDonald and Wooden observe, is to elicit religious zeal and passion (or even hysteria) sufficient to pry youth from the clutches of the devil.[11] These rhetorical strategies come

---

8. Nathanael Vincent, *The Principles of the Doctrine of Christ; Or, A Catechism unto Which Is Added a Catechism for Conscience* (London: Parkhurst, 1691), n.p.

9. So expressed by Ruth K. MacDonald, *Literature for Children in England and America from 1646 to 1774* (Troy, N.Y.: Whitson, 1982), 27; and Warren Wooden, *Children's Literature of the English Renaissance* (Louisville: University of Kentucky Press, 1986), 140–41. The term *Puritanism* refers to a reactionary movement beginning in the fifteenth century within Protestantism in Britain and colonial America. The movement initially sought to purge the Church of England of its Roman Catholic elements: the wearing of vestments and the position of church furnishings suggesting a sacrificial priesthood; belief in the real presence of Christ in the Eucharist; the governance of the episcopate; and so forth. Puritan thought emphasized the sovereignty of God against the Arminian tendencies within the Church of England, recognition of the innate depravity of the individual, and temperance in conduct. Many Puritan preachers developed a graded morphology of religious transformation, moving from election through vocation, justification, and sanctification to glorification. For a brief introduction to the history of the movement and its main ideals with bibliography, see Francis J. Bremer, "Puritanism," *ER* 12:102–6.

10. MacDonald, *Literature for Children*, 23–27; James Janeway, *A Token for Children: Being an Exact Account of the Conversion, Holy, and Exemplary Lives, and Joyful Deaths of Several Young Children* (London: n.p., 1671–72); Cotton Mather, *A Token for the Children of New England* (Boston: Nicholas Boone, 1700); Thomas White, *A Little Book for Little Children* (London: n.p., 1693).

11. MacDonald, *Literature for Children*, 26–27; Wooden, *Children's Literature of the English Renaissance*, 140–41.

from a fervent desire for the regeneration of the child and the conviction that there is an inherent human affinity for iniquity and waywardness.[12]

The second essential quality of catechistic texts is the use of dialogue. While the recitation of codes and creeds often is an integral component in the exchange, the concern goes beyond an emphasis upon memorization and adherence to a code. For Demers, the constant interchange is an invitation to readers to find their own voice. Catechistic texts, according to her, "resemble the declension and conjugation paradigms that all of us have probably struggled with in second-language classes: a necessary grid by which to verbalize, translate and interpret."[13] As with the study of grammatical declensions and conjugations, the effort to discern the structure of a paradigm and its possibility for application across a range of circumstances must follow the ability to recite the various religious propositions. This demonstrates the ability to penetrate into the sense of the code and to derive principles of significance beyond the particularities of the subject. The success of catechistic literature, for Demers, hinges upon its ability to cultivate in the reader knowledge of, and interaction with, Christian doctrine.

As a consequence of its focus on the uninitiated (mostly youth), catechistic literature tends to find analogies for its claims to truth among the more mundane and common aspects of life. This is a feature that is shared with children's religious literature from the period leading up to the nineteenth century. MacDonald demonstrates, for example, that Bunyan's poetry for children is replete with examples from experience familiar to children.[14] The intention of the poet is to persuade children to set their sights on things heavenly by speaking through images and objects at home in a nursery. Another example of a focus on common experience comes from Benjamin Keach's animated catechism in *War with the Devil* in 1676.[15] The character, Youth, as Demers points out, considers the biddings of Conscience and Truth quite out of step with the trends of seventeenth-century London: lost would be the delights of play houses and sexual services for sale should relentless attention to financial profit cease.[16] The demands of the Christian conscience in opposition to the ways of the world become clear in the dialogue. Keach and Bunyan supply vivid illustrations of biblical truths from the world of their readers.

As a consequence of the concern of catechesis for engendering a correct understanding of belief, the Christian canon is never far from view. The consistent allusion to Scripture is the third defining feature of catechistic literature.

---

12. Wooden, *Children's Literature of the English Renaissance*, 140.
13. Demers, *Heaven upon Earth*, 54.
14. MacDonald makes her argument, illustrating her point with reference to select portions of Bunyan's poem (*Literature for Children*, 29).
15. Benjamin Keach, *War with the Devil; Or, the Young Man's Conflict with the Powers of Darkness: In a Dialogue* (London: Harris, 1676).
16. Demers, *Heaven upon Earth*, 64.

Care is taken to clarify the meaning of Scripture for the common person in the pew. John Cotton's brief catechism for the youth of Boston published in 1646 provides one example. The catechism begins with questions requiring answers of a straightforward nature:

> Q: What is sinne?
> A: Sinne is a transgression of the Law.
> Q: How many commandments of the Law be there?
> A: Ten.
> Q: What is the first Commandement?
> A: Thou shalt have no other Gods but me.[17]

As the catechism proceeds in its exploration of the Decalogue, the degree of interpretation required for the respondent increases.

> Q: What is the eighth commandement?
> A: Thou shalt not steal.
> Q: What is the stealth here forbidden?
> A: To take away another man's goods, without his leave: or to spend our own without benefit to ourselves or others.
> Q: What is the duty here commanded?
> A: To get our goods honestly, to keep them safely, and to spend them thriftily.[18]

The response to the second question includes taking another person's property without permission as theft. Even irresponsibly spending one's resources is included. The misuse of any part of creation is tantamount to an act of theft against the Creator. Cotton's catechism carefully interprets Scripture and extends the teachings of biblical texts.

In sum, it may be said that catechistic literature represents an artful and intelligent effort to inculcate readers into the fundamentals of the Christian religion. Based on a Christian understanding of the unregenerate state of humankind, catechistic texts aim to produce an understanding of doctrine that engages the contemporary experience of the believer. The formal characteristics of catechistic literature—the focus on volition, the consistent allusion to Scripture, and the preference for dialogue—implement these ideals and purposes.

---

17. Patricia Demers and Gordon Moyles, eds., *From Instruction to Delight: An Anthology of Children's Literature to 1850* (Oxford: Oxford University Press, 1982), 24.

18. Ibid., 25.

Transformations in the Genre:
The Form and Function of Hall's Catechism

In expressing the struggles of a young reader encountering the Bible, young Fanny requests "a simple connected narrative of the story, with its general relation to the several parts of the Bible."[19] Mother responds by congratulating young Fanny and her siblings for their interest as well as by acknowledging the difficulty. Thus begins Mother's paraphrase and interpretation of the grand narrative of Israel's formation and demise, and Hall's introduction of the Hebrew Bible to young readers.[20] In her preface to the original edition, Hall is critical of the church's neglect of the Hebrew Scriptures, considering both Testaments to display in tandem "the treasure in the clearest point of view" (v). *Conversations on the Bible* is an attempt to clarify the various cultural and historical elements that render the Hebrew Scripture obscure for nineteenth-century Americans, pointing out such difficulties in the questions raised by the three youngsters. In form and function, the work maintains the element of dialogue, the consistent allusion to Scripture in the service of religious pedagogy, and the exhortation to choose well. It conforms to the hallmarks of the genre.

The work differs in its conscious departure from a topical format and preoccupation with questions pertaining to doctrine. These differences are the result of attending to the chronological sequence of the narrative in Scripture and to problems in interpretation directly related to the agenda of the text. Hall's work is not a series of questions and answers addressing a series of theological topics; it is a narration of the events of the Hebrew Bible, punctuated by questions on interesting or difficult points in the story. The book informs the reader's memory and facilitates an understanding of the connections among the parts of the Hebrew Bible (14). Hall's choice of a domestic setting for the unfolding dialogue, another difference from earlier works, is shared by several other catechistic texts emerging in the early part of the nineteenth century.[21] Of the numerous pieces displaying this transformation in the genre, several match Hall's preference for attending to the structure and the literary agenda of larger segments of the biblical text. For example, Favell Mortimer's *Line upon Line* presents a family's discussions

---

19. Hall, *Conversations on the Bible*, 13. Subsequent references to *Conversations on the Bible* will be provided within the text.

20. Hall's work by and large follows the sequence of the Christian Old Testament. However, there are exceptions. Chronicles is treated in conjunction with Kings in the same chapter. Daniel is inserted between Chronicles and Ezra. The Latter Prophets, which stand outside the grand narrative complex in its treatment of events, are dealt with at the end of the work after Nehemiah and before Job. The rest of the Writings are omitted.

21. This designation of a domestic setting for the characters in the book exceeds the tendency of earlier works merely to imply a familial relationship between author and reader in their vocabulary.

of religious matters that provide occasions for retelling episodes in the Bible.[22] Other examples of a similar attention to biblical narratives within the context of domestic religious instruction occur in Lucy Wilson's *Mamma's Bible Stories* and Mrs. Thomas Dalby's *Dutch Tiles*.[23] All three examples share Hall's concern for explaining difficulties in biblical interpretation to a child. Engaging a child's curiosity in religious matters replaces the focus in earlier works on the catechumen's ability to supply answers to questions concerning theology and the moral life. In light of these examples of catechistic texts from the early part of the nineteenth century, it is evident that Hall's application of the genre is part of a larger literary movement within the period.

Conversations on the Nature of Narrative

In accordance with her interest in the narrative structure of the Hebrew Bible, Hall pays close attention to the element of motivation. She notes both the biblical author's selection of events for coverage and the reasons for the actions of characters. The focus upon the latter is especially pronounced. At various points the children interrupt their mother, raising questions concerning choices made by individual biblical characters. Catherine expresses incredulity at Israel's lack of resolve at the Red Sea despite the visible and palpable presence of God (85; see Exod 14:10–14). Elsewhere Catherine inquires about the extent of Aaron's participation in Israel's apostasy with the forging of the golden calf. In response, Mother proposes that the act is understandable as a reflex of the pagan impulse to adopt a visible representation of divinity in religious adoration (94; see Exod 32:1–35). On Jacob's motivations in stealing his brother's blessing (Gen 27:1–40), Mother is torn between ascribing selfish ambition to the patriarch or an admirable zeal to succeed to the spiritual legacy ordained by God (45). Greater certainty characterizes Mother's claim that the careless consumption of strong drink prior to approaching God is the cause of the demise of Nadab and Abihu in Lev 10:1–7. Mother finds support for this interpretation in the following command in verse 8 for priests to avoid strong drink before entering the tent of meeting. Moses is motivated to speak on the issue because of the preceding disaster involving Aar-

---

22. Favell Lee (Bevan) Mortimer, *Line upon Line; Or, A Second Series of the Earliest Instruction the Infant Mind Is Capable of Receiving* (2 vols.; London: Hatchards, 1876–77).

23. Lucy Wilson, *Mamma's Bible Stories, for Her Little Boys and Girls: A Series of Reading Lessons Taken from the Bible, and Adapted to the Capacities of Very Young Children* (7th ed.; London: Grant & Griffith, 1842); Mrs. Thomas Dalby, *Dutch Tiles: Being Narratives of Holy Scripture* (London: Mason, 1842). Dalby's work displays the unusual feature of rehearsing biblical stories by pointing to a series of ornamental tiles around a fireplace depicting scenes from the Bible. All three examples are cited by Demers (*Heaven upon Earth,* 66), who provides a more extensive list of cases that display the preference for conversations between adults and children at this point in the development of the genre.

on's sons. In this last example, Hall joins the debate within scholarship (modern and premodern) over God's motivation in meting out punishment on Aaron's sons.[24] The exchange between mother and children consistently pays attention to the elements of choice that move the plot of the narrative along. Where ambiguities in the motives of characters exist, Hall does not shrink from supplying one or more possibility. The assumption is that the actions of the characters must make sense.

This penchant for filling in the gaps in motivation is especially important in diffusing the appearance of injustice in biblical narrative. For example, when relating Israel's practice of genocide in Jericho and other cities, Mother absolves Israel of any guilt by pointing out the sanction of divinity behind the course of action (128–29). Israel acts in order to effect the justice of God, not out of any inherent right to the land by virtue of righteousness before God. In another example, Mother reflects on the parting discourse of Moses in Deuteronomy. Here the requirement that Israel take the land from the Amorites is coupled with the description of a land rich with produce (Deut 3:25), in contrast with the barrenness of the wilderness (Deut 1:19–20). Moses' description of the land is presented as a stratagem that anticipates Israel's fear of obeying by appealing to their baser instincts. In a single stroke of interpretive genius, Israel's entrance into the land is justified, and Moses is portrayed as a rhetorician of the highest order. In seeking to justify or explain the actions of characters in biblical narrative, Hall draws upon her understanding of human experience.

A concomitant feature of Hall's reliance on the correspondence between the events of the narrative and those of common human experience is a tendency to defend the historicity of the historical narratives. For Hall, the motivations and the actions of the characters are true to life because the Bible is a reliable record of events from the past. This concern for historicity emerges in Mother's reference to ancient customs when explaining the abhorrence of the Egyptians to dine with the Hebrews in the Joseph story (66; see Gen 44:32). In her interpretation, the Bible presents an authentic view on the ancient world. Elsewhere Hall implies the historical reliability of Scripture by ascertaining, with reference to modern works of scholarship, the geographical location of Sodom (32; see Gen 18:16–19:26) as well as of Ararat and the fertility of its soil as being suitable for the sustenance of the postdiluvian population (24; see Gen 8:1–9:28).[25] In response to a query by

---

24. The variety of opinion on the reason for divine action in this episode includes the following: Aaron's sons intruded upon the most holy portion of the tabernacle; the offering was not in accordance with the established timetable of the cult; the sons were not properly attired; the conflagration was an act of sanctification, God displaying his favor upon those closest to him. For a survey of the various scholarly perspectives on the episode, see John E. Hartley, *Leviticus* (WBC 4; Dallas: Word, 1992), 132–35.

25. The authority referred to on the location of Sodom is a certain Mr. Maundrel. On the location of Ararat and the nature of its environs, Hall uses a dictionary compiled by William

Charles as to the literal (i.e., historical) truth of the transformation of Lot's wife into a pillar of salt (Gen 19:24–26), Mother responds that it is the infidel who would suggest a metaphorical interpretation, because "history was written for the instruction of the common people, and all classes were commanded to teach it to their children" (31). Hall's insistence on the comprehensibility of motives and actions in the biblical text, therefore, is tied to the literal and historical reliability of Scripture and the identification of a target audience.

Conversations on Christology and Intertextuality

If common human experience sheds light on the actions of characters, an intertextual approach explains the selection of events for inclusion in the Hebrew Bible. Hall's approach, articulated through the words of Mother, is to view the process as culminating in the text under the superintendence of divinity. Scripture consists of "a whole, harmonious in all its parts" (15). Its purpose is to reveal "the defection of man from the righteousness in which he was created, and the consequent forfeiture of eternal life … and the mode of his restoration by the unmerited favor of the Sovereign Creator and Disposer of all things" (15). This plot overrides the limited understanding and the intentions of the individual authors. Hence, as Mother points out, even Balaam, a prophet at odds with Israel, may be brought to profess the word of God (117; see Num 23:1–24:25).

Many of the intertextual connections forged by Mother have a christological focus. Thus, for example, beyond the representation of faith in action, Abraham's attempted sacrifice of his son in Gen 22 prefigures the sacrificial death of Jesus Christ (37). Elsewhere Hall's christological interpretation is manifested in her reading of Leviticus; the sacrifices delineated in Lev 1–7, of course, are analogous to the crucifixion of Jesus (98). This explanation is Mother's response to Fanny's inquiry as to the reason for reading about laws and rituals no longer practiced by Christians. A christological approach employing typology explains the selection of events and obscure practices (to the nineteenth-century American Christian) that are included within the canon of Scripture.

Hall also employs an intertextual approach within the Hebrew Bible in her attempt to resolve issues in interpretation. For example, when Charles disrupts the narration of events in Joshua to protest the destruction of Achan's children by God (Josh 7:16–26), Mother suggests that the innocence of children cannot

---

Young (*Brown's Dictionary of the Bible* [Philadelphia: Young, 1792]). Elsewhere, in a chapter entitled "Biblical Criticism" (Hall, *Selections from the Writings*, 36–37), Hall defends the authenticity of the words of Jesus praying in the Garden of Gethsemane (Mark 14). She argues that the disciples were able to hear and remember the words because they were close by (Mark 14:35; Luke 22:41) and, subsequently, were aided by the Holy Spirit in recalling the words of Jesus (John 14:26). Furthermore, Hall points to the lack of a statement in the Gospels that the disciples were asleep for the entire duration of the prayer in the garden.

be assumed because the text is silent on that subject (143). As a counterargument to Charles's suggestion that God has punished the innocent along with the guilty, Mother denies the proposition by referring to Deut 24:16. Only the guilty bear the consequences of their own transgressions. By deduction, Mother concludes that the family shared in the guilt of Achan by concealing the stolen items. Confidence that Scripture is formed under divine inspiration and superintendence allows Hall to answer these challenges. At the heart of the undertaking is the unwavering assurance in the consistency of Scripture regarding the nature of God and the requirements for faithful religious practice.

Conversations on the Roles of Women

In her interpretation of biblical narratives, Hall attends to women's interests. For example, in recounting the suffering of the Israelites at the hands of Amalek in 1 Sam 30:1–6, Hall laments the lack of attention in biblical commentaries to the perspective of the Israelite women, among others, in the narrative:

> Although the pen and the pencil have borrowed some of their finest subjects from the Bible, it yet contains many that remain untouched. The story before us is one of these. The distress of the Israelitish women on the irruption of the barbarians—the conflagration of their dwellings before their eyes, and their own captivity; the desolate scene on the return of fathers, lovers, husbands—the united cries of grief and rage—the tumultuous rush of desperate men to pursue the spoilers, and the sudden recovery of all their treasures, are affecting circumstances, on which genius might delight to dwell. (209)

Hall's focus on the effect of the destruction and the captivity of the women is prominent. Of greater import, perhaps, is her observation that the dismay and desperation of the men (fathers, lovers, husbands) in discovering the loss of their households, including their women, spurs them on to the pursuit of the enemy. In a later narrative, the writer's attention to the loss (1 Sam 30:5) and recovery (30:18) of David's two wives supports Hall's suggestion that loyalty to the women motivated the pursuit. The perspectives of women and their importance to men are highlighted in Hall's reading of Scripture. Elsewhere Hall praises Abigail for her role in averting disaster for her husband Nabal in 1 Sam 25:1–18 (205–6). In Mother's account of eliminating David's hostility against Nabal, David's repentance is not due to his mercy (v. 35) or even directly to the grace of God (v. 34). Rather, it is the divinely ordained ingenuity of Abigail as a mediator between violent and impetuous men that saves the day. The words of David (v. 33) acknowledge the superiority of Abigail's judgment in the matter.

Perhaps the most significant discussion of women's roles occurs in the conversation about Deborah and Jael in Judg 4:1–5:31. Fanny comments that the appointment of Deborah as judge over Israel is an indication of the equality of the feminine to that of the masculine intellectual capability (159). Mother agrees, with the additional note that the appearance of inequality in nineteenth-century America is due to the lack of investment in the education of women. The complaint addresses the observation that women's education, by and large, is allotted less than half of the twenty-one years afforded men. Women, thus, are forced to rely on meager educational resources to discharge their duties within the domestic sphere.[26] Notwithstanding this injustice, it remains the will of God, in Hall's perspective, that women remain under the authority of their husbands and fathers and that they focus their energies on domestic matters.

In other writing, Hall expands her views on women's roles and women's education. An examination of these will provide a more complete picture of how she understands the separate spheres and roles that are assigned to women and men and what needs to be reformed in nineteenth-century America.

HALL's VIEWS ON WOMEN's ROLES

Hall's designation of the domestic realm as the primary responsibility of women stems from her observation of women's diminished physical capacity in relation to that of men.[27] For Hall, "the delicate texture of the female frame" is indicative of her suitability for "the discharge of all those interesting duties" that flow from the "employments of social and domestic life." The command of Scripture—the second source of the communication of divine will in the matter—in accordance with the image of the good wife in Prov 31:10–13 is for women to attend faithfully to the management of the household.[28] Men are to be engaged in intercourse with the world, braving the storms of public life and pursuing wealth and honors. Women, however, are to be content with "the modest shade of retirement," eschewing "display and notoriety."[29] Even within the domestic realm, women are to surrender all authority to their husbands in the government of the family in accordance with scriptural doctrine.[30] All power resides in the hands of the man; the husband is to exercise jurisdiction in whatever proportion he should choose. Any attempt to usurp this prerogative is "degrading to the dignity of her character." With regard to a husband's pleasure, the good wife "knows no pleasure equal to the pleasure of pleasing him." The husband's "convenience" is "the object of her cares and labours." Toward this end, she is "to spend and be spent in his ser-

---

26. Hall certainly has in mind here the task of educating youth in the home. In the following discussion of her work, this task clearly falls within the female sphere according to Hall's definitions.

27. Hall, "On the Extent of Female Influence," 1–2.

28. Ibid., 5.

29. Ibid., 2.

30. Ibid., 4.

vice."[31] The dominion of a woman ought to be perceived indirectly, through the lives of her husband and her sons.[32] For Hall, this is the dictate of Scripture and the witness of nature in the designated physical form of women.

One of the domestic tasks that fall to women is the education of young children. This task builds on the natural affection a child holds for the mother and the consequent influence the mother has over the child. According to Hall, this attachment often is severed only by death.[33] The child's affection leads to concern for how one's actions will affect one's mother. Moreover, the intimacy of the relationship allows a mother to discern the unique dispositions of each child for particular vices and to correct that propensity in its early stages.[34] Early training through such corrective measures gives rise to healthy dispositions, intellectual or moral, well into adulthood. A mother's influence cannot be gainsaid.

For Hall, competence in running the household and education of the young is the goal of education for females. Any objective beyond this is regarded as a departure from the norm. On the subject of the study of the classical languages, for example, Hall deems that the female intellect certainly is capable of such study. Notwithstanding this capability, Hall's definition of the purpose of education for females excludes such study, placing it beyond the practical requirements of the curriculum:

> Let it not be imagined that we are enemies to the language of Homer or Virgil, or even that we think lightly of their value. We commend, not only them, but the whole circle of science, to every *man* to whom they can be useful. We are merely contending, that they are not necessary to the fulfilment of a woman's duties; nor would they add to the graces of her conversation—consequently, they are not essential to her complete education.[35]

The study of Greek and Latin, according to Hall, is for the enrichment of literary appreciation, an aspect of children's education under the auspices of more formal modes of education outside the domestic realm.[36] A second purpose for the cultivation of the knowledge of classical terminology and imagery is the formation of

---

31. Ibid., 3. It should be noted that the general tenor of Hall's writing clarifies and restricts the nature of this authority of the husband. In an allegorical work on the challenges of marriage ("The Garden of Wedlock," in *Selections from the Writings*, 38–42) Hall, for example, speaks in a disparaging tone of a husband who "thinks *submission* comprises the whole of a woman's duty!" The husband is warned, if he means to reach the "temple" (the place of marital harmony and bliss), that he must allow his wife to pursue her own interests beyond domestic duties, as these interests are dictated by her talents.

32. Hall, "On the Extent of Female Influence," 5.

33. Ibid., 6.

34. Ibid., 7.

35. Hall, "On Female Education," 21–22.

36. Ibid., 20.

an author's imagination, a vocation beyond the ambitions of proper women.[37] On a positive note, Hall considers geography, grammar, arithmetic, French, certain aspects of astronomy, and the best of literature in English essential for the education of women.[38]

While Hall is supportive of such domestic roles for women, her criticism of the social practices that prevent a woman from fulfilling her vocation erodes her argument for such a calling specific to women. Can domestic tasks be sustained solely by women? Hall's perspective in "On the Extent of Female Influence" attributes the inadequacy of female education to cutting short a young girl's education because of the "peculiar and paramount duties" required of young women.[39] She goes on to recommend that the entertainment of guests, one of the duties of the domestic realm, ought to be curtailed in favor of allotting more time for the education of young girls. Elsewhere Hall discloses in more detail the barriers to the completion of women's education. A young girl is often obliged to attend to training in the requirements of etiquette and dress, the prerequisites of entertaining in polite society. Sewing and the general upkeep of a home absorb the rest of time not devoted to such duties. With the plethora of tasks set before young women, according to Hall, they may become only superficially competent in academic subjects.[40] The onset of marriage and the arrival of children multiply these labors, with the result that an hour taken to pore over a book is a rare occurrence. Can a woman charged with educating her young children, acquiring and maintaining the skills to do so, and maintaining the other elements of domestic order accomplish her goals given the social expectations placed upon her? It should be noted that the context for Hall's complaints in "On Female Education" is an argument to exclude women from the study of the classical languages, in order to uphold their traditional roles.[41] Hall is supportive of a traditional interpretation of the distinction between the genders. However, the incompatibility of domestic responsibilities with the acquisition of a thorough education adequate to the tasks of the home (even without the study of the classical languages) is implicit to Hall's

---

37. Hall's knowledge of the classical languages (and Hebrew) and her status as an author, presumably, are exceptions to her prescribed norms for the roles of women in society.

38. Hall, "On the Extent of Female Influence," 10.

39. Ibid., 9.

40. Hall, "On Female Education," 22–24. A similar conflict between a woman's preparation for domestic duty and the burdens of that duty is seen in another essay defending the virtues of American women to a British audience ("Defence of American Women," in *Selections from the Writings*, 43–53). The task of assisting their mothers in household chores and the acquisition of the "ornamental" skills of drawing, dancing, and music (for the entertainment of the household) take away precious time required for academic instruction, a necessary component in fostering the ability "to think, and act, in all the vicissitudes, and on every occasion of life" (46).

41. Hall, "On Female Education," 17–21.

argument. Hall accepts the prescribed roles for women while decrying the heavy burden of family duties.

Contributing to the weariness of women's tasks in the household is the husband's lack of involvement. Hall's proposal of a distinct calling for women to the domestic realm does not absolve husbands of responsibility in running the affairs of the home. The distinction between the sexes in regard to the duties of the home, in Hall's view, is a difference in the degree of responsibility. Hall stipulates that the obligation for the nurture of the young is distributed between parents, even if the bulk of the duties fall to the female.[42] Hall exhorts husbands to assume a more supportive role in raising children, and she admonishes them for their tendency to undermine the efforts of their wives in the instruction of the young:

> Now, how distressing is the embarrassment of a conscientious woman, who must in her conversations with her children, either censure their father, or concur in his errors; we will use no harsher term, for we are willing to believe, that such conduct arises from a thoughtless compliance with the ways of the world. A man of any reputation would be shocked to be told that he was an instructor in vice.[43]

When the tasks of maintaining domestic efficiency and acquiring the skills to do such are combined with the requirement that the husband share in household responsibilities, a more egalitarian approach to the division of labor results. The solution to women's woes, according to Hall, is that men assume more domestic duties. Hall's theory of women's affinity for domestic duty by natural design and biblical prescription is compromised in her call for husbands to participate more in family life.

Another element that threatens Hall's theory on the roles of the sexes occurs in her recognition of exceptions to the divine summon of women to marriage, motherhood, and domestic duty.[44] Hall recognizes the contribution of women who pursue other vocations, exercising the talents bestowed upon them for the benefit of society. Specific examples of such beneficial employment include "the diffusion of knowledge, the relief of the indigent, and the promotion of Christianity."[45] The means to carry out such duties, in Hall's estimation, are teaching through Sunday schools and the distribution of religious literature through tract

---

42. Hall, "On the Extent of Female Influence," 7.

43. Ibid., 8.

44. Ibid., 12–13.

45. Ibid., 12. Lawrence Cremin (*American Education: The National Experience, 1783–1876* [New York: Harper & Row, 1980], 60–61) speaks of the use of the women's auxiliary by the Bible Society, the Tract Society, and the Sunday-School Union for selling subscriptions to and collecting funds from rural households. The opportunities afforded women in such evangelistic activities, according to Cremin, were seen by women as a relief from strict adherence to domestic duties in the early part of the nineteenth century. These evangelical auxiliaries spawned institutions for the education of women for the support of their ministries.

societies. While maintaining the legitimacy of a general exclusion of women from the profession of writing, Hall attests to the unique contributions of women's writing. For Hall, the female pen is devoid of pretension and most suitable for popular communication across the distinctions of class. This natural ability of female writers and the flagrant need to spread Christianity through literature leads Hall to exhort women not to withhold from society their talent for writing.[46]

While it may be said that exceptions prove the rule, it is true also that they weaken its validity. Does this departure from Hall's norms regarding the roles of the sexes represent a gradual erosion in the author's views for the division of labor within the Christian home? Hall's positive evaluation of the extension of a woman's influence beyond the household goes hand in hand with references to the improvement of women's education, meager as they are, as an advancement of her time. The contributions of women beyond the domestic realm and society's designation of resources to meet those tasks stand out, by Hall's assessment, as the achievements of her generation.[47] These advances are seen by Hall to be products of a genuine Christian piety.[48] Such remarks have led Hardesty to view Hall's advocacy as contributing to the wave of change that expanded women's opportunities and rights.[49] However, it remains unclear whether Hall's opinions on gender roles are a thoughtful defense of an older position in the face of challenges by recommending minimal concessions from a traditional position, or if they are calculated statements advancing the newer egalitarian perspective.

---

46. Hall, "On the Extent of Female Influence," 15–16.

47. Ibid., 2–3; Hall, "On Female Education," 17–18. According to these two essays, these achievements include a shift in public opinion allowing for an increase in the participation of women in public life in schemes for moral advancement and improved educational opportunities for women. An expanded curriculum for female education had provision for instruction in grammar, geography, history, modern languages, and the natural sciences. For an overview of the ideals in educational reform in the nineteenth century as exemplified by the Common School Movement, see H. Warren Button and Eugene F. Provenzo Jr., *History of Education and Culture in America* (Englewood Cliffs, N.J.: Prentice-Hall, 1983), 84–112. It is almost certain that Hall is speaking of the emphases upon the cultivation of a responsible citizenry and social equality in postcolonial America that stand behind the educational reforms in the early nineteenth century. The Common School Movement advocated public financial support for a system of schools to cultivate a skilled and disciplined workforce with an informed (and uniformed) political consciousness. Riding the momentum of an egalitarian spirit seeking to narrow the gap between socioeconomic classes, the number of women's academies grew in the nineteenth century. In addition to the purpose of education for domestic duties, women were trained with a view toward the distinct possibility of a profession in teaching. Indeed, certain advocates for change, as noted by Cremin (*American Education*, 120), saw the proper education of women as being crucial for the intellectual and moral propagation of subsequent generations of citizens in the new independent nation.

48. Hall, "On the Extent of Female Influence," 12–13.

49. Hardesty, "Sarah Ewing Hall," 225.

A Summary Description of Hall's Catechism
and Views on Women's Roles

Conversations on the Bible is a positive contribution to the genre of catechistic literature that strikes a balance between the fundamental aspects of the genre and the innovative features of Hall's time. It may be said that the book maintains the essential components of dialogue, Scripture reference, and exhortation. An examination of the book's distinctive features reveals its unique functions. In terms of the degree of prominence, reference to Scripture dominates in Hall's catechism. The general chronological progression of narrative in the Hebrew Bible is the backbone of the catechism. Mother's aim is to tell the story of Scripture, not to examine the children on points of theology and dogma. This approach, as well as the domestic setting, is of course in line with Hall's concern for women as educators in the home, as opposed to catechism through examination in an ecclesiastical setting. In a form contrary to most catechisms, the questions are not posed by the catechizer. Like most catechisms, the questions explore theological matters, but only as these arise from the narrative. Where exhortation occurs, it does so on occasions where biblical characters provide positive or negative examples. Thus, the dialogue and the acts of exhortation respectively serve and are determined by the narrative. The paraphrase of the Hebrew Bible pays attention to matters pertaining to motivation and intertextuality. In assessing Hall's contribution, it may be said that her encouragement to readers to attend to the narrative, to enter the world of the story, is an improvement to the isolated engagement with doctrinal formulation in some earlier works.

In addressing matters of significance in the world of the author, the subject of the function of gender in society is of interest. This subject is discussed briefly in commentary on biblical narratives and receives fuller attention in two essays. There, despite a rigorous defense of a predominantly domestic role for women, Hall's articulations on the subject display a drift toward a more egalitarian perspective on the division of labor in the home. This burgeoning egalitarian perspective is endemic to Hall's demand for greater attention to women's education and for an expanded role for women in affairs beyond the home.

Bibliography

Bremer, Francis J. "Puritanism." *ER* 12:102–6.

Button, H. Warren, and Eugene F. Provenzo Jr. *History of Education and Culture in America.* Englewood Cliffs, N.J.: Prentice-Hall, 1983.

Cremin, Lawrence. *American Education: The National Experience, 1783–1876.* New York: Harper & Row, 1980.

Dalby, Mrs. Thomas. *Dutch Tiles: Being Narratives of Holy Scripture.* London: Mason, 1842.

Demers, Patricia. *Heaven upon Earth: The Form of Moral and Religious Children's Literature to 1850.* Knoxville: University of Tennessee Press, 1993.

Demers, Patricia, and Gordon Moyles, eds. *From Instruction to Delight: An Anthology of Children's Literature to 1850*. Oxford: Oxford University Press, 1982.

Hall, Harrison, ed. *Selections from the Writings of Mrs. Sarah Hall, Author of Conversations on the Bible*. Philadelphia: Harrison Hall, 1833.

Hall, Sarah (Ewing). *Conversations on the Bible*. 4th ed. Philadelphia: Harrison Hall, 1827.

Hale, Sarah Josepha. *Woman's Record; Or, Sketches of Distinguished Women from the Creation to A.D. 1854: Arranged in Four Eras with Selections from Female Writers of Every Age*. 2nd ed. New York: Harper & Brothers, 1855.

Hardesty, Nancy. "Sarah Ewing Hall." Pages 224–25 in vol. 2 of *American Women Writers*. Edited by Lina Mainiero. 4 vols. New York: Ungar, 1980.

Hartley, John E. *The Book of Leviticus*. WBC 4. Dallas: Word, 1992.

Janeway, James. *A Token for Children: Being an Exact Account of the Conversion, Holy, and Exemplary Lives, and Joyful Deaths of Several Young Children*. London: n.p., 1671–72.

Keach, Benjamin. *War with the Devil; Or, The Young Man's Conflict with the Powers of Darkness: In a Dialogue*. London: Harris, 1676.

Kunitz, Stanley Jasspon, and Howard Haycraft. *American Authors 1600–1900: A Biographical Dictionary of American Literature*. New York: Wilson, 1938.

MacDonald, Ruth K. *Literature for Children in England and America from 1646 to 1774*. Troy, N.Y.: Whitson, 1982.

Mather, Cotton. *A Token for the Children of New England*. Boston: Boone, 1700.

Mortimer, Favell Lee (Bevan). *Line upon Line; Or, A Second Series of the Earliest Instruction the Infant Mind Is Capable of Receiving*. 2 vols. London: Hatchards, 1876–77.

Vincent, Nathanael. *The Principles of the Doctrine of Christ; Or, A Catechism unto Which Is Added a Catechism for Conscience*. London: Parkhurst, 1691.

White, Thomas. *A Little Book for Little Children*. London: n.p., 1693.

Wilson, James Grant, and John Fiske, eds. *Appleton's Cyclopaedia of American Biography*. 7 vols. New York: Appleton, 1888.

Wilson, Lucy. *Mamma's Bible Stories, for Her Little Boys and Girls: A Series of Reading Lessons Taken from the Bible, and Adapted to the Capacities of Very Young Children*. 7th ed. London: Grant & Griffith, 1842.

Wooden, Warren. *Children's Literature of the English Renaissance*. Louisville: University of Kentucky Press, 1986.

Young, William. *Brown's Dictionary of the Bible*. Philadelphia: Young, 1792.

Wisdom and Mercy Meet: Catherine McAuley's Interpretation of Scripture

Elizabeth M. Davis

Introduction

Catherine McAuley (1778–1841) lived in a time when lay Catholics did not read the Bible. In fact, there is no direct evidence that McAuley had her own Bible. She was not a "Scripture scholar." Yet Scripture significantly influenced McAuley and the community of religious women she founded. That influence has extended over 170 years, to more than thirty countries and approximately thirty thousand women who have been Sisters of Mercy and millions of people whose lives the sisters have touched in their ministries of health care, education, parish work, social services, justice, housing, administration, catechetics, and communications.

McAuley's interpretation Scripture is evident in her own words and in her adaptations of the words of others and is reflected in the use of Scripture in the works of the first sisters in her community. Her engagement with the text anticipates emerging directions in biblical hermeneutics today.

Historical Context

McAuley's interpretation is situated in the contexts of early nineteenth-century Ireland and Catholic biblical interpretation. This is how Helen Marie Burns and Sheila Carney describe McAuley's Ireland:

> Catherine, born in 1778, matured in the early decades of the nineteenth century in Ireland. Unemployment was high, especially in urban areas where poorhouses and workhouses multiplied as fast as factories. Rapid industrialization as well as crop failure impelled hundreds of farmers to migrate toward urban areas for assistance and employment. Uneven educational opportunities, neighborhood decay and urban and rural tensions resulted from both discrimination and migration. Modern progress eased life's burdens for some, while

civil war, political unrest and disease weakened the support systems of many others, mainly women and children.[1]

McAuley realized that this desperate social situation, especially for women and children, demanded leadership. She gave and inspired such leadership through a new community of women who helped poor people find new ways to address the challenges they faced.

The second contextual element involves the attitude of lay Catholics to the Bible in nineteenth-century Ireland. The Roman Catholic Church had become a church of law and sacraments rather than a church of the gospel and the word, with the result that Catholics often neglected the spiritual riches contained in the Bible.[2] There was a popular misconception that Catholics were forbidden to read the Bible and that indeed the Bible was a Protestant book. In nineteenth-century Ireland, few Catholics who were not theologians, women or men, would have had any familiarity with the Bible.[3] Therefore, scholars have assumed that McAuley would not use Scripture as a resource in creating a community focused on alleviating the social inequities of her time. In fact, the opposite is true. Scripture became an essential element in her establishment of a religious community designed to influence social development in Ireland and beyond.

McAULEY'S LIFE

McAuley was born into a prosperous middle-class Catholic family in Dublin. From her father, she learned to respond personally to the needs of those around her; from her mother, she learned to function graciously in society. As a young adult, she became a companion for a Quaker woman, Mrs. Callaghan, with whom she lived for twenty-five years. After Mr. and Mrs. Callaghan died, McAuley established a large house in central Dublin with money she had inherited from them. She gathered a number of young, often wealthy women to help the young women who came into Dublin for work but who were without skills or protection. In 1831, following the direction of Church leaders, she founded the Congregation of the Sisters of Mercy.[4]

---

1. Helen Marie Burns and Sheila Carney, *Praying with Catherine McAuley: Companions for the Journey* (Winona, Minn.: Saint Mary's, 1985), 15.

2. Avery Robert Dulles, *The Reshaping of Catholicism: Current Challenges in the Theology of Church* (San Francisco: Harper & Row, 1988), 23.

3. In this chapter, the terms *Protestant* and *Catholic* will be used, reflecting the usage of the terms in the publications of nineteenth-century Ireland.

4. For facts about the life of Catherine McAuley, see further Mary Bertrand Degnan, *Mercy unto Thousands: Life of Mother Mary Catherine McAuley, Foundress of the Sisters of Mercy* (Westminster, Md.: Newman, 1957); and Mary Austin Carroll, *Life of Catherine McAuley* (New York: Sadlier, 1890).

McAuley's Own Words

In assessing McAuley's use of Scripture, we look first to her own words found in her letters and writings describing the purpose and nature of the Sisters of Mercy. In personal letters, McAuley used quotations from the Bible in many different ways: direct citations such as, "Oh, death, where is thy sting?" (1 Cor 15:55 DRV);[5] citations with modified grammar to accommodate the statement she was making, as in, "His ways are not like our ways, nor His thoughts like our thoughts" (Isa 55:8);[6] citations modified to accommodate the completion of the quotation in the situation she was describing: "The Sun never, I believe, went down on our anger" (Eph 4:26);[7] allusions to a verse or theme in Scripture: "Since to the obedient victory is given, may God continue his blessings to you" (Prov 21:28);[8] and echoes of scriptural themes, such as, "May God bless and animate you with His own divine Spirit" (Rom 8:14; Gal 4:6).[9] She also used the ending of Paul's letters as her way of ending her own letters: "May God preserve and bless you,"[10] or "God bless you and send you every comfort and restore you to health."[11] In these letters written to guide her first communities, she deliberately appropriated the language and authority of Scripture.

Her purposes in quoting or alluding to Scripture were clear. She wanted her community to "consecrate themselves to the service of the poor for Christ's sake,"[12] and she believed that they would be best prepared to do this if they would "labour to impress humility and meekness by example more than precept—the virtues recommended most by our Saviour and chiefly by example."[13] She was not using biblical proof texts to support doctrinal positions; she was seeking to shape a community that had "the same mind that was in Christ Jesus" (Phil 2:5).

These themes are visible in her adaptation of the Rule of the Presentation Sisters[14] for use by her newly formed community:

---

5. Letter to Mary Francis Ward dated August 1837 in Mary C. Sullivan, ed., *The Correspondence of Catherine McAuley: 1818–1841* (Dublin: Four Courts, 2004), 91.

6. Letter to Mary Catherine Leahy dated 13 November 1840, in ibid., 321.

7. Letter to Mary Elizabeth Moore dated 13 January 1839, in ibid., 180.

8. Letter to Mary Francis Ward dated early 1839 in Mary Angela Bolster, ed., *The Correspondence of Catherine McAuley, 1827–1841* (Cork: Congregation of the Sisters of Mercy, 1989), 79.

9. Letter to Mary Francis Ward dated 23 October 1837, in Sullivan, *Correspondence of Catherine McAuley*, 101.

10. Letter to Mary Francis Ward dated 23 December 1837, in ibid., 116.

11. Letter to Mary Francis Ward dated ca. 25 April 1838, in ibid., 134.

12. Letter to Mary Elizabeth Moore dated 28 July 1840, in ibid., 282.

13. Letter to Mary Elizabeth Moore dated 28 July 1840, in ibid., 283.

14. Each religious institute adopts a rule as its foundation document subject to approval from Rome and developed on the basis of a previous rule from a religious institute that shares a similar ministry or way of life. McAuley, the founder of a new institute, completed her initial formation with the Presentation Sisters and adapted their rule for her community.

> In undertaking the arduous, but very meritorious duty of instructing the poor, the Sisters whom God has graciously pleased to call to this state of perfection, shall animate their zeal and fervor by the example of their Divine Master Jesus Christ, who testified on all occasions a tender love for the poor and declared that He would consider as done to Himself whatever should be done unto them (Matt 7:12).[15]

The original Presentation Rule had spoken about Jesus' "tender love for little children" supported by the Gospel reference "whosoever receiveth these little ones in his name, receiveth himself" (Matt 18:5),[16] a narrow emphasis on the education of children that McAuley broadened to the instruction of poor people by substituting the reference to Matt 7:12.

The themes of a community consecrated to the service of the poor and of sisters formed in the image of Christ are reiterated in *The Spirit of the Institute*, which McAuley adapted from the Jesuit theologian Rodriquez:[17]

> In order to excite and animate us in our daily occupation, let us imagine that God says to us, as we read in Holy Scripture "Fear nothing, it is I who have called you, take courage, and be of resolution" (2 Kgs 13:28) for in the execution of the duties to which I have called you, you are safe, and may confidently say with holy David, "Though I should have to walk in the midst of the shades of night, I will fear nothing because thou are with me" (Ps 22:4).
>
>   The first means by which the saints have recommended to render us most useful to others, is to give good example and to live in sanctity.... It was for this reason that our Blessed Savior marked the way to Heaven by His example. "Jesus Christ," says Saint Luke, "began to do and to teach" (Acts 1). Thus signifying to us that we should do first what we would induce others to do.[18]

---

15. "Rule and Constitutions," in Mary C. Sullivan, *Catherine McAuley and the Tradition of Mercy* (Notre Dame, Ind.: University of Notre Dame Press, 1995), 295. The rule is the foundational document of a religious institute in which members pronounce public vows and live a life in common as brothers or sisters. Constitutions embody the charism and theology of a religious community and set down norms to govern its life and activities.

16. Ibid., 262.

17. *The Practice of Christian and Religious Perfection*, written by the Spanish Jesuit theologian Alonso Rodriquez and published at Seville in 1609 (with multiple editions and translations), is a book of practical instructions on all the virtues that make up the perfect Christian life, whether lived in the cloister or in the world. *The Spirit of the Institute*, using theology and language from Rodriquez's book, is the work in which McAuley describes the vocation of the Sisters of Mercy. Undated and untitled manuscripts of the essay now known as *The Spirit of the Institute* are found in McAuley's handwriting at archives in the Convent of Mercy in Bermondsey, London, and in the Convent of Mercy in Carysfort Park, Blackrock, Dublin.

18. Quotations from McAuley, *The Spirit of the Institute*. See Mary C. Sullivan, "Catherine McAuley's Theological and Literary Debt to Alonso Rodriguez: The 'Spirit of the Institute' Parallels," *Recusant History* 20 (1990): 98–99. Sullivan refers to the copy of the essay in Mary Ignatia Neumann, ed., *Letters of Catherine McAuley, 1827–1841* (Baltimore: Helicon, 1969), 385–91.

She had slightly modified the reference from 2 Kgs 13:28 by substituting "I who have called you" for "I that command you" and by deleting "men" in "be of resolution," reflecting the choice her sisters had in their response to the call to religious life and the inclusivity inherent in that call.

Scriptural references were woven throughout McAuley's directions to her trusted companions. In acknowledging the early deaths of the first sisters and the resistance from the clergy that her young community faced, McAuley said, "Without the Cross the real portion of the Crown cannot come" (Rev 2:10).[19] She expressed her desire that her sisters love one another by saying, "If the number full I find united in one heart and mind, I'll bless my store" (Acts 4:32).[20] She constantly relied on trust in God's providence and reminded the sisters to "put your whole confidence in God (1 John 3:21). He will never let you want necessities for yourself or your children."[21] Despite the crosses of their ministry, she emphasized joy in doing God's work with the words, "If He looks on us with approbation for one instant each day it will be sufficient to bring us joyfully on to the end of our journey" (Ps 94:1).[22] McAuley cited Scripture authoritatively to direct, motivate, and support her new community. She confirmed her leadership by weaving Scripture through all her letters and using Scripture-like blessings at the conclusion of each letter.

A tract that highlights both the social and religious reality of nineteenth-century Ireland and the misconceptions about Catholics and the Bible has been attributed to McAuley.[23] Written after the repeal of the British Penal Laws when the Catholic Church once again had legitimate standing in Ireland, *Cottage Controversy* avoids language of prejudice and self-righteousness.[24] It presents a series of conversations between Margaret Lewis, a humble Catholic cottager, and Lady P., the Protestant lady of the manor. In a discussion on the Catholic practice of confession, the following conversation takes place:

---

19. Letter to Mary Elizabeth Moore dated 21 March 1840, in Sullivan, *Correspondence of Catherine McAuley*, 259.

20. Letter to the Sisters at Baggot Street dated 12 May 1840, in ibid., 267.

21. Letter to Mary Angela Dunne dated 20 December 1837, in ibid., 115.

22. Letter to Mary deSales White dated 20 December 1840, in ibid., 332.

23. Although the term *tract* has several meanings, ranging from a lengthy theological discourse to a short written work of either political or religious nature, in the nineteenth century tracts generally were religious works written in small pamphlets and used by both Catholics and Protestants to defend their religious positions.

24. Catherine McAuley, *Cottage Controversy* (1883; repr., Baltimore: Lowry & Lubman, 1964). In a letter to Mary Josephine Warde, dated 18 October 1839, McAuley wrote: "Tell dear Sr. M. Vincent that I am quite disappointed that she never writes me one little note. I fear she will not patronize my next work, I dare not venture to dedicate it to her, if she does not give me more encouragement." To date, most published copies of McAuley's life or writing infer that this is a reference to *Cottage Controversy*. However, an original copy of the tract has not yet been found. See Sullivan, *Correspondence of Catherine McAuley*, 123.

Lady P.: We should depend on the holy Bible, and not on the voice of men or tradition, as you Roman Catholics term it.

Margaret: Sure it is in the Protestant Bible that Thomas[25] has—nothing can be plainer—when our blessed Saviour, rose from the dead, and came into the room where the disciples were, though the doors and the windows were shut, standing in the midst of them; that when he had saluted then and said, "My peace be with you," he breathed on them, saying "Receive ye the Holy Ghost; whose sins ye forgive, they are forgiven" (John 20:22).[26]

In typical Protestant fashion, Lady P. elevates Scripture over tradition. Margaret's response shows that she can engage the issues within the parameters set by Lady P. as she defends the sacrament of confession on the basis of Scripture teaching.

In another example, Lady P. and Margaret speak about the Catholic devotion to Mary. Here again Lady P. criticizes, and Margaret defends by quoting Scripture:

Lady P.: Speak truly, are you not taught to believe that she has the same power as Christ himself?

Margaret: Sure, the Blessed Virgin never thought it, for when she said, "All generations shall call me blessed," she added, "Because he that is mighty has done great things for me" (Luke 1:48-49).[27]

The tract illustrates the depth of theology understood by the two women, the respect they show each other, and their knowledge of the words of the Bible as well as doctrines regarding its authority. These two women from different social and economic classes are presented as reading the Bible and conversing on theological and scriptural issues, activities rarely attributed to women in the nineteenth century and certainly not women from different religious traditions. The association of the tract with McAuley highlights her understanding of the religious and social realities of her time. Even more, it shows that she knew the Bible and applied its teachings in the real world with the conviction and confidence that such was legitimately women's work.

WORDS OF MCAULEY'S FOLLOWERS

The centrality of Scripture in McAuley's teaching is reflected in the written and artistic works of the first members of her community. After McAuley's death, Mary Clare Moore and Mary Vincent Harnett wrote their memories of her, often associating moments of her life with Scripture. Moore noted that, on an occasion when the sisters were deeply saddened by the illness of one of their number,

---

25. Thomas, Margaret's husband, had become a Catholic when he married Margaret.
26. McAuley, *Cottage Controversy*, 33.
27. Ibid., 43–44.

McAuley "repeated aloud the verse of the *Benedicite* said in the Refectory at Easter: 'This is the day the Lord hath made; let us rejoice and be glad therein' (Ps 117:24), reminding them that the trial came from Him Whose will we ought not only to obey but love with our whole hearts."[28] When speaking about her death, Moore said McAuley could die saying, "Now Thou dost dismiss Thy servant, O Lord, according to Thy word in peace. Because mine eyes have seen Thy salvation" (Luke 2:29).[29] She described how McAuley prepared herself for her last hour, trusting in Jesus' words: "Blessed are the merciful for they shall obtain mercy" (Matt 5:7).[30]

Harnett, in describing the pressure placed on McAuley to establish a religious institute, remembered that McAuley found strength in Jesus' words, "Blessed are ye when they shall revile you, and persecute you, and speak all that is evil against you untruly for my sake, be glad and rejoice for your reward is very great in heaven" (Matt 5:11).[31] She recalled McAuley's frequent exhortations on "St. Paul's description of charity" (1 Cor 13) and her dwelling on Jesus' words, "Learn of me because I am meek and humble of heart" (Matt 11:29).[32] According to Harnett, "Revd. Mother was a great enemy to that spirit of sadness which destroys true devotion, and to inculcate the contrary used often to quote the Scripture which describes our Divine Lord as being neither 'sad nor troublesome' (Isa 42:4)."[33]

These sisters authored other documents that reflect McAuley's influence on their interpretation of Scripture. Based on her memory of McAuley's words, Moore compiled *A Little Book of Practical Sayings* that was to be used by the sisters in their prayer and community life.[34] Among the biblically based references in the *Sayings* are those that provide advice about the struggles of living in community. When faced with incompetent church leaders, McAuley advised, "We may feel assured that however unworthy the persons duly appointed to direct us may appear, God will not fail to enlighten them and give them the necessary graces since Christ saith, 'He who heareth you, heareth me'" (Luke 10:16).[35] In the trials of adjusting to the limitations imposed by the Church for all religious communities, she encouraged the sisters with the words, "Is this restraint, this self-denial, to make us gloomy, sad or peevish? No, such is not His intention for it is to those who deny themselves He has declared that 'his yoke is sweet and His

---

28. Mary Clare Moore, *Excerpts from the Annals of the Convent of Our Lady of Mercy, Bermondsey,* in Sullivan, *Catherine McAuley and the Tradition of Mercy,* 110.

29. Ibid., 124.

30. Ibid.

31. Mary Vincent Harnett, *The Limerick Manuscript,* in ibid., 166.

32. Ibid., 173.

33. Ibid., 180.

34. Mary Clare Moore, *A Little Book of Practical Sayings, Advices and Prayers of Our Revered Foundress, Mother Catherine McAuley* (London: Burns, Oates & Co., 1868).

35. Ibid, 9.

burden light'" (Matt 11:30).[36] Consistent with her emphasis on following the way of Jesus, she stated, "we find those who can enumerate very particularly all that Jesus Christ said and did, but what does He care for that? He said and did so, not that we should recount it in words, but shew Him in our lives, in our daily practice" (Matt 23:1-12).[37] This last reference reinforces the fact that McAuley was less interested in critically analyzing the Bible than she was in using it intentionally to strengthen her community for their ministry.

In a similar attempt to preserve the valued words of their deceased founder, Mary Teresa Purcell recorded from her own memory and the memories of others the *Retreat Instructions* of McAuley.[38] Purcell said of McAuley, "she seemed to inherit the great gift bestowed by God on the Prophet Isaias who said, 'The Lord hath given me a learned tongue, whereby to support with a word him that is weary'" (Isa 50:4).[39] The book shows the differing approaches McAuley used in interpreting specific texts. She used Scripture to lead the sisters to identify personally with the example of the first followers of Jesus: "With the Apostle a religious must consider herself a stranger and pilgrim on earth, having her conversation in heaven" (Phil 3:20).[40] She used a maternal image of God from the Old Testament as a source of comfort for the sisters in their struggles: "God says He will comfort and console us as the loving mother cherishes her child (Isa 49:15), the greatest example of affection he could give."[41] She directly quoted the words of Jesus again as a source of comfort to encourage the sisters: "By practice it will not only become easy but delightful, for Jesus Christ has said, 'My yoke is sweet and My burden light' (Matt 11:30)."[42] She reiterated the need for action rather than words through the sayings of one of Jesus' followers: "It is not sufficient that Jesus Christ be formed in us; he must be recognized in our conduct.... 'let us love not in word nor in tongue but in deed and in truth' (1 John 3:18)."[43] She quoted one of the few Old Testament references to the behavior of women to reinforce that same lesson: "All the glory of the king's daughter is within" (Ps 44:14).[44]

For McAuley, the words of Scripture were decisive, yet they were often presented by her in ways that determined how they should be interpreted. We saw above her adaptation of the words of 2 Kgs 13 in *The Spirit of the Institute*. We read in *Retreat Instructions*, "Look, and make it according to the pattern" (Exod

---

36. Ibid., 14.

37. Ibid., 25.

38. Mary Teresa Purcell, *Retreat Instructions of Mother Mary Catherine McAuley* (ed. M. B. Degnan; Westminster, Md.: Newman, 1952).

39. Sullivan, *Catherine McAuley and the Tradition of Mercy*, 67.

40. Purcell, *Retreat Instructions, 32.*

41. Ibid., 51.

42. Ibid., 51, 144.

43. Ibid., 71.

44. Ibid., 82.

25:40).[45] She rhetorically contrasted what Jesus did not say with what he did say to teach an important lesson: "Jesus Christ did not say, 'Come to me, you that are free from faults' but 'Come to Me, all you that labor and are burdened and I will refresh you' (Matt 11:28)."[46] She commented on the Lukan story of Martha and Mary, subtly using a reference to Matthew to modify the intended lesson of Luke: "The functions of Martha should be done for Him as well as the choir duties of Mary (Luke 10:38–42). He requires that we should be shining lamps giving light to all around us (Matt 5:16). How are we to do this if not by the manner we discharge the duties of Martha?"[47] McAuley's authoritative and confident interpretation permeated these biblically based instructions to the newest community members.

Another document pointing to Scripture's decisive shaping of the thinking of McAuley and the Sisters of Mercy is Harnett's *Catechism of Scripture History*.[48] Using a question-and-answer method, this text was in the tradition of the "penny catechism," a compendium of theological information intended for use in schools.[49] Given the presumed attitude to the Bible by Catholics at this time, it is remarkable that this *Catechism* was ever written and even more that it was extensively used. Indeed, it was revised and published in the United States in 1854.[50] The preface of the *Catechism*, in giving the reason why the text was published, highlights the extensive use of the original material prepared by Harnett:

> The "Catechism of Scripture History" has been some years used in Manuscript in the Schools of the Sisters of Mercy, Limerick, having been compiled by them for the more easy instruction of their pupils. It was commenced in rather a limited form, was gradually added to as the children advanced. It is now deemed advisable to print it, both to prevent the inaccuracies likely to arise from frequent transcripts, and to meet the wishes of those who desired to use copies.[51]

The fourfold purpose of the *Catechism,* outlined in the preface, is to give the children an accurate knowledge of the principal events recorded in Scripture, to give them a clear idea of the time in which each of these events occurred, to familiarize them with the prophecies relating to our divine Lord, and to lead them to

---

45. Ibid., 68.

46. Ibid., 91.

47. Ibid., 155.

48. Mary Vincent Harnett, *A Catechism of Scripture History Compiled by the Sisters of Mercy for the Use of Children Attending Their Schools* (rev. E. O'Reilly; London: Dolman, 1852).

49. J. P. Marmion, "The Penny Catechism: A Long Lasting Text," *Paradigm* 26 (October 1998): n.p. [cited 23 February 2006]. Online: http://w4.ed.uiuc.edu/faculty/westbury/Paradigm/Marmion3.html.

50. The *Catechism of Scripture History* was revised by M. J. Kerney and published by J. Murphy & Co. in Baltimore in 1854.

51. Harnett, *Catechism of Scripture History,* iii.

regard the Old Testament as a figure and a foreshadowing of the New.[52] In other words, the purpose as stated shows a balance between the interpretation of the plain sense of the text and a typological interpretation.

This balance is reinforced in other ways throughout the *Catechism*. The predictions of the prophets and their fulfillment in the coming of Jesus are not included in the chapters about the prophets but are added in a separate chapter.[53] Dates in the Old Testament are given in two forms: A.C. (*Anno Christi*), commonly used by Christians, and A.M. (*Anno Mundi*), commonly used by the Jewish community.[54] Considerable attention is given to history, to genealogies, to the ages of patriarchs and reigns of kings, and to geography. For example, lesson 28 has an exercise on the map of Palestine with questions such as, "What description of climate has Palestine? What are its productions? How is it situated for commerce?"[55] While this *Catechism* still presents the Bible as God's Word and is far from incorporating a historical-critical approach, there is a move away from a purely typological approach and toward an appreciation of the influence of the study of history, travel, archaeology, and social science on the understanding of the biblical texts.

Extensive passages from Scripture are quoted, often including stories in which women play a significant role. The creation story from Gen 1, the story of Ruth, Solomon's wisdom, the marriage of the young Tobias and Sarah, the story of Esther, and the narrative of the martyrdom of the seven Maccabees in the presence of their mother all appear in the *Catechism*. Eve is described as having "yielded to the temptation of the devil," but all other references to events in the Garden of Eden relate to "our first parents" and do not assign Eve any particular blame. The answer to the question of how Jephthah fulfills his vow (Judg 12:39) recalls the dilemma that interpreters have always faced: "some suppose that he consecrated her to God by a vow of perpetual virginity, others that he offered her a holocaust to God."[56] The latter takes a footnote, "Supposing him to have done so, we must say either that what he did was wrong, although perhaps excusable on the ground of ignorance; or that it was justified in a special inspiration of God."[57]

In the New Testament chapters, although the majority of the answers are taken directly from the scriptural texts, there are several interesting asides. There are comments by John Chrysostom on Jesus' hesitancy in responding to the Canaanite woman in Matt 15:22 in order to teach us faith and perseverance in

52. Ibid., iv.

53. Ibid., 179–96.

54. For example, from creation to the flood is from A.M. 1 to 1656 or A.C. 4000 to 2344; the law is given on Sinai in A.M. 2453 or A.C. 1547, in ibid., v.

55. Ibid., 62.

56. Ibid., 74.

57. Ibid., 75.

prayer,[58] and there is a footnote on the identity of the woman who anointed Jesus' feet: "Some commentators think that this Mary and Mary the sister of Lazarus are two distinct persons."[59] All the women in the Old and New Testaments are identified and presented as they are portrayed in the biblical texts. The reader perceives that careful attention is being drawn to the presence of these women.

McAuley's interpretation of Scripture is also reflected in the visual art of the early sisters. Mary Clare Agnew was inspired by the work of the Sisters of Mercy in the poorest parts of Dublin to illustrate the spiritual and corporal works of mercy,[60] and her work was made available in a printed volume, *Illustrations of the Spiritual and Corporal Works of Mercy.*[61] Further study needs to be completed on the extent of the scriptural scenes and allusions used by another sister, Mary Clare Augustine Moore, in her illustrations, which are deemed to be among the best of the illumined works of nineteenth-century Ireland.[62]

While it is not within the scope of this essay to examine the interpretations of subsequent generations of McAuley's community, it is significant that Scripture was formalized in ritual in every Mercy convent after McAuley's death. The Little Office of the Blessed Virgin was said daily in Latin until 1965; since then the Divine Office has been said in the vernacular. Until the 1960s, Ps 129 (130) was recited as the sisters went to meals; Ps 50 (51), as the sisters returned to the chapel after the noon meal; the Magnificat (Luke 1:46–55), with the return to chapel after the evening meal; and the full Grace (with verses from Pss 21, 144, and 116) before and after all meals.[63] McAuley's intentional use of Scripture to form the first sisters was so definitive that it was embedded in the formation and community life of all the sisters who followed in her footsteps.

SOURCES OF SCRIPTURE USED BY MCAULEY

Scholars have still not found the actual Bible that McAuley used. However, Harnett wrote that, when McAuley cared for Mrs. Callaghan during her three-year illness,

---

58. Ibid., 221.

59. Ibid., 262.

60. Corporal and spiritual works of mercy are a Catholic tradition of charitable practices based in Scripture and dated to the early Middle Ages. The spiritual works are to admonish the sinners (Luke 15:7), instruct the ignorant (Mark 16:15), counsel the doubtful (John 14:27), comfort the sorrowful (Matt 11:28), bear wrongs patiently (Luke 6:27–28), forgive all injuries (Matt 6:12), and pray for the living and the dead (John 17:24). The corporal works, based in Matt 25:31–46, are to feed the hungry, give drink to the thirsty, clothe the naked, shelter the homeless, visit the sick, visit the imprisoned, and bury the dead.

61. *Illustrations of the Corporal and Spiritual Works of Mercy, by a Sister of the Religious Order of Our Lady of Mercy, with Descriptive Anecdotes in Four Languages* (London: Dolman, 1840).

62. Sullivan, *Catherine McAuley and the Tradition of Mercy,* 195.

63. Personal conversations with Sisters of Mercy who lived in Mercy convents prior to the 1960s.

"she often read for her some book of moral and religious instruction."[64] Because Mrs. Callaghan was a Quaker, it would be reasonable to assume that most of this reading came from her Bible. It was in those years, according to Doyle, when McAuley had some doubt about her faith, "she had recourse to the celebrated Dr. Beatie who quite convinced her."[65] This priest's name was on the list of subscribers for Ward's *Errata*,[66] a book owned by McAuley, thus implying that she had knowledge of the Protestant Bible. It is likely that McAuley inherited Mrs. Callaghan's books, including her Bible, but to date these books have not been located.

There is substantial evidence that McAuley had access to texts that were biblically based. On the day after McAuley was professed as a religious sister, "The *Little Office of Our Blessed Lady* was recited by all the Sisters together, and in English, according to the Approbation of the Archbishop previously received."[67] In *Cottage Controversy*, Margaret and Lady P. discuss the *Office* in this way:

> Lady P.: Is this a prayer book?
> Margaret: Yes, my lady, the Primer with the office of our blessed lady.
> Lady P.: Oh, Margaret, all the prayers in this great book to the Virgin! You cannot but offend her Creator.
> Margaret: It is odd that you should say that, my lady, for almost the whole office is taken from the Bible.[68]

Mary Clare Augustine Moore noted, "The Archbishop [Murray] ordered that the *Office* should be said in English, and as long as he lived we were not permitted to say it in Latin."[69] The wording is ambiguous, not indicating if the sisters saw this

---

64. Harnett, *Limerick Manuscript*, in Sullivan, *Catherine McAuley and the Tradition of Mercy*, 145.

65. Letter from Mary Ann Doyle to Mary Clare Augustine Moore dated 1844, in Sullivan, *Catherine McAuley and the Tradition of Mercy*, 43.

66. Thomas Ward, *Errata of the Protestant Bible; Or, The Truth of the English Translations Examined* (London: n.p., 1688) (many editions). Texts such as Ward's reflected the Roman Catholic Church's fear that Scripture was being translated by the Reformers to distort the original meaning by changing a few key words with the intention of undermining the authority of the clergy and negating tradition (e.g., *altar* became *table*, *priest* became *elder*, *church* became *congregation*, *grace* became *favor*). Such translations, often accompanied by commentaries that reinforced the differences in theology, were referred to as "Protestant" Bibles.

67. Mary Ann Doyle, *The Derry Manuscript*, in Sullivan, *Catherine McAuley and the Tradition of Mercy*, 60. The Little Office, a shorter version of the Divine Office, contains seven, hours each of which is divided into three psalms, hymns, canticles (Benedictus [Luke 1:68–79], Magnificat [Luke 1:46–55] and Nunc Dimittis [Luke 2:29–32]), anthems and versicles from the psalms, lessons and chapters taken from the Bible, and prayers. See J. M. Lelen, ed., *The Little Office of the Blessed Virgin Mary* (New York: Catholic Book Publishing, 1946), 7–10.

68. McAuley, *Cottage Controversy*, 96.

69. Mary Clare Augustine Moore, *A Memoir of the Foundress of the Sisters of Mercy in Ireland*, in Sullivan, *Catherine McAuley and the Tradition of Mercy*, 206.

as a good direction or as a sign that they were somehow inferior to those congregations who prayed the Office in Latin, the official language of the church. It is not known how long the sisters continued to recite the Office in English before changing to Latin, but we do know the Office was recited every day. Chapter 11 of the Rule and Constitutions says, "As the Sisters of the Institute must employ a great part of their time instructing the poor, they shall be obliged only to the short *Office of Our Blessed Lady* which they shall daily recite together."[70] The extent of McAuley's devotion to the Office was shown when, as she lay dying with extreme soreness in her mouth, "she would go on reading the public lectures, and reciting the *Office* until absolutely incapable of uttering a word."[71]

The public lectures referred to above usually involved reading from *A Journal of Meditations for Every Day in the Year*,[72] a series of biblically based meditations collected from unidentified ascetical writers. At the beginning of her copy dated 1823, McAuley had written a prayer, "Come Holy Ghost, take possession of our hearts and kindle in them the fire of thy divine love."[73] These words recall her description of five young English women who were entering her community: "This is some of the fire He cast on the earth—kindling" (Luke 12:49).[74] In Doyle's words, the sisters "at 6 o'clock assembled in the chapel within the grate for morning prayer which consisted chiefly of the Act of Oblation followed by a meditation from the *Journal* 'till 7,"[75] a practice also described by Moore.[76]

The introduction to the *Journal* notes, "The matter is solid and for the most part grounded on Divine Scripture."[77] An excerpt from the *Journal* gives a sense of the tone of the book, its use of texts from both the Old Testament and the New Testament, and its application of the texts to the daily life of the reader:

Fourth Sunday of Advent—introductory quotation from Luc.19.5 ("Zacheus, come down in haste; because this day I must abide in thy house"), consideration

---

70. Rule and Constitutions 11:1, in Sullivan, *Catherine McAuley and the Tradition of Mercy*, 306.

71. Harnett, *Limerick Manuscript*, in Sullivan, *Catherine McAuley and the Tradition of Mercy*, 188.

72. Nathaniel Bacon, *A Journal of Meditations for Every Day in the Year Gathered out of Divers Authors* (trans. E. Mico; 1669; repr., Ann Arbor: University Microfilms, 1984), A3. Although the title refers to "Divers Authors," the names of these writers are not recorded in the text.

73. Sisters of Mercy of the Americas, ed., *Praying in the Spirit of Catherine McAuley* (Chicago: Institute of the Sisters of Mercy of the Americas, 1999), 53–54.

74. Letter to Mary Elizabeth Moore dated 28 July 1840, in Sullivan, *Correspondence of Catherine McAuley*, 282.

75. Doyle, *The Derry Manuscript*, in Sullivan, *Catherine McAuley and the Tradition of Mercy*, 54.

76. Letter from Mary Clare Moore to Mary Clare Augustine Moore dated 1844, in ibid., 90.

77. Bacon, *Journal of Meditations*, A3.

on Christ's desire to become the guest of your souls ("I stand at the dore and knock" Apoc. 3.20), consideration on your making ready the room of your heart ("prepare the way" Luc.3.4, and "Lord I am not worthy" Luc. 7.6), and consideration on those who "anciently did entertain their guests" (Abraham the three Angels—Gen.18.3&c, the Sunamite woman, the Prophet Elizeus—4 Reg.4.8 and Martha Christ himself—Luc.10.38) with a final quotation from Prov.23.26 ("my son, give me thy heart").[78]

This interweaving of texts, meant for a day that celebrated the coming of Jesus, is an interesting intertextual approach to Scripture. The New Testament references use Jesus' words to speak about his presence in the life of a person. The Old Testament references are not used typologically or allegorically but give concrete examples of hosts (men and women) who show respect for their guests. The reader is invited to envision the narratives of the Old and New Testaments and to emulate the women and men associated with them as a preparation for the coming of Christ.

Two other biblically based devotional texts favored by McAuley were *The Following of Christ* and *A Paraphrase on the Seven Penitential Psalms*.[79] *The Following of Christ* was written about 1530 by Thomas à Kempis. Of Scripture, Thomas wrote:

> Charity and not eloquence is to be sought in Holy Scripture, and it should be read in the same spirit with which it was first made. We also ought to seek in Holy Scripture spiritual profit rather than eloquence of style.... Almighty God speaks to us in His Scriptures in various manners, without regard for persons.... if you will profit by reading Scripture, read humbly, simply and faithfully.[80]

This way of approaching Scripture was a model for McAuley, about whom Moore relates: "She did not like the Sisters to use long words in speaking or writing, remarking that in the Psalms and other parts of Holy Scripture inspired by divine wisdom, there was scarcely a word more than three syllables."[81] McAuley's favorite chapters from *The Following of Christ* contained quotations from and multiple allusions to the Gospels, Deuteronomy, the historical books, and the Psalms.[82]

78. Ibid., 66–67.

79. Moore, *Annals of Convent of Our Lady of Mercy,* in Sullivan, *Catherine McAuley and the Tradition of Mercy,* 116; repeated in Moore, *Little Book of Practical Sayings,* 34.

80. Thomas à Kempis, *The Imitation of Christ* (ed. H. C. Gardiner; 1530; repr., New York: Hanover House, 1955), 37.

81. Moore, *Little Book of Practical Sayings,* 28.

82. Ibid., 35.

A Paraphrase on the Penitential Psalms begins with quotations from Ezekiel, Isaiah, and Luke, all focusing on the sinner doing penance.[83] The author reflects on each verse of the seven psalms (6, 31/32, 37/38, 50/51, 101/102, 129/130, and 142) with paraphrases such as the following:

> *Psalm 50(51):14*–I will teach thy ways to the Unjust, and the Wicked shall turn to Thee. Grant me this favour, my GOD; that I may make some Amends for the Scandal I have to often given to Others. Hear me but, Lord; and I will teach thy Ways to the Unjust, as well in my Practice as in my Discourse. And so exemplary shall my Conduct be that, not only They to whose Crimes I have been any ways accessory, but All the Wicked, who see it, charmed with the sweet Effects of thy Grace and Mercies in me, shall forsake their evil Courses and turn to Thee by a sincere Repentance.[84]

An appendix in the book gives a more scholarly analysis of the seven psalms,[85] using Hebrew and Greek references as exemplified by this discourse on the title of Ps 6:

> Now if we compare this and other like titles with 1 Chronicles xv.21 where the two Synonymous terms *Cinnorath* and *Sheminith* are used, the One for a Harp, the Other, for an Octave … it is highly probable that both senses are true; and that the Royal Psalmist composed this sacred Canticle, to be sung to a particular instrument on a particular Key.[86]

The tradition of using the *Paraphrase* in Lent was common within Mercy communities until the 1960s, when, under the influence of Vatican II, the approach to the prayer and spirituality of religious congregations changed significantly.

COMPARISON WITH SCRIPTURAL INTERPRETATIONS TODAY

An emerging direction in scriptural scholarship is a focus on the meaning of the biblical text not only as intended by the original author or editor but as shaped by the reader or reading community. While it is not the purpose of this essay to explore this approach in detail, it is helpful to consider McAuley's interpreta-

---

83. Francis Blyth, *A Devout Paraphrase on the Seven Penitential Psalms; Or, A Practical Guide to Repentance* (3rd ed.; Dublin: Lamb, 1749). Blyth was an English Carmelite who wrote expositions on many parts of the Bible, including the penitential psalms. Together with Bishop Challoner, he revised the Douay Bible.

84. Ibid., 38.

85. Blyth says in the appendix, "If we follow the sentiments of St. Augustin, and many other considerable Interpreters, they were All composed by David himself. But St. Jerom and Others are of a contrary opinion" (ibid., A3).

86. Ibid., A7.

tion of Scripture in a trajectory with three biblical scholars who share McAuley's Roman Catholic tradition.

Reflecting on the task of biblical interpretation, Raymond Brown differentiates the literal meaning, the canonical meaning, and the meaning over time:

> "Biblical meaning" is not simply what a passage meant to the author who wrote it (literal meaning), or what it meant to those who first accepted it into a normative collection (canonical meaning); biblical meaning is also what the passage means today in the context of the Christian Church. The very existence of the Bible understood as a normative collection of books supposes an ongoing community willing to shape itself by responding to that norm. I would contend that the way in which the Church in its life, liturgy and theology comes to understand the Bible is constitutive of "biblical meaning", because it is chiefly in such a context that this collection is serving as Bible for believers. We are not dealing merely in such an instance with application, accommodation, or eisegesis; we are dealing with the issue of what a biblical book *means*, as distinct from what it *meant*.[87]

Sandra Schneiders understands interpretation in the context of a dialectic involving the worlds of the text and the reader, with neither the meaning of the text nor the reader emerging from the encounter unchanged.[88] She says:

> Appropriation of the meaning of the text, the transformative achievement of interpretation, is neither a mastery of the text by the reader (an extraction of its meaning by the application of method) nor a mastery of the reader by the text (a total submission to what the text says) but an ongoing dialogue with the text about its subject matter. This dialogue is never-ending because of the text's surplus of meaning, which allows it to generate an effective history in interpretation with the historical consciousness of the believing community.[89]

"Rhetorical-emancipatory" is the term by which Elisabeth Schüssler Fiorenza designates a paradigm of biblical interpretation used to interrogate biblical texts, questions, methods, and strategies of interpretation as to their function in political and personal self-understandings and public convictions.[90] She explains this approach to interpretation:

---

87. Raymond E. Brown, *The Critical Meaning of the Bible* (New York: Paulist, 1981), 20, 34–35.

88. Sandra M. Schneiders, *The Revelatory Text: Interpreting the New Testament as Sacred Scripture* (San Francisco: HarperSanFrancisco, 1991), 16.

89. Ibid., 177.

90. Elisabeth Schüssler Fiorenza, *Wisdom Ways: Introducing Feminist Biblical Interpretation* (Maryknoll, N.Y.: Orbis, 2001), 44.

The critical interpretative process or "hermeneutical dance" has as its goal and climax a hermeneutics of transformation and action for change. It explores avenues and possibilities for changing and transforming relations of domination inscribed in texts, traditions and everyday life. It also seeks to articulate religious and biblical studies as a site of social, political, and religious transformation.[91]

Brown's reference to "an ongoing community willing to shape itself by responding to that norm," Schneiders's description of "an ongoing dialogue with the text about its subject matter," and Schüssler Fiorenza's identification of a "hermeneutics of transformation and action for change" are more developed ways of expressing the manner in which McAuley consciously used Scripture to form her community. In the scriptural references woven into her written communications with her sisters living throughout Ireland and the British Isles, in her biblically based descriptions of the purpose and nature of the Sisters of Mercy, and in her assumption of authoritative leadership in interpreting Scripture for her community, this nineteenth-century Irish woman intentionally used the Bible to shape a community of women motivated by the life and teachings of Jesus and dedicated to the service of "the poor, the sick and the ignorant."[92] McAuley's interpretation of Scripture, undertaken to influence the lives of women so that they would in turn influence the world around them, was indeed a moment when wisdom and mercy met and made a difference.

BIBLIOGRAPHY

Bacon, Nathaniel. *A Journal of Meditations for Every Day in the Year Gathered Out of Divers Authors.* Translated by Edward Mico. 1669. Repr., Ann Arbor: University Microfilms International, 1984.

Blyth, Francis. *A Devout Paraphrase on the Seven Penitential Psalms; Or, A Practical Guide to Repentance.* 3rd. ed. Dublin: Lamb, 1749.

Bolster, Mary Angela, ed. *The Correspondence of Catherine McAuley, 1827–1841.* Cork: Congregation of the Sisters of Mercy, 1989.

Brown, Raymond E. *The Critical Meaning of the Bible.* New York: Paulist, 1981.

Burns, Helen Marie, and Sheila Carney. *Praying with Catherine McAuley.* Companions for the Journey. Winona, Minn.: Saint Mary's, 1985.

Carroll, Mary Austin. *Life of Catherine McAuley.* New York: Sadlier, 1890.

Degnan, Mary Bertrand. *Mercy unto Thousands: Life of Mother Mary Catherine McAuley, Foundress of the Sisters of Mercy.* Westminster, Md.: Newman, 1957.

Dulles, Avery Robert. *The Reshaping of Catholicism: Current Challenges in the Theology of Church.* San Francisco: Harper & Row, 1988.

---

91. Ibid., 186–87.

92. Traditional phrase used by the Sisters of Mercy to describe their focus in ministry.

Harnett, Mary Vincent. *A Catechism of Scripture History Compiled by the Sisters of Mercy for the Use of Children Attending Their Schools*. Revised by Edmund O'Reilly. London: Dolman, 1852.

Illustrations of the Corporal and Spiritual Works of Mercy, by a Sister of the Religious Order of Our Lady of Mercy, with Descriptive Anecdotes in Four Languages. London: Dolman, 1840.

Kempis, Thomas à. *The Imitation of Christ*. Edited by Harold C. Gardiner. 1530. Repr., New York: Hanover House, 1955.

Kerney, M. J. *A Catechism of Scripture History*. Baltimore: Murphy, 1854.

Lelen, J. M., ed. *The Little Office of the Blessed Virgin Mary*. New York: Catholic Book Publishing, 1946.

Marmion, J. P. "The Penny Catechism: A Long Lasting Text." *Paradigm* 26 (October 1998). No pages. Cited 23 February 2006. Online: http://w4.ed.uiuc.edu/faculty/westbury/Paradigm/Marmion3.html.

McAuley, Catherine. *Cottage Controversy*. New York: O'Shea, 1883. Repr., Baltimore: Lowry & Lubman, 1964.

Moore, Mary Clare. *A Little Book of Practical Sayings, Advices and Prayers of Our Revered Foundress, Mother Catherine McAuley*. London: Burns, Oates & Co., 1868.

Muldrey, Mary Hermenia. *Abounding in Mercy: Mother Austin Carroll*. New Orleans: Habersham, 1988.

Neumann, Mary Ignatia, ed. *The Letters of Catherine McAuley 1827–1841*. Baltimore: Helicon, 1969.

Purcell, Mary Teresa, and Mary Bertrand Degnan, eds. *Retreat Instructions of Mother Mary Catherine McAuley, 1834–1853*. Westminster, Md.: Newman, 1952.

Schneiders, Sandra M. *The Revelatory Text: Interpreting the New Testament as Sacred Scripture*. San Francisco: HarperSanFrancisco, 1991.

Schüssler Fiorenza, Elisabeth. *Wisdom Ways: Introducing Feminist Biblical Interpretation*. Maryknoll, N.Y.: Orbis, 2001.

Sisters of Mercy of the Americas, ed. *Praying in the Spirit of Catherine McAuley*. Chicago: Institute of the Sisters of Mercy of the Americas, 1999.

Sullivan, Mary C. *Catherine McAuley and the Tradition of Mercy*. Notre Dame, Ind.: University of Notre Dame Press, 1995.

———. "Catherine McAuley's Theological and Literary Debt to Alonso Rodriguez: The 'Spirit of the Institute' Parallels." *Recusant History* 20 (1990): 81–105.

———, ed. *The Correspondence of Catherine McAuley: 1818–1841*. Dublin: Four Courts, 2004.

Ward, Thomas. *The Errata to the Protestant Bible; Or, The Truth of Their English Translations Examined*. London: n.p., 1688.

Mary Anne SchimmelPenninck:
A Nineteenth-Century Woman as Psalm-Reader

Lissa M. Wray Beal

Mary Anne SchimmelPenninck (née Galton, 25 November 1778–29 August 1856) was raised in affluence in Staffordshire, England. Her childhood home welcomed people of refinement who represented varying streams of thought and belief. She was exposed to new scientific and philosophic thought, as well as examples of Christian life and sentiment from Roman Catholic, Church of England, and Dissenting perspectives.

Each of these influences affected SchimmelPenninck's adult convictions. Examination of her interpretation of the Psalms reveals deeply held assumptions and the hermeneutical practices informed by these assumptions, which place her in the precritical interpretive stream. Not unaware of the new historical-critical approaches, she rejects them, reaching back into Roman Catholic thought of the seventeenth and eighteenth centuries and Reformation commitments to form her hermeneutical stance. These influences were joined to her own Dissenting commitment to individual interpretation, contemplative spirituality, and thoroughly evangelical social action. Thus, while a precritical interpreter, her work reveals a unique blend of influences. Moreover, she wrestled hermeneutically with some of the issues common in today's interpretive milieu, yet the outcomes are vastly different, separated as they are by two centuries of historical-critical interpretive models.

This essay examines SchimmelPenninck's life, noting influences that shaped her interpretive work. Then, working with her major writings on the Psalms, it recovers her hermeneutical method. Finally, brief comments will draw connections between her method and the questions and issues of today's interpreters.

Life and Influences

Family

SchimmelPenninck's parents and paternal grandfather were strong influences in her early life. Her mother instilled in her a reverence for the Scriptures through daily Christian instruction and life example. For these, SchimmelPenninck remembers her with respect and warmth. Her paternal grandfather's home was filled with the graces and simplicity of the Quaker faith. There she participated often in the Friends' meetings and remembers that "scarcely knowing it, I felt the influence of that holy presence of God."[1] Despite these early religious influences, she did not come to personal faith in Christ until she was twenty-two years old. While staying in Bath in a Moravian home she came to "know the Lord."[2] Although discipled by Moravians, she also associated herself with the Wesleyan Methodists in her thirties. In 1818, she joined the Moravian church and remained there throughout her life.

SchimmelPenninck remembers her father as a kind man, considerate of her frequent ill-health. He was a man of "superior intellectual endowments ... [interested in] the exact sciences,"[3] and a member of the Royal Society, Linnaean Society, and Lunar Society. Through him, the family circle admitted several men of intellectual stature who excelled in diverse scientific and religious fields (e.g., Joseph Priestly, Benjamin Franklin, and Erasmus Darwin [grandfather of Charles]). This early intellectual exposure did much to shape SchimmelPenninck and is apparent in the hermeneutical underpinnings of her interpretive work of Scripture.

In 1806, SchimmelPenninck married Lambert SchimmelPenninck of Bristol. He was involved with shipping interests that provided a comfortable financial life even after his death. He was variously described by family and friends as "sensible, amiable, well read, but not brilliant," "a religious and a very worthy man," and an "affectionate husband."[4] Although the couple remained childless, SchimmelPenninck educated children from her home. Her husband greatly encouraged SchimmelPenninck's literary endeavors, and her biographer, Christiana Hankin, asserts that "it was mainly owing to his sympathy and wishes that several of her books were published."[5] In 1815, she published *Theory on the Classification of Beauty and Deformity.*[6] *Biblical Fragments*[7] appeared in 1821,

1. Christiana C. Hankin, ed., *Life of Mary Anne SchimmelPenninck* (2 vols.; London: Longman, Brown, Green, Longmans, & Roberts, 1858), 1:55.

2. Ibid., 2:24.

3. Ibid., 1:36.

4. Ibid., 2:57–59.

5. Ibid., 2:85.

6. A philosophical discussion from a Christian perspective of the theories of aesthetics and the sublime expressed in nature and physiognomy. A revision was published posthumously as *Principles of Beauty.*

7. Mary Ann SchimmelPenninck, *Biblical Fragments* (London: Ogle, Duncan, & Co., 1821). A publication "to encourage amongst her own sex a taste for scriptural reading," it arose from SchimmelPenninck's long habit of "noting down in her Bible whatever occurred to her as

demonstrating her Hebrew language skills. *Psalms according to the Authorized Version* followed in 1825.[8]

Widowed in 1840, SchimmelPenninck continued (despite decreasing health that confined her to the home) to pursue her studies, charitable work (including the abolitionist movement), teaching, and counseling. During these years, the Psalms were her constant companions. Many were committed to memory in Hebrew, and she often would recite them, even during the final days of her life. She noted the blessings of her whole life as "more than can be numbered" and quoted Ps 23 as indicative of her feeling: "Mercy and goodness have followed me all the days of my life; and I shall dwell in the house of the LORD for ever."[9]

RELIGIOUS AND EDUCATIONAL INFLUENCES

SchimmelPenninck was an educated woman. The study of classics, poetry, languages (Latin, Greek, Hebrew, Anglo-Saxon), the arts, physiognomy and phrenology, and biblical geography and history indicate the breadth of her education and interests. She was committed to the education of young people, and in the preface to *Biblical Fragments* she encourages parents consciously to educate their children in the Scriptures as the only sure means of inculcating Christian values.

Her commitment to children's education included the education of young women. This was not due to incipient feminism; SchimmelPenninck held conventional societal norms regarding the role of women. She affirmed that a man's education must prepare him for a determinate destination such as a statesman, philosopher, poet, or divine, but a woman's education had a very different object:

> [Woman] has no fixed destiny but the blessed one of being a helper. Her education then, must be a continued training of all her faculties and powers; to be ready with each, to take up or lay down this that or the other, as may be the future pursuit of her husband her father or her brother; or the future calls of

---

throwing light upon the text" (*Biblical Fragments,* vii). Topics discussed are as varied as the two lights of Gen 1:16 and the image of gold in Dan 3:1.

8. Mary Ann SchimmelPenninck, *Psalms according to the Authorized Version; With Prefatory Titles, and Tabular Index of Scriptural References, from the Port Royal Authors, Marking the Circumstances and Chronologic Order of Their Composition: To Which Is Added, An Essay upon the Psalms, and Their Spiritual Application* (London: Arch, 1825). The preface reveals SchimmelPenninck's purpose, intended audience, and sources for this book: "Having found the Port Royal Introduction to the Psalter very useful…; and having found it to furnish a peculiarly interesting and valuable course of family reading to my own household, I thought it might likewise prove acceptable to those of other persons, and more especially so to families in which there were many young people" (*Psalms,* vii).

9. Hankin, *Life of Mary Anne SchimmelPenninck,* 2:271.

the sick-room, the school-room, the dispenser to the poor, or the claims of the social or domestic circle.[10]

Although writing primarily for a female audience and the family circle, her interpretive interests are not undertaken with any self-conscious reflection on her role as a woman interpreter of the Psalms. Her use of the Port Royal authors, her hermeneutical assumptions, and the passages selected for interpretation show she simply takes up the interpretive traditions she inherits and writes as an educated scholar.

Through the family's intellectual circle, young SchimmelPenninck was exposed to developing historical-critical tendencies within the church and academy. Her writings make it clear that such exposure was not a positive influence but introduced doubt into her childhood faith.[11] A pivotal experience came when studying the writings of the family's Unitarian friend, Dr. Joseph Priestly.[12] His works appear, from SchimmelPenninck's account, to have a historical-critical methodology; she also recounts that "my heart sank within me ... his writings set forth produced on me at this time an evil effect."[13] These early experiences were instrumental in her eschewal of a critical hermeneutic. She remarks that Dr. Priestly's works were a "turning point in her own life" and that she had since seen "many ... who have groaned under the same unhappy teaching."[14]

SchimmelPenninck's hermeneutical assumptions cannot be construed without recognizing that she lived through the French Revolution. She viewed the philosophical abandonment of God promulgated during the revolutionary years as a powerful negative force within society. This stood in contrast to the peace and simplicity of her weekly visits to her Quaker grandfather's house.[15] She was profoundly affected by the enduring truthfulness of the faith encountered there, and this was perhaps another influence that encouraged her to disregard a critical hermeneutic.

Throughout her life, SchimmelPenninck associated and conversed with Quakers, Moravians, Methodists, Anglicans, and Roman Catholics and developed an ecumenical spirit. In her writings on the Psalms, she uses several Roman Catholic sources, owning that these writers demonstrated the Roman Catholic

---

10. Ibid., 2:131.

11. Ibid., 1:274–75.

12. Ibid., 1:300. Priestly's *An History of the Corruptions of Christianity* (Birmingham: Johnson, 1782) and *History of Early Opinions Concerning Jesus Christ, Compiled from Original Writers; Proving That the Christian Church Was at First Unitarian* (Birmingham: Johnson, 1786) attack the concept of the Trinity and other tenets of orthodox Christianity.

13. Hankin, *Life of Mary Anne SchimmelPenninck*, 1:302–3.

14. Ibid., 1:306.

15. Ibid., 1:223.

principle of loyal love and faith that she considered indispensable to a correct interpretation of Scripture and to which she committed herself:

> I own I have more predilection for that principle of loyal love, which urges [the soul] on to merge itself in its central sun, than for that principle of self-reliance which tempts us to start off at a tangent, and wander in lonely isolation amidst the wilderness of unexplored thought, or to rush with headlong precipitancy into the wild chaos of conflicting speculation.[16]

One wonders how much of this commitment is also a commentary upon the Protestant Unitarian and historical-critical thought she had encountered as a child and the rising philosophies of unbelief that had so troubled her and that she found unhelpful in addressing her personal questions of faith.

THE INFLUENCE OF PORT ROYAL

SchimmelPenninck's spiritual life and writings were significantly influenced by the Bible translators and annotators of the Cistercian convent of Port Royal. Established in the thirteenth century southwest of Paris, it had by the seventeenth century a reputation for thought and piety that attracted prominent French intellectuals and ecclesiastics. From this religious center came a translation of the Bible in French.[17] In the religious and political storms of the seventeenth century, Port Royal aligned with the Jansenist movement, and this association led to its eventual dissolution by papal bull.[18]

During an 1814 visit to the convent site, SchimmelPenninck added to her existing collection of Port Royal works by acquiring several volumes that were little-known in England. She subsequently published much of the Port Royalists' work and information about the convent in a volume entitled *Select Memoirs of Port Royal*.[19] SchimmelPenninck's work on the Psalms relies heavily upon Port

---

16. Excerpted from correspondence by SchimmelPenninck in which she extols the virtues found in both the Roman and Protestant Churches. See Hankin, *Life of Mary Anne Schimmel-Penninck*, 2:141–44.

17. Sacy's Bible, published 1672–93.

18. Cornelius Jansen, a Dutch theologian, wrote *Augustinus* (published posthumously in 1640). Jansen asserted that Counter-Reformation and Jesuit theology had erred and moved the church into Pelagianism. Port Royal's refusal to condemn Jansenism, as well as its work in education and Bible translation, brought papal discipline and eventual dissolution in 1709. See "Port Royal" *Encyclopaedia Britannica Online*, n.p. [cited 7 March 2006]. Online: http://search. eb.com/eb/article-9060943; "Roman Catholicism, History Of," *Encyclopaedia Britannica Online*, n.p. [cited 7 March 2006]. Online: http://search.eb.com/eb/article-43752.

19. The original edition appeared in 1829 as *Select Memoirs of Port Royal: To Which Are Appended Tour to Alet, Visit to Port Royal, Gift of An Abbess, Biographical Notes, etc. Taken From Original Documents* (London: Arch, 1829).

Royal authors, who are often incorporated into her writing without specific credit (through marginal annotations she made in her Bible). She acknowledges her indebtedness to the Port Royal authors,[20] particularly the value of their annotations regarding the historical occasion for individual psalms.[21] The esteem in which she held the Port Royal authors is broached in a footnote found in *Biblical Fragments*:

> Nothing is more astonishing to the reader of the Port Royal authors than to hear the confident manner with which it is so common for Protestants to deny to *all* their Catholic brethren any acquaintance with Scripture; yet the Port Royal writers alone could furnish some hundred volumes of commentaries, whose elaborate learning has not, perhaps, often been exceeded, and whose spirituality it would, perhaps, be almost impossible to equal.[22]

INTERPRETATION OF THE PSALMS

SchimmelPenninck's work on the Psalms clearly displays her hermeneutical assumptions. Besides the references in her biographical material, two main published works reveal these hermeneutics. The first is a lengthy chapter in *Biblical Fragments* on the spiritual interpretation of the Psalms entitled "Preliminary Observations, Intended to be Prefixed to a Version of the Psalms." Published in 1821, this chapter reappears appended to her second publication, *Psalms*, in 1825. *Psalms* contains the text of the Psalms in the Authorized Version, each with an extensive prefatory title and scriptural references indicating the asserted historical circumstances of the psalm's composition. These two works form the basis for analysis in this paper.

ASSUMPTIONS REGARDING THE HERMENEUTICAL TASK

In *Biblical Fragments* and *Psalms*, SchimmelPenninck affirms the inspiration of revealed Scripture. She takes this for granted and gives no proof.[23] Three corollaries arise from this assumption, each of which is paramount in Schimmel-Penninck's interpretive work. The first corollary is practical: "If it [Scripture] be the only infallible guide, follow it alone."[24] Here we have the impetus for Schimmel-Penninck's lengthy exhortation to biblically based education, for all thought and action must, for a Christian, be founded upon the Scriptures.

---

20. SchimmelPenninck, *Biblical Fragments*, xxxiii; *Psalms*, xvii.
21. SchimmelPenninck, *Psalms*, vii.
22. SchimmelPenninck, *Biblical Fragments*, 114–15.
23. Ibid., xxxii.
24. Ibid.

The second corollary is that inspiration is linked to prophetic authorship. All but fifteen psalms are thus attributed to David as a prophetic figure,[25] and, for those psalms referring to events *after* the life of David, she attributes their authorship to "those who are mentioned, in sacred writ, as invested with the prophetic character at that period."[26] I will take this up later, as I discuss her particular hermeneutics.

The third corollary to her assumption of the inspired text is that of christological interpretation. Quoting 2 Tim 3:16, she concludes from this that inspired Scripture teaches of the fall of humanity and the savior who is the means of recovery from that fall. The goal of the inspired text is Christ, the "living temple in whom all the avenues of Scriptural truth terminate."[27] Again, I will explore later this corollary to her assumption of an inspired text.

SchimmelPenninck assumes that the true goal of interpretation is the spiritual meaning of the text, that is, how the text speaks to our relationship to God. An interpretation that did not reveal the spiritual sense was a "mere dead letter."[28] On the other hand, the spiritual meaning was not a "mere pious adaptation; but…, in every case, the true, substantial, spiritual sense of each passage."[29] The spiritual sense was not divorced from the literal sense but was related to the literal sense as soul is to body. Only an accurate literal interpretation provided the basis upon which to found "a rational and enlightened, as well as a devotional spiritual interpretation."[30] The discovery of the true, intended spiritual sense rather than pious adaptation was much on SchimmelPenninck's mind:

> The literal sense should first be strictly ascertained, and then the spiritual senses should be solidly given, after which any adaptations may be added; but then they must be carefully distinguished from the intended sense, and must be given only as what they are, namely, as the effusions of some pious mind, awakened by the subject in hand. For a sound spiritual, as well as a sound critical, interpretation, should seek the precise spiritual meaning that was designed, and not excurse into those merely pious applications the subject might suggest, and which, though edifying and pleasing as the fruit of the pious author, are yet not the object of sound biblical interpretation, not being the object of faith presented to us in that passage by the inspiration of the Holy Spirit himself.[31]

SchimmelPenninck's emphasis on the spiritual meaning as the interpreter's goal is evident from the fact that *Biblical Fragments*, her first work on the Psalms,

---

25. Ibid., 83–84; *Psalms*, xii–xiii.
26. SchimmelPenninck, *Psalms*, xiii.
27. SchimmelPenninck, *Biblical Fragments*, 76.
28. Ibid., 31.
29. Ibid., 34.
30. SchimmelPenninck, *Psalms*, ix.
31. SchimmelPenninck, *Biblical Fragments*, 75.

addresses spiritual interpretation. Her later work, *Psalms*, which sets each psalm in its historical context in the life of David as a means to the correct literal interpretation, has appended to it the essay from *Biblical Fragments*. This appendix directs the interpreter to move beyond literal interpretation to the ultimate goal of spiritual interpretation "lest a work so entirely on the literal sense of any portion of scripture [i.e., *Psalms*], should unfortunately prove a means of tempting some to stop short of the living truth."[32]

Spiritual interpretation was to determine the meaning that was "definitely intended," "literally and solidly true," and "as capable of a fixed interpretation, as the literal sense."[33] Throughout her work, she assumes this intended, spiritual interpretation is the revelation of Christ in all of Scripture.

HERMENEUTICAL PRINCIPLES FOUNDED ON SCHIMMELPENNINCK'S ASSUMPTIONS

The above assumptions form the bedrock for SchimmelPenninck's hermeneutical principles. I will now explore those principles, with examples taken from her work on the Psalms.

SchimmelPenninck bases spiritual interpretation upon literal interpretation, making the discovery of the literal meaning imperative. Revealing her precritical stance toward Scripture, she relies on three sources of data for determining authorship and occasion:[34] (1) the text of the psalms themselves; (2) the psalms' superscriptions in the Hebrew and Greek (SchimmelPenninck understands these as original to the inspired text);[35] and (3) diligent comparison of the first two data with the historic books of the Old Testament.

SchimmelPenninck assumes Davidic authorship for all those psalms that bear his name, together with many of the unascribed psalms contiguous to them. For all other psalms that are not attributed to David, she looks for authors of "prophetic character" (as required by her model of inspiration) as follows:

Psalm 90—Moses
Psalm 1—Samuel at the consecration of David
Psalm 45—Nathan or some other prophet on Solomon's marriage
Psalm 132—Solomon

---

32. SchimmelPenninck, *Psalms*, xx.

33. SchimmelPenninck, *Biblical Fragments*, 34.

34. SchimmelPenninck, *Psalms*, xi.

35. In the 1820s, when SchimmelPenninck wrote on the Psalms, historical-critical work had already undermined the authenticity of the psalm titles and their interpretive validity. Brevard Childs (*Introduction to the Old Testament as Scripture* [Philadelphia: Fortress, 1979], 509) states, "By the middle of the nineteenth century the Psalm titles ... had been almost universally abandoned as late, inauthentic, and insignificant. The last major scholarly commentary to defend completely the traditional stance was that of Hengstenberg in 1842."

Psalm 82—Asaph, Jehazeal, or King Jehoshaphat
Psalm 83—Jehazeal
Psalm 48—Jehoshaphat
Psalm 80—Hezekiah
Psalm 76—Hezekiah or Isaiah
Psalm 74, 79—Jeremiah
Psalm 85, 102, 137—prayers by pious Jews in Babylonian captivity
Psalm 126—Ezra

Psalm 42 exemplifies how SchimmelPenninck fits many psalms into the life of David. Her interpretation is contained in the prefatory title and notes that she appends to the psalm. She sets the reference in verse 6 to Jordan, Mizar, and Hermon as the place of composition and then searches David's life for a period when he could be found in such a location. She concludes the psalm was:

> composed by David when, quitting the cave of Adullam, he left his native country, and sought a refuge in Mizpeh of Moab.... Having passed the river Jordan, and being now arrived at the little mountain of Hermon, he takes a last view of the Holy Land, and pours out his soul in this beautiful psalm. 1 Sam xxii. 3, 4[36]

Similarly, she attributes several psalms to David's flight from Jerusalem during Absalom's revolt: Ps 3 is David's complaint upon hearing of the revolt; Ps 55 is David's psalm at he ascends the Mount of Olives and learns of Ahithophel's deceit; Ps 25 is David's prayer upon gaining the summit of the mountain; and Ps 41 is David's thanksgiving when Hushai joined him at the summit of the mountain.

With respect to occasion, SchimmelPenninck begins with clues within the text itself, followed by reliance upon the psalm headings and comparison to the records of the historic books. She rarely used commentaries, preferring to interpret Scripture by Scripture. Therefore, she "most zealously sought for every parallel passage that could by possibility throw light on the subject which engaged her."[37] With the Port Royalists, SchimmelPenninck required that the instigating event must be of a public nature because "a psalm enrolled in the public service of the Jewish nation, must be supposed to have been composed on some occasion of public interest and notoriety."[38]

SchimmelPenninck's concern with historical questions of authorship and occasion is apparent,[39] but her approach is not a historical-critical one. Her

---

36. SchimmelPenninck, *Psalms*, 125.
37. Hankin, *Life of Mary Anne SchimmelPenninck*, 2:232.
38. SchimmelPenninck, *Psalms*, xiii.
39. See appendix A for excerpted examples of the notations in the two sections of *Psalms* for Pss 3 and 8. Revealing her concern with historical matters, each section references the chronological placement of the psalms in the life of Israel.

precritical interpretation equated the literal sense of Scripture with historical referentiality, and because this literal sense was already prescribed by her assumption of Davidic authorship and occasion, her use of such research is bound by her assumptions. When she speaks favorably of historical criticism, it is only in respect of work done to ascertain the "peculiar customs, manners, or facts, which constitute the literal sense of scripture."[40]

After the exploration of prophetic authorship and historical occasion, SchimmelPenninck moves toward a spiritual interpretation, that is, one that reveals Christ. In this section I will explore three of her christological interpretive methods, which I will call (1) a prophetic-christological hermeneutic; (2) a canonical-christological hermeneutic; and (3) an ecclesiological-christological hermeneutic.

The foremost application of her christological hermeneutic is that she interprets the Psalms as ultimately speaking not of David (that is, historically) but of Christ (that is, prophetically). She argues that the New Testament writers and even David himself understood his writings to be prophetic (Matt 13:35 cites Ps 78, and Matt 27:35 cites Ps 69 as spoken by a prophet; similarly, David refers to himself as a prophet in 2 Sam 23:1-2).[41] She does not deny the historical referentiality to David but asserts:

[I]n point of fact, the Psalms are continually quoted in the Gospels and Acts as testimonies to Christ, and *never* as relative to David. We do not mean to deny, that they in an inferior sense may relate to [David]; but we would wish clearly to establish, that this was decidedly not esteemed by the evangelists their principal sense. (84)

SchimmelPenninck credits the New Testament with fifty quotations of the Psalms in which the writers interpret literal references to David as prophetic references to Christ (84, 105).[42] By extension, other psalms (although not quoted in the New Testament) should follow the interpretive example of the New Testament writers and also be interpreted prophetically. Psalms to be so interpreted are determined primarily from the psalm titles. Those psalms that refer in their title to David (meaning "Beloved") are literally understood to reference King David and spiritually understood to reference Christ, the Beloved of God.[43] Similarly, psalms without Davidic authorship inscriptions are still prophetic in character (as

---

40. SchimmelPenninck, *Biblical Fragments,* 72.

41. Ibid., 84. Subsequent references to *Biblical Fragments* will be provided within the text.

42. She does not cite these New Testament references.

43. That these references to David should be understood as references to Christ she argues by extension from the prophets. There (e.g., Isa 55; Ezek 34; Hos 3) references to David are made that cannot refer to King David (who was by that time dead) and must refer to Christ. In a *qal wahomer* argument, she holds that the same prophetic, spiritual understanding applies in the Psalms (*Biblical Fragments,* 98).

discussed above), and the inscriptions are interpreted to refer spiritually to Christ. For instance, titles that cite Asaph ("gatherer") refer to a literal member of David's band but are spiritually "given to Christ ... who should gather his elect from the four winds of heaven" (100); psalms that cite the Sons of Korah ("sons of mourning") refer spiritually to Christ, who is best able to comfort those who mourn (102). Psalms of ascent are literally psalms by which the Israelites "beguiled the tediousness of the road, as they went up to Jerusalem," but are spiritually referring to "the risen and ascending Saviour" (100). In this way, she builds a basis for the spiritual interpretation of all the psalms as prophetically speaking of Christ.

Her work with the psalm titles becomes even more complex and shows SchimmelPenninck's continuity with the precritical interpretive tradition. A fascinating element of her work arises in her charge of an error to the Authorized Version in attributing the psalms to the literal David and not to the spiritual antitype, Christ. She first traces the error back to the Reformers, who, in their zeal to correct the perceived interpretational errors of the church fathers and the Roman Catholic Church, abandoned all but a literal interpretation. She then argues that the Authorized Version has consistently erred in the translation of the psalm titles, thus offering a false key to their interpretation. Because the translators understood the psalms in relation to literal David, their translation of the titles reflected that assumption. Under this misconception,

> [They] uniformly mistranslate the title, to ascribe the psalm to David, in violation of the plainest grammatical rules of Hebrew.... they insert words of their own coining, to which the original gives not the least countenance.... [they leave] Hebrew words untranslated, as they stand, without affixing to them any meaning whatever; thus leaving the English reader to imagine them the names of persons or of places. (85–86)

The ascription of Ps 8 is a cameo example of SchimmelPenninck's work on the psalm titles (see appendix A). She argues that the translation "A Psalm *of David*" is incorrect and should be understood as a psalm *to* or *for* David, not specifying a psalm written *by* David. *David* could also be translated as *The Beloved*, and, by various intertextual references, SchimmelPenninck argues that the prophets use this name to refer to Christ-as-David, the Beloved of God. The reference in the psalm title is to be understood as written *about* or *regarding* Christ (86–89).

SchimmelPenninck also employs etymology to demonstrate that the psalm titles refer to Christ. She makes definitive statements as to the meaning of several Hebrew words, particularly the so-called "musical notations" (which even today are held as uncertain and left untranslated). In Ps 8, she claims the etymology of למנצח (*lamnaṣṣēaḥ*) suggests "To the overcomer" or "To the victor." Then she translates גתית (*gittit*) as "wine-press" or "oil-press," asserting that this is the same word as the New Testament גת שמן (*gat šemen*), that is, "Gethsemane." Through her christological lens, the meaning of the title of Ps 8 is "To the Conqueror on Gethsemane. A Psalm to the Beloved." Similar etymological work runs throughout her interpretation, carrying all the flaws for which such work was largely abandoned. Yet all this is done in service to her christological commitment.

SchimmelPenninck also derives the psalm's spiritual interpretation by translating proper names within the titles according to the root of the name. For instance, the title of Ps 51 in the Authorized Version reads, "To the chief musician; a Psalm of David. When Nathan the prophet came to him after he had gone to Bathsheba." SchimmelPenninck interprets Nathan and Bathsheba etymologically so that the title becomes, "To the Conqueror, a Psalm for the Beloved, when the *given prophet* [נתן (*nātān*) 'he gave'] went forth from him after he went to the *daughter of the oath* [בת שבע (*bat šăba'*) 'daughter of the oath/covenant']" (95). SchimmelPenninck credits the meaning of the title as "representing ... the confession of the sin of Christ [the given prophet], when, going forth from his Father, he came to rescue his Church [the daughter of the oath/covenant]" (95).

SchimmelPenninck further employs a christological hermeneutic through an approach that reads each psalm in light of the canon of Scripture. She holds that Pss 1 and 2 together form an introduction to the Psalter, describing the twin revelation of Christ that will be revealed throughout the Psalms: Christ in his suffering and Christ in his glory. Through this lens, SchimmelPenninck reads the Psalms with the Gospel accounts in mind: while the Gospels describe Christ's "outward walk and suffering; the psalmist portray[s] his inmost heart, describing his internal conflicts and anguish" (79). For instance, SchimmelPenninck finds psalms that describe Christ's suffering in the garden (Ps 38), his abandonment by his disciples (Ps 27), and his suffering on the cross (Pss 22; 69). The great Hallel (Pss 112–118) takes up the themes of "the last supper ... the atonement ... the breaking the power of Satan ... the call of the Gentiles; the eucharistic sacrifice, the peace in believing, and the call of the individual believer" (80). Schimmel-Penninck even finds psalms that treat the eighteen silent years of Christ, from his Jerusalem journey at age twelve to the commencement of his public ministry (81).[44] Here, while the Gospel accounts are silent, the Psalms speak to his "interior course" (81), so that diligent contemplation of the Psalms may yield "every crumb of the bread of life ... to the abundant feeding of their souls" (81). Where the Gospel accounts end the narrative with the resurrection and ascension, the body of Psalms "goes on with the history, portrays the fruit of these blessings on the call of his church" (80).

While SchimmelPenninck's canonical reading certainly differs from a canonical reading today that addresses the theological concerns of the redactors of the Psalms corpus, it does seek to read the canon in such a way that its very shape has meaning. The meaning, rather than revealing the theological concerns, social

---

44. She does not indicate which of the psalms she refers to, nor do I find this indicated in the prefatory titles or in the biographical works.

setting, or historical circumstances of the redactor, reveals instead a spiritual revelation of Christ; it is a symbolic representation of Christ on a canonical scale.

To the above canonical-christological interpretation in which Christ's suffering and glorification is revealed, SchimmelPenninck adds another hermeneutical key that I will label an ecclesiological-christological hermeneutic. By this key SchimmelPenninck finds in the Psalms a dual type in which every line contains the "double but indissoluble portraitures of Christ, the Son of GOD; and the church, his inseparably united bride" (37). Both of these interpretations are part of the spiritual interpretation, but it is the portraiture of Christ that is paramount:

> The first of these spiritual interpretations, revealing the great object of the believer's faith [i.e., Christ]; the latter, unfolding the vast treasury of the church's experience. But as Christ is the head of his body, the church; so is the first spiritual sense, as applied to him, pre-eminent in dignity to the second, as applied to his church. (37)

It is the indissolubility of Christ and his bride in which SchimmelPenninck finds incontrovertible ground for such a double spiritual interpretation. This indissolubility is echoed in the Psalms themselves, for they present a blend of confession, innocence, lamentation, and triumph, often intermingled within a single psalm. Faced with such a phenomenon in the Psalms, SchimmelPenninck concludes that no consistent sense can be given the Psalms if read on the literal level only. If read literally, the expressions of sinfulness and guilt in the Psalms (e.g., Pss 14:1–2; 53:1–2) necessitate the author to be an unbeliever while yet claiming his innocence—and SchimmelPenninck recoils that such a person's writing would be included in Scripture (38). The key to interpreting such passages in which the psalms blend guilt with innocence or lamentation with triumph must instead be spiritual interpretation that envisions both Christ and his church:

> [W]e must unlock the passage by this key: That *Christ Jesus is of God made to us righteousness, sanctification, and redemption*; and thus may the church appropriate to herself all the triumphant passages; because, *whilst glorying, she glories in her Lord*. By this means every passage applies both to Christ and to the church. To Christ literally the passages of triumph; and by imputation the humiliating ones: and to his bride, the converse. (38)

Christ and his church, then, appear in every psalm. Christ is figured in the words of triumph and (as sin bearer for the world) by imputation in the words of humiliation and lament. In the same way, the church is found in the Psalms in its humiliation and by imputation shares in the triumphs of Christ.

SchimmelPenninck gives a short list of hermeneutical guidelines by which she sought to ascertain the spiritual interpretation of the Psalms. Each works toward a christological hermeneutic to render a spiritual sense for the Psalms (76–78):

1. Sound spiritual interpretation finds Christ in every passage.
2. A christological reading of a particular verse in the Old Testament enables the whole of the passage to be read christologically.
3. If a passage has been explained by the Lord or the Evangelists as referring to Christ, when that same passage, image, type, or custom is taken up or alluded to by another Evangelist, a similar christological key is to be applied.
4. Apostolic interpretation (i.e., the interpretive methods outlined in the methodology of guidelines 1–3) stands as a methodological precedent for the ongoing church's interpretation of all parallel passages—not as a definitive list of interpretational models but merely as examples. Subsequent interpretation seeks to "copy their manner, and imbibe their spirit."

ASSESSING SCHIMMELPENNINCK'S WORK IN LIGHT OF MODERN AND POSTMODERN INTERPRETATION

SchimmelPenninck's work, read in the context of her life, reveals a woman who was interpreting the Psalms on the cusp of the historical-critical wave. The assumptions and hermeneutical choices she made, however, placed her firmly in the precritical interpretational era. She undertook historical study to determine authorship and occasion but turned to the psalms, their titles, and the historical books of the Old Testament as determinative of this question. Although aware of theories of compositional development of the biblical text (such as Dr. Priestly's work), she nowhere engages this question.[45] Additionally, she was committed to christological interpretation of the Psalms—again a precritical emphasis.

While SchimmelPenninck used Reformation principles such as interpreting Scripture by Scripture, she married her interpretational method to that of the Port Royal authors (and through them to the church fathers), feeling that the Reformers had uncritically shunned all interpretational methods associated with the Roman Church. Her work in bringing the Port Royalists to the English public reveals an openness to past interpretive work when it revealed the spiritual meaning of the Psalms. As well, it reveals an ecumenical spirit that thoughtfully and irenically assessed the contributions of both Protestants and Catholics to the work of interpretation.

SchimmelPenninck's understanding of the relationship of literal and spiritual meaning again reveals her as a precritical interpreter. The basic interpretation upon which she bases her spiritual interpretation is labeled literal in that it purportedly represents the past history of David. Precritically, this literal-realistic

---

45. See above, n. 35. Wilhelm Martin Lebrecht de Wette's critical commentary (*Commentar über die Psalmen* [Heidelberg: Mohr & Zimmer, 1811]) refuted much traditional interpretation of the Psalms and influenced critical discussion for the century.

reading of Scripture was indissolubly joined to a figurative reading of Scripture,[46] and this is precisely the approach that SchimmelPenninck takes.

Many of SchimmelPenninck's hermeneutical choices and their underlying assumptions and questions sound like linear ancestors of some questions, assumptions, and hermeneutical approaches today. For instance, her insistence upon both literal and spiritual meanings inherent in the text echoes in the questions that abound today regarding the place of meaning and the possibility of multiple meanings. As well, when she finds this spiritual meaning via types and symbols in service of a christological interpretation, she is using the means of her day by which the two Testaments were held in unity—again, a concern that still abounds today. Further, some recent Psalms scholarship, like Schimmel-Penninck's work, focuses on asking theological questions of the text and not merely historical questions.[47] Unlike SchimmelPenninck, who worked early in the historical-critical era, today's scholarship cannot easily reject or ignore the findings of historical criticism, and often theological observations arise out of historical-critical findings or at least demonstrate an awareness of such findings. Finally, as SchimmelPenninck attempted to read the Psalms for spiritual meaning, she affirmed the hermeneutic of Christ and the apostles as a model to be taken up by subsequent interpreters. Her adoption of the apostolic model of interpretation echoes today in writers who are returning to such precritical hermeneutical models in the quest for meaning that integrates the Old and New Testaments.[48]

Mary Anne SchimmelPenninck's work on the Psalms is shaped by diverse Christian communities within Protestantism and Roman Catholicism. Additionally, her personal experience of faith in Jesus Christ—its reality and effectiveness in all her life and decisions—became the bedrock upon which every assumption and hermeneutical principle was hammered out. Each was then either abandoned or integrated, depending on its ability to render the Psalms as part of the Scripture that revealed Christ. That the Psalms were a vital part of her daily faith-walk is attested by her constant reference to them in her writings and letters, her com-

---

46. Hans Frei's introduction to *The Eclipse of Biblical Narrative: A Study in Eighteenth and Nineteenth Century Hermeneutic* (New Haven: Yale University Press, 1974), 1–16, details the precritical connection of literal-realistic and figurative readings. Read in light of Frei's assessment, SchimmelPenninck is clearly a precritical interpreter in her assumption of the indissoluble connection between literal-realistic readings and figurative readings.

47. E.g., Gerald Wilson, *The Editing of the Hebrew Psalter* (SBLDS 76; Chico, Calif.: Scholars Press, 1985); J. Clinton McCann, *A Theological Introduction to the Book of Psalms* (Nashville: Abingdon, 1993); James L. Mays, *The Lord Reigns: A Theological Handbook to the Psalms* (Louisville: Westminster John Knox, 1994).

48. E.g., Richard B. Hays, *Echoes of Scripture in the Letters of Paul* (New Haven: Yale University Press, 1989); Ellen F. Davis and Richard B. Hays, eds., *The Art of Reading Scripture* (Grand Rapids: Eerdmans, 2003).

mitment to learn the Psalms by heart in Hebrew, and her use of them even in her final days.

While much of her interpretation of the Psalms, particularly her Hebrew and etymological work, appear fantastical in the light of subsequent linguistic and historical-critical scholarship, they do represent sincere and prayerful study given the tools and philosophical commitments of the Christian community of her day. She made conscious interpretive choices that constrained her to a precritical interpretive model, yet, in light of her personal journey and the impact of new historical-critical thought upon her, such choices appear understandable. What shines through, in both her interpretive work and her life, is an individual who thoughtfully married diligent study with a commitment to walk in daily relationship with Christ. This relationship, arrived at through much distress and great thought, was finally the sustaining joy through her whole life.

Appendix A

Excerpts from sections 1 and 2 of *Psalms*, for Pss 3 and 8. The two sections are separated in *Psalms*. Here the two sections are presented sequentially for each psalm examined. SchimmelPenninck's own translation of the ascription is given in italics. Archaisms of punctuation and spelling have been preserved as they appear in *Psalms*.

Psalms, section 1, is entitled: "Tabular Index; or List of Psalms, Classed according to their dates; arranged according to the order, and referred to the circumstances in which they are supposed to have been written. NB, The Arabic numeral, marks the number of the Psalm in its chronologic order; the Roman numeral, its order as arranged in the Book of Psalms. The scripture reference, points out the circumstances under which it is supposed to have been composed."

Psalms, section 2, is entitled: "The Books of Psalms. Each Psalm being headed by a prefatory title; and scriptural reference to the historic books of the Old Testament; pointing out the circumstances under which it appears probable it was composed. NB. Observe. The Roman numeral, marks the number of the Psalm as arranged in Holy Writ; the Arabic numeral, points out its number in the preceding Tabular Index; by consulting which, the Reader may at pleasure find the Psalms which precede, or which succeed, it in historical and chronologic order."

PSALM 3   SECTION 1; CHRONOLOGICAL SEQUENCE

> This psalm appears chronologically with this notice: "Psalms composed by David during the revolt of his son Absalom. David was sixty-two years of age when it commenced. The judgment denounced by Nathan, (2 Sam. xii. 10.) upon David's great crime having thus commenced twenty-two years after the sin which had occasioned it had been par-

doned; probably to mark the continual humiliation which should abide on the heart before God, even for long past offences. According to St. Jerome, the revolt of Absalom lasted only six months. Year of the world 2980. Of David 62. Before Christ 1021."

"SECTION I: Psalms composed by David on being first informed of the conspiracy of Absalom; when he fled from Jerusalem, and passed the brook Kedron to avoid falling into his hands. 2 Sam. xv. 1–30.
Psalm 96. III. Complaint and prayer of David to implore the Divine protection, and to reanimate his own confidence in God, on being first informed, by an especial messenger, that the hearts of all the people were gone after his son Absalom. 2 Sam. xv. 1-13."

SECTION 2; CANONICAL SEQUENCE

"[substantially the same as per section 1].... A Psalm of David, when he fled from Absalom his son."

PSALM 8   SECTION 1; CHRONOLOGICAL SEQUENCE

This psalm appears grouped chronologically with this notice: "Psalms composed from the year of the world 2934 to 2942. From before Christ 1066 to 1058. From the consecration of David, at the age of sixteen, till his persecution by Saul, after slaying Goliath, at the age of twenty-four. Reign of Saul, 26th to the 34th year."

"SECTION II: Psalms composed by David after his consecration, whilst he tended his flocks at Bethlehem. Including the period of his short stay with Saul, to whom he ministered during his malady; after which he again returned to keep his sheep. See 1 Sam. xvi. 13–23. and xvii. 13–15. This period includes about eight years.
Psalm 3. VIII. Psalm for the midnight watch.
Psalm 4. XIX. Psalm for the morning watch.
Psalm 5. CIV. Psalm for removing from place to place, according to the season, with his flocks.
Psalm 6. CXLVIII. Composed after David's return from the court of Saul to Bethlehem. 1 Sam. xvi. 19-23. and xvii. 15."

SECTION 2; CANONICAL SEQUENCE

"Psalm VIII. 3. David's anthem of praise, whilst he kept watch by night in those plains of Bethlehem where, so many years after, the Saviour was announced by the angelic hosts to the shepherds. It was a frequent custom with shepherds to sing responsively; partly to beguile the time, and partly to keep within hearing, that they might be ready to assist each other in case of attacks of wild beasts or of robbers. See 1 Sam. xvii. 34–36. John x. 1–13. Nor did they omit to join their anthem of praise with the hours of the temple or tabernacle watch. The sun not being alluded to, but only the moon and stars being mentioned, seems to point out this psalms as the midnight watch hymn.

To the chief Musician upon Gittith. A Psalm of David [Authorized Version].

To the giver of victory concerning presses. A Psalm of David"

BIBLIOGRAPHY

Childs, Brevard. *Introduction to the Old Testament as Scripture.* Philadelphia: Fortress, 1979.

Davis, Ellen F., and Richard B. Hays. *The Art of Reading Scripture.* Grand Rapids: Eerdmans, 2003.

Frei, Hans. *The Eclipse of Biblical Narrative: A Study in Eighteenth and Nineteenth Century Hermeneutic.* New Haven: Yale University Press, 1974.

Hankin, Christiana C., ed. *Life of Mary Anne SchimmelPenninck.* 2 vols. London: Longman, Brown, Green, Longmans, & Roberts, 1858.

Hays, Richard B. *Echoes of Scripture in the Letters of Paul.* New Haven: Yale University Press, 1989.

Jansenius, Cornelius. *Cornelii Jansenii Episopi Iprensis Augustinus....* Jacobi Zegeri, 1640.

Mays, James L. *The Lord Reigns: A Theological Handbook to the Psalms.* Louisville: Westminster John Knox, 1994.

McCann, J. Clinton. *A Theological Introduction to the Book of Psalms.* Nashville: Abingdon, 1993.

Priestly, Joseph. *An History of the Corruptions of Christianity.* Birmingham: Johnson, 1782.

————. *An History of Early Opinions Concerning Jesus Christ, Compiled from Original Writers; Proving That the Christian Church Was at First Unitarian.* Birmingham: Johnson, 1786.

SchimmelPenninck, Mary Anne. *Biblical Fragments.* London: Ogle, Duncan, & Co., 1821.

————. *Psalms according to the Authorized Version; With Prefatory Titles, and Tabular Index of Scriptural References, From the Port Royal Authors, Marking the Circumstances and Chronologic Order of Their Composition: To Which Is Added, An Essay upon the Psalms, and Their Spiritual Application.* London: Arch, 1825.

————. *Select Memoirs of Port Royal: To Which Are Appended Tour to Alert, Visit to Port Royal, Gift of an Abbess, Biographical Notices, etc. Taken from Original Documents.* London: Arch, 1829.

Wette, Wilhelm Martin Leberecht de. *Commentar über die Psalmen.* Heidelberg: Mohr & Zimmer, 1811.

Wilson, Gerald Henry. *The Editing of the Hebrew Psalter.* SBLDS 76. Chico, Calif.: Scholars Press, 1985.

Harriet Beecher Stowe and the Mingling of Two Worlds: The Kitchen and the Study*

Marion Ann Taylor

Harriet Beecher Stowe was a nineteenth-century interpreter of Scripture who stood in the interstices of two worlds: the male world of the academy and church and the female world of women's culture. This essay will show how Stowe was uniquely positioned to interpret Scripture using the resources traditionally associated with the world of men and at the same time to read through the eyes of a woman who was very much a part of the women's culture of her day.[1] Examples of Stowe's biblical interpretation will be drawn from her novel, *The Minister's Wooing* (1859); her poetry; and her later prose works that focused more particularly on the Bible, *Woman in Sacred History* (1873) and *Footsteps of the Master* (1878).

Born to Preach

Harriet Beecher Stowe (1811–96) was the seventh of nine children born to Lyman Beecher (1775–1863), a famous Congregational (later Presbyterian) minister, theologian, and seminary president, and his first wife, Roxanna Foote (1775–1816); four more children would be born to his second wife, Harriet Porter (1790–1835).[2] Stowe's parents had a formative influence on her life. Around the dinner table, Lyman Beecher would school and test all his children on their logic and precision in thinking by posing arguments for them to prove. He made sure

* I am grateful for the generous support of an ATS Lilly Theological Research Grant, an ATS Travel Grant, and a Louisville Summer Stipend Fellowship that enabled me to carry out the research that stands behind this essay. I also want to thank those who assisted me in this project and read drafts of this essay.

1. Stowe endorsed the cult of domesticity, valuing especially women's spirituality, power, and motherhood.

2. Lyman Beecher's third wife was Lydia Beals Jackson (1789–1869). They had no children. See the Beecher family tree in Milton Allan Rugoff, *The Beechers: An American Family in the Nineteenth Century* (New York: Harper & Row, 1981), xvi–xvii.

all his children could discuss any sort of exegetical debate, essay, or sermon.[3] His children also knew that they belonged to the chosen race. He once said of his daughter Harriet; "No Jewish maiden ever grew up with a more earnest faith that she belonged to a consecrated race, a people especially called and chosen by God for some great work on earth."[4] Not surprisingly, seven of Lyman Beecher's sons became preachers; his daughter Catharine made her mark as an educator, philosopher, and theologian;[5] and as Mary Kelley has suggested, "Had [Harriet Beecher] Stowe been a male she undoubtedly would have followed her father's example and embarked upon a ministerial career."[6] When she was nineteen, she confessed to her brother, "I was made for a preacher—indeed I can scarcely keep my letters from turning into sermons.... Indeed it is as much my vocation to preach on paper as it is that of my brothers to preach *viva voce*."[7] As Kimball observed, "To be a Beecher meant to be a preacher."[8] Arguably, Harriet Beecher Stowe had a ministerial career—she preached with her pen. Her text was the Bible; her congregation was the world.[9]

3. Lyman Beecher later wrote about how "all the great theological problems of Calvinism" influenced his daughter Harriet (cited in Helen Petter Westra, "Confronting Antichrist: The Influence of Jonathan Edwards's Millennial Vision," in *The Stowe Debate: Rhetorical Strategies in Uncle Tom's Cabin* [ed. M. I. Lowance Jr.; Amherst: University of Massachusetts Press, 1994], 141). I am indebted to Gladys Lewis for her insights into the role Lyman Beecher played in the intellectual, theological, and vocational formation of his children.

4. Edward Wagenknecht, *Harriet Beecher Stowe: The Known and the Unknown* (Oxford: Oxford University Press, 1965), 135. Lyman Beecher also recognized his daughter's intelligence and wished she were a boy. When she was seven, he wrote in a letter: "Hattie is a genius. I would give a hundred dollars if she was a boy. She is as odd as she is intelligent and studious" (cited in Joan D. Hedrick, *Harriet Beecher Stowe: A Life* [Oxford: Oxford University Press, 1994], 29–30).

5. Mark David Hall, "Catharine Beecher: America's First Female Philosopher and Theologian, *Fides et Historia* 32 (2000): 65–80. See also Catherine Villanueva Gardner, "Heaven-Appointed Educators of Mind: Catharine Beecher and the Moral Power of Women," *Hypatia* 19/2 (2004): 1–16.

6. Mary Kelley, *Private Woman, Public Stage: Literary Domesticity in Nineteenth-Century America* (Oxford: Oxford University Press, 1984), 82.

7. Letter to George Beecher, 20 February [1830?], cited in Gail Katherine Smith, "Reading the Word: Harriet Beecher Stowe and Interpretation" (Ph.D. diss., University of Virginia, 1993), 9.

8. Gayle Kimball, *The Religious Ideas of Harriet Beecher Stowe: Her Gospel of Womanhood* (New York: Mellen, 1982), 2.

9. Smith broadens the scope of Stowe's preaching to include sermons on nature, art, and politics. She writes: "Throughout her life she [Stowe] took on the preaching role, in letters outlining sermon ideas for her minister son Charles, in biblical exegesis for her twin daughters in school in Paris, in published reflections on the possibility of 'Christian art,' in meditations on Czar Nicholas' assassination as a parable about divine government.... Whether she was 'reading' the significance of a flower, a painting, a passage from St. Paul, or a legal statute from Missis-

Enmeshed in the Academic Study of Scripture

In 1836 Harriet Beecher married Calvin Ellis Stowe (1802–86), professor of Sacred Literature at Lane Theological Seminary in Cincinnati. Theological books,[10] students, and discussions about the latest German critical theories and rabbinic exegesis filled their home. The books Calvin Stowe read, as well as the lectures, articles, and books he wrote, indelibly shaped his wife's approach to reading Scripture. She constantly relied on her husband's literary and scholarly judgments and used him as a resource for her own writing.[11] He even "read and criticized her drafts, suggested lines of investigation and brought many sources, including apocryphal and traditional ones, to her attention."[12] Even when his wife was wrestling with personal issues relating to the afterlife following their son's premature death, Calvin directed her to commentaries and translated relevant texts. In a letter to her sister, Harriet Beecher Stowe writes:

> Mr. Stowe says the text "By which he (Christ) went and preached unto the spirits in prison" [1Peter 3:19] can by no means be interpreted without great violence to the text to mean any thing more or less than that Christ's soul [,] while his body lay in the grave [,] went and declared the news of salvation to those spirits who were disobedient in the time of Noah.... This you see opens a wide field of thought.[13]

With the help of her personal "Rabbi," as she affectionately called her husband, Stowe added a critical dimension to the exegetical and practical homiletical skills she had learned from her father.

Calvin Stowe, recognizing his wife's abilities as a writer and interpreter of Scripture, encouraged her to become a student at Andover Theological Seminary, where he taught from 1852 to 1864. He dreamed of having his wife help him "break the old Andover fetters and make the pieces fly." He wanted her to agree

---

sippi, she continually preached, interpreting her 'text' and encouraging her audience to do this kind of interpretation for themselves" (Smith, "Reading the Word," 9).

10. The only personal property that Calvin Stowe brought into his marriage was his library of thousands of scholarly volumes. See Hedrick, *Harriet Beecher Stowe: A Life*, 98.

11. In a letter to her children following Calvin's recovery from malaria in 1872, Harriet expressed her great relief that his mental faculties remained intact: "I am so grateful to God that he is spared to me a little longer for I am so dependent on his superior knowledge & judgment in my profession, that I hardly feel that I could ever be much without him" (Harriet Beecher Stowe to Hatty and Eliza Stowe, 19 December 1872, folder 156, Beecher-Stowe Collection SchL, cited in Hedrick, *Harriet Beecher Stowe: A Life*, 385).

12. Marie Caskey, *Chariot of Fire: Religion and the Beecher Family* (New Haven: Yale University Press, 1978), 183.

13. Passage taken from Stowe's letter to Catharine Beecher and Mary Beecher Perkins, 1858 cited in ibid., 183.

to "get Greek enough just to read the Greek New Testament, and then attend the entire course of my lectures.... I know you will enjoy it beyond any study you were ever engaged in, and you could help me amazingly to write out a most interesting series by your rich suggestions."[14] Harriet Beecher Stowe, however, was not willing to "break the old Andover fetters" and refused her husband's offer of a place at Andover.[15] The reasons for her decision were many, including her intimate knowledge of the world of theological education and its excesses.

Harriet Beecher Stowe recognized that the academic study of theology could adversely affect a person's spiritual life. She criticized her husband for spending too much time keeping up to date with his scholarship and not enough time fostering his devotional life. In a letter that shows Stowe functioning as "the priest of the home," she chastises her husband:

> If you studied Christ with half the energy that you have studied Luther ... If you were drawn toward him & loved him as much as you loved your study & your books then would he be formed in you, the hope of glory.... But you fancy that you have other things to do.... you must write courses of lectures.... you must keep up with the current literature ... & and read new German books—all these things you must do & then if there is any time, any odds & ends of strength & mental capability left, why they are to be given occasionally to brushing up matters within, & keeping a kind of a Christian character.[16]

Harriet Beecher Stowe's poem "Summer Studies," which satirizes a student of Greek and Hebrew who "ignores the beauty of nature and nature's God which surround him," reflects similar critical sentiments.[17] Yet, however negatively Stowe viewed an academic approach to the study of the Bible, she recognized the usefulness of resources such as knowledge of the original languages of Scripture, the history of the interpretation of Scripture, and contemporary German critical

---

14. Letter to Harriet Beecher Stowe 9 February 1870, as cited in Smith, "Reading the Word," 59.

15. Harriet Beecher Stowe may have been influenced by the common notion that "woman as a sex ought not to do the hard work of the world, either social, intellectual, or moral. There are evidences in her physiology that this is not intended for her" (Stowe, *House and Home Papers*, 306, cited in Kimball, *Religious Ideas*, 153). Similarly, Bushnell argued that women's physiology would change if they left the home's seclusion; they would "become bigger, angular, abrupt, lank and lean" (Horace Bushnell, *Women's Suffrage: The Reform against Nature* [New York: Scribner & Sons, 1869], cited in Kimball, *Religious Ideas*, 157).

16. Letter of Calvin E. Stowe [ca. 21 May 1844]), cited in Smith, "Reading the Word," 58.

17. Harriet Beecher Stowe and John Michael Moran, *Collected Poems of Harriet Beecher Stowe* (Hartford: Transcendental Books, 1967), 14: "Why shouldst thou study in the month of June / In dusky books of Greek and Hebrew lore, / When the great Teacher of all glorious things / Passes in hourly light before thy door? ... / Wilt thou, then, all thy wintry feelings keep, / The old dead routine of thy book-writ lore, / Nor deem that God can teach, by one bright hour, / What life hath never taught to thee before?"

scholarship with its emphasis on sources and historical development. Sometimes she even participated directly in her husband's scholarly work:

> My poor *Rab.* has been sick with a heavy cold this week, and if it hadn't been for me you wouldn't have had this article, which I send in triumph. I plunged into the sea of Rabbis and copied Mr. Stowe's insufferable chaldaic characters so that you might not have your life taken by wrathful printers.... Thus I have ushered into the world a document which I venture to say condenses more information on an obscure and curious subject than any in the known world—Hosanna![18]

Stowe also encouraged her husband to write his highly successful book, *The Origin and History of the Books of the Bible* (1868). Indeed, she advised the publisher directly as to how to deal with her husband:

> You must not scare him off by grimly declaring that you must have *the whole manuscript complete* before you set the printer to work; you must take the three quarters he brings you and at least make believe begin printing, and he will immediately go to work and finish up the whole; otherwise what with lectures and the original sin of laziness, it will all be indefinitely postponed. I want to make a crisis that he shall feel that *now* is the accepted time and that this must be finished first and foremost.[19]

Thus, although Harriet Beecher Stowe received no formal theological training, she had direct access to the resources of the academy. Her writings demonstrate that she took full advantage of these resources.

INTERPRETING THE BIBLE AS A WOMAN

Harriet Beecher Stowe's message, however, was not that preached by her father, her brothers, or even her husband, for she was a woman shaped by the distinctive women's culture of the nineteenth century. Harriet's mother Roxanna, regarded by Lyman Beecher as his intellectual and moral superior, died of tuberculosis when Harriet was only five. Roxanna Beecher's powerful influence lived on, however, as the family remembered her as a perfect mother and ideal woman: gentle, sensitive, pure, modest, pious, and self-denying. She "became pure symbol with them all, an ideal, the family's virgin Mary, the symbol of all that was most perfect in womanhood." [20]

---

18. Annie Fields, ed., *Life and Letters of Harriet Beecher Stowe* (Boston: Houghton Mifflin, 1889), 379.

19. Ibid.

20. Forrest Wilson, *Crusader in Crinoline: The Life of Harriet Beecher Stowe* (Philadelphia: Lippincott, 1941), 32. Stowe was especially drawn toward the Virgin Mary, the quintessential

Catharine Beecher[21] also had a formative influence on her younger sister's life, having raised her from the age of five.[22] At thirteen, Stowe became a student at Hartford Female Seminary, a school her sister had founded. Stowe's experiences at Hartford Female Seminary, where she was first a student and later a teacher, preacher, and peer counselor, were especially formative.[23] Joan Hedrick suggests that the pastoral letters Harriet wrote between 1826 and 1832 reveal "the emergence of a non-judgmental and non-hierarchical value system that is implicitly at odds with the authoritarian methods of her father."[24] Lyman Beecher, for example, counseled his daughter Catharine "to set aside her 'wrong feelings' and murmurings" and submit to God's will following the death of her fiancé.[25] By contrast, Harriet Beecher Stowe used her experience to empathize and "to acknowledge rather than to brush aside those feelings of insupportable loss."[26]

Stowe's early experiences as a daughter, sister, and teacher brought her into the center of women's culture. Marriage and motherhood deepened these experiences. Together they became the basis for her critique of the male world of the church and academy. More positively, Stowe's experiences of women's culture gave a distinctively feminine hue to her exegesis and exposition of Scripture. Stowe preached about "the redeeming power of women," or what she called "the gospel of womanhood."[27]

Many of Harriet Beecher Stowe's writings extolled women. In her novel *The Minister's Wooing* (1859), Mary Scudder embodies Stowe's ideal woman:

---

perfect mother. She includes two chapters on Mary in *Woman in Sacred History* and models the character Mary after the Virgin (and likely her own mother) in *The Minister's Wooing*.

21. Kathleen Berkeley lists the following achievements of Catharine Beecher: "founder of several institutes of higher education for women, including the once prestigious Hartford Female Seminary; the driving force behind the American Woman's Educational Association; and the author of close to thirty publications on such pressing social issues as educational reform, religion and ethics, slavery and abolition, the condition of women's health, dress, diet, calisthenics, the principles of domestic science, and the rights and duties of American women" (Kathleen Berkeley, "Catharine Beecher and Domestic Relations," in *Against the Tide: Women Reformers in American Society* [ed. P. A. Cimbala and R. Miller; Westport: Praeger, 1997], 1).

22. See Joan D. Hedrick, "'Peaceable Fruits': The Ministry of Harriet Beecher Stowe," *American Quarterly* 40 (1988): 308.

23. Ibid.

24. Ibid., 309.

25. Ibid.

26. Ibid., 310.

27. Kimball, *Religious Ideas*, 1. Stowe's portrayal of women as saviors developed over time. In her early writings, "women are devoted wives or magical, pretty fairies who twinkle about, but they don't have the power to transform lives in the same way as they do in later novels" (ibid., 14).

The fair poetic maiden, the seer, the saint, has passed into that appointed shrine for woman, more holy than cloister, more saintly and pure than church or altar—a Christian home. Priestess, wife, and mother, there she ministers daily in holy works of household peace, and by faith and prayer and love redeems from grossness and earthliness the common toils and wants of life.[28]

Not all her female characters are so typical of the nineteenth-century ideal woman. Stowe often pushes the boundaries of the cult of domesticity when she creates female characters who preach, offer effective pastoral care, theologize, and even perform salvific acts much more effectively than her male characters. Stowe's character Candace, a black slave, for example, preaches more effectively to a grieving mother than the learned minister and theologian, Dr. Hopkins:

Now honey, ... I knows our Doctor's a mighty good man, an' larned, — an' in fair weather I ha' n't no 'bjection to yer hearin' all about dese yer great an'mighty tings he's got to say. But, honey, dey won't do for now; sick folks mus'nt hab strong meat.... *Look right at Jesus.* Tell ye, honey, ye can't live no other way now. Don't ye' member how He looked on His mother, when she stood faintin' an' tremblin' under de cross, jes' like you? He knows all about mothers' hearts; He won't break yours.... Look an' see what He is! —don't ask no questions, and don't go to no reasonin's,—jes' look at *Him*, hangin' dar, so sweet and patient, on de cross! ... Dar's a God you can love, a'nt dar? Candace loves Him, —poor, ole, foolish, black, wicked Candace,— and she knows He loves her.[29]

By showing that Candace delivers more effectual pastoral care than Dr. Hopkins, Stowe subtly and yet intentionally favors lay ministry and removes hierarchies of privilege, gender, and education.[30]

Stowe's female characters not only function as pastoral caregivers, but they are also theologians, priests, and prophets. Their theology is practical, hands-on, lived theology.[31] In *The Minister's Wooing*, Stowe's female characters adeptly move from the high to the low, from theological discourse and biblical exegesis to mundane household tasks, from discussions about the millennium to taking a perfect cake out of the oven and cutting material for a dress.[32] In addition, Stowe argues for women's priestly and prophetic ministries. She designates her young heroine, Mary, as one of God's real priests "whose ordination and anointing are from the Holy Spirit's unction; and he who hath not this enthusiasm is not ordained of

28. Harriet Beecher Stowe, *The Minister's Wooing* (1859; repr., Boston: Osgood, 1875), 567–68.

29. Ibid., 348–49.

30. Kimball, *Religious Ideas*, 279–80.

31. Stowe, *The Minister's Wooing*, 294.

32. Ibid., 204–5.

God, though whole synods of bishops laid hands on him."[33] In one of her sermonic asides to the reader following Mary's inspired reading of Scripture, Stowe opines that "one verse in the Bible read by a mother in some hour of tender prayer has a significance deeper and higher than the most elaborate of sermons, the most acute of arguments."[34] Stowe uses a conversation between the learned theologian and Mary's mother on the apostle Peter's sermon in Acts 2:7 as a further opportunity to advocate for women's prophetic ministry.[35] Stowe's experiences of women's culture where she witnessed women exercising traditionally male ministries became the basis for her argument for change. She clearly believed that women could do theology and exercise priestly and prophetic gifts.

Stowe's familiarity with women's culture also gave her a fresh perspective on such important hermeneutical questions as to whether gender, race, and class affect how a person reads a text. In a conversation between Candace, a black slave, and a church deacon, Stowe intimates that such variables as experience, class, race, and gender influence interpretation.

> "You must remember, Candace," said a good deacon to her one day, when she was ordering him [Cato, her husband] about at a catechizing, "you ought to give honor to your husband; the wife is the weaker vessel."
>
> "I de weaker vessel?" said Candace, looking down from the tower of her ample corpulence on the small, quiet man whom she had been fledging with the ample folds of a worsted comforter, out of which his little head and shining bead-eyes looked, much like a blackbird in a nest, —"I de weaker vessel? Ump!"
>
> A whole women-rights' convention could not have expressed more in a day than was given in that single look and word. Candace considered a husband as a thing to be taken care of, —a rather inconsequent and somewhat troublesome species of pet, to be humored, nursed, fed, clothed, and guided in the way that he was to go, —an animal that was always losing off buttons, catching colds ... but she often condescended to express it as her opinion that he was a blessing, and that she didn't know what she should do, if it wasn't for Cato.[36]

Candace's challenge of the notion of the weaker vessel opens up the woman question. Moreover, through Candace, Stowe suggests that women can challenge traditional interpretations of Scripture and interpret Scripture for themselves. Carolyn Haynes suggests further that Stowe intimates here that "if anything—

---

33. Ibid., 131.

34. Ibid., 396.

35. Advocates for women's right to preach publicly in the church such as Phoebe Palmer, Josephine Butler, and Catherine Booth often used Acts 2:7 as a platform for their position. See Phoebe Palmer, *The Promise of the Father* (Boston: Degen, 1859); Josephine Butler, *Prophets and Prophetesses* (Newcastle-on-Tyne: Mawson, Swan & Morgan, 1898); and Catherine Booth, *Female Ministry; Or, Woman's Right to Preach the Gospel* (London: Morgan & Chase, ca. 1859).

36. Stowe, *The Minister's Wooing*, 178–79.

women have a more critical and insightful ability to comprehend the Bible than do men."[37]

Stowe's experiences of women's culture were the basis of her critique of the male world of ministry, theology, and biblical interpretation that she knew so well. Her experiences also became the lens through which she read and interpreted Scripture. In her most mature writings as a female exegete, *Woman in Sacred History* (1873) and *Footsteps of the Master* (1878), Stowe seamlessly blends the world of women's culture, memorialized in her mother and experienced as a student, a teacher, a wife, and a mother, with the male world of the academy and church into which she was born and wed.

Two Worlds Together: *Woman in Sacred History*

Like a number of nineteenth-century women, Stowe recognized that women were often missing from accounts of history. To the question, "Are there any lives of women?" Stowe's character Mr. Sewell in *The Pearl of Orr's Island* (1862) answers: "No, my dear ... in the old times, women did not get their lives written, though I don't doubt many of them were much better worth writing than the men's."[38] In her book *Woman in Sacred History*, Stowe tries to redress history's wrongs by presenting "a history of Womanhood under Divine culture," which she thought moves toward "that high ideal of woman ... in modern Christian countries."[39] To do this, she appropriates the tools of contemporary biblical scholars. She follows the "modern fashion of treating the personages of sacred story with the same freedom of inquiry as the characters of any other history."[40] This approach allows her to set aside traditional theological categories, to reinterpret stories in fresh ways, to criticize traditional readings of texts (even those in the New Testament), and to write for a broad audience.

Stowe's fashionable and scientific approach allows her to discern "a *system* progressively developing from age to age," through which "the Creator revealed himself to man [*sic*]."[41] She romanticizes "the artless simplicity of the primi-

---

37. Carolyn A. Haynes, *Divine Destiny: Gender and Race in Nineteenth-Century Protestantism* (Jackson: University of Mississippi, 1998), 78.

38. Harriet Beecher Stowe, *The Pearl of Orr's Island*, cited in Hedrick, *Harriet Beecher Stowe: A Life*, vii.

39. Harriet Beecher Stowe, *Woman in Sacred History* (New York: Fords, Howard, & Hulbert, 1873) 11.

40. Ibid., 12. Stowe cites Michaelis's *Laws of Moses* and Smith's *Dictionary of the Bible*. She is aware of the work of de Wette, a prominent German critical scholar. She begins *Footsteps of the Master* with a translation of de Wette's hymn that reveals his struggles with doubt.

41. Stowe, *Woman in Sacred History*, 11. Stowe knew of Darwin's work and was very close to her brother Henry Ward Beecher (1818–87), who popularized the theory of evolution in America, making it a cornerstone of his theology.

tive period" upon which the "dew of earth's early morning lies … sparkling and undried; and the men and women speak out of their hearts with the simplicity of little children."[42] She assesses each character according to his or her place in God's system of education and revelation. Accordingly, she proposes that Abraham's "falsehoods" about his relationship with Sarah be judged "by the ancient standard" which deemed "skill in deception … as one of the forms of wisdom."[43] Moreover, she explains Sarah's "real flesh and blood … foibles weaknesses, and variabilities" (such as Sarah's lie about laughing when she heard the announcement that she would have a son in Gen 18:9–15) as appropriate "to womanhood, in an early age of imperfectly developed morals" (29).

Stowe also uses the "principle of *selection,* much talked of now in science" instead of the traditional theological language of election and predestination to explain God's operating plan (51). She likens God to a "skilful husbandman" who perfected "a certain seed" or "stock" by separating it out from others to grow on its own and produce "the sacerdotal race, through which should come his choicest revelations to man … [i.e.,] Jesus" (40–41). Stowe believes the fittest survived the selection process. She explains: "The thoughtful, patient, meditative Isaac is chosen; the wild, hot-blooded, impetuous Ishmael is rejected,—not as in themselves better or worse, but as in relation to their adaptation to a great purpose of future good to mankind" (41). Similarly, the choice of Jacob over Esau illustrates the principle that "the peaceable, domestic, prudent and conservative elements are uniformly chosen, in preference to the warlike and violent characteristics of the age" (51).

Stowe often draws on tradition to fill in gaps in the biblical stories or address contentious theological or moral issues in the stories of women. For example, Stowe wrestles with the relatively short biblical portrayal of Miriam and looks to rabbinic tradition and legend for further proof of her importance: "It is remarkable that while Jewish tradition regarded Miriam with such veneration, while we see her spoken of in Holy Writ as a divinely appointed leader, yet there are none of her writings transmitted to us, as in the case of other and less revered prophetesses" (81). Following the lead of Hebrew lore and using her own assumptions about women's moral influence on men, Stowe fleshes out Miriam's story, positing her influence on the Mosaic laws. She felt that Moses "must have gained much of that peculiar knowledge of the needs and wants and feelings of women" from "the motherly heart of this sister" (81). Specifically, Stowe saw Miriam's influence on laws that protected an unloved wife from a husband's partiality, mandated the consideration of the rights of captive women, and "secured the marriage-rights

---

42. Ibid., 25. See Kimball's discussion of Stowe's "romantic evangelicalism" in Kimball, *Religious Ideas,* 95–126.

43. Stowe, *Woman in Sacred History,* 27. Subsequent references to *Woman in Sacred History* will be provided within the text.

of the purchased slave and forbade making merchandise of her" (82). Like the rabbis, then, Stowe fills out the biblical story of Miriam. Her unique embellishments, however, come out of her experiences of women's culture.

Like most nineteenth-century interpreters, Stowe felt it important to read texts in their historical contexts. She uses all available traditional and contemporary resources to provide historical background. Regarding the details of Moses' childhood and education, for example, she draws on the speech of Stephen in Acts; information from the ancient historians Strabo, Philo, and Josephus; and data on the life and training of Egyptian priests from Wilkinson's *Egypt* (67–68). Stowe posits that Moses appropriated his Egyptian education and then presses the homiletical point that God uses worldly wisdom (68). The illustrations Stowe chooses to accompany her biblical retellings, which represent different schools and periods of art, also suggest her desire to read the Bible in light of its ancient setting; they provide another interpretive lens through which to read the stories.[44]

Stowe combines her scholarly approach to Scripture with a more devotional approach that allows her to preach the text. In her exposition of Hagar's encounter with the angel in the desert, for instance, Stowe reads the story figuratively, suggesting that it is "so universally and beautifully significant of our every-day human experience, that it has almost the force of an allegory." She asks, "who of us has not yielded to despairing grief, while flowing by us were unnoticed sources of consolation? The angel did not *create* the spring in the desert" (38). Stowe's husband would have approved heartily of his wife's attempts to make the biblical stories relevant to her readers. In his "Introduction to the American Edition" of Charles J. Ellicott's *Commentary on St. Paul's Epistle to the Galatians*, Calvin Stowe criticizes what he calls "severe and strictly linguistic exegesis" and commends an approach that, "though less pure … furnishes the material more ready for immediate use."[45]

Stowe's desire to draw practical and spiritual lessons from the stories of women forced her to wrestle with such questions as the relationship of the Testaments and the authority of tradition and Scripture. Her exposition of the story of Sarah shows Stowe's willingness to face difficult interpretive issues, to use her own experiences to criticize tradition, and to offer fresh interpretations. Stowe contrasts the traditional Christian reading of Sarah as an exemplary model of meekness and wifely submission[46] with the Sarah she finds in the Old Testament. Taking her cue from the meaning of the Hebrew name Sarah, "princess,"

---

44. Stowe was very interested in art and had written a book on the subject. See "Toward an Ecumenical Art," in Smith, "Reading the Word," 209–81.

45. Calvin E. Stowe, "Introductory Notice to the American Edition," in Charles J. Ellicott, *Commentary on St. Paul's Epistle to the Galatians* (Andover: Draper, 1888), 11.

46. 1 Pet 3:6. "Even as Sarah obeyed Abraham, calling him lord; whose daughters ye are, so long as ye do well, and are not subject to a slavish fear."

Stowe concludes that Sarah "crowned with the power of eminent beauty, and fully understanding the sovereignty it gave her over man ... was virtually empress and mistress of the man she called 'lord'" (25). Stowe thought that the strong, domineering, and even despotic wife Sarah, who expected Abraham "to use his authority in the line of her wishes," modeled a type of submission few women could find objectionable (25).[47]

Doubtless, Sarah's submission mirrored the experience of many nineteenth-century women who ruled the home and expected their husbands to use their authority in accordance with their wives' wishes. Stowe herself wrestled with the notion of wifely submission. Her biographer, Joan Hedrick, writes of Stowe's unhappiness with her husband's decision to accept two academic positions in two different cities while teaching at a third college.[48] Stowe advised her husband that he should stay at Bowdoin, a place where she was particularly happy. However, Calvin Stowe disregarded his wife's wishes and accepted the prestigious position of chair of Sacred Literature at Andover Theological Seminary in Andover, Massachusetts. This decision, Hedrick notes, was "the last significant decision Calvin Stowe made as head of the family."[49] Like Sarah, Harriet Beecher Stowe was a very powerful woman and expected her husband to follow her wishes. Like many women, Stowe used various methods of persuasion to get her way in marriage. Sarah's type of submission, which did not seem like submission at all, appealed to Stowe. Edward Wagenknecht writes that Stowe "knew that on the domestic front women are more than a match for men and always have been, that if a man loves a woman she has a hold over him which no legal privilege that he may hold can possible counter-balance, and that if he does not wish to kill her or discard her, he *must* please her."[50] Stowe's views of women's power then pushed her to reinterpret the story of Sarah and undercut the traditional Christian teaching about female submission included in most nineteenth-century wedding ceremonies.[51]

---

47. In the Genesis story itself, Sarah is portrayed as the domineering spouse. She orders Abraham, for example, to have sexual intercourse with her maid Hagar, and he readily complies (Gen 16:1–50).

48. A correspondent of the *New York Independent* commented sarcastically: "How far Dr. Stowe approximates to the faculty of omnipresence, we are not informed; but if, as the papers have stated, he is to have an actual and effectual connection with one college and two theological seminaries at the same time, he must stand in need of something like it" (Hedrick, *Harriet Beecher Stowe: A Life,* 207).

49. Ibid., 208.

50. Wagenknecht, *Harriet Beecher Stowe,* 56.

51. In her novel *My Wife and I,* Harry Henderson tells Eva Van Arsdale, who has conscientious misgivings about promising to "obey" her husband-to-be, that "there can be no obeying where there is no commanding, and as to commanding you I should as soon think of commanding the sun and moon" (ibid., 55).

Stowe's experiences of women's culture enabled her to recognize Sarah's humanity. Following the narrative clues in Genesis, Stowe contends that Sarah was little more "than a beautiful princess of a nomadic tribe, with many virtues and the failings that usually attend beauty and power" (28). Stowe casts Sarah in a particularly dark light in her "domestic broil" with Hagar. She suggests that the biblical narrative "in its usual naïve way ... represents Sarah as scolding her patient husband for the results which came from following her own advice" (28). Thus, Stowe characterizes Sarah as "the eager, impulsive, hot-hearted woman, accustomed to indulgence, impatient of trouble, and perfectly certain that she is right, and that the Lord himself must think so" (28). Still she tries to find some redeeming qualities in Sarah. Following a rabbinic tradition that Sarah loved Hagar before Hagar's pregnancy caused a rift between them, Stowe suggests that the women were reconciled following Hagar's return (29). Stowe also makes the novel supposition that "Sarah, like most warm-hearted and passionate women, was in the main, a kindly, motherly creature, and ... that she should at times have overwhelmed Hagar with kindness, and helped her through the trials of motherhood, and petted the little Ishmael till he grew too saucy to be endured" (29). Finally, Stowe sees in "the simple and touching announcement" of Sarah's death—especially Abraham's mourning and tears and his purchase of her burial place—and the subsequent veneration of her sepulcher evidence for a more positive memory of Sarah, "the beautiful princess, the crowned mother of a great nation, the beloved wife" (30).

Stowe's sketches of the women in sacred history illustrate her ability to blend her own distinctively female reading of the text with insights and resources traditionally associated with the male world of the academy and church. By combining these approaches, she produces readings that sometimes challenge traditional interpretations of texts and women's roles and often encourage readers in their spiritual lives.

THE WEDDING OF TWO WORLDS: *FOOTSTEPS OF THE MASTER*

In 1878 Stowe published *Footsteps of the Master,* a book that is neither written for women nor concerns women as its subject. Stowe wrote *Footsteps of the Master* to feed the soul and the intellect of both seekers and believers as they reconsider the person of Christ. Stowe uses the liturgical calendar as the organizing principle of the book and, beginning with Advent, considers Christ's role in the Old Testament and prophecy, his birth and childhood (Christmas and Epiphany), events of his adult life and crucifixion (Lent and Passion Week), and his resurrection and ascension (Easter and Ascension). *Footsteps of the Master* demonstrates Stowe's strengths as an exegete, apologist, and pastor—typically male roles. Her particular interest in women, however, also surfaces unobtrusively in this book, showing Stowe's ability to wed traditionally separate spheres.

Stowe came to her study of the life of Christ with pastoral concerns for the spiritual life of her readers. In her chapter "The Prayer-Life of Jesus," for example,

Stowe addresses those who regard "all protracted seasons of prayer and periods spent in devotion" as wasted time.[52] Using an exemplary hermeneutic, she argues that if Jesus Christ deemed it important to spend considerable time in prayer, how much more should we who are "feeble and earthly, with hearts always prone to go astray, living in a world where everything presses us downward to the lower regions of the senses and passions" (107). Stowe also speaks to those wrestling with such intellectual issues as the supernatural elements of the temptation narratives. She acknowledges different ways of reading texts, suggesting that "whatever we may think of the mode and manner of that mysterious account of the temptations of Christ, it is evident that they were met and overcome by the spiritual force gained by prayer and the study of God's word" (107). At the same time, Stowe warns that a strictly academic encounter with the story of Jesus' wilderness experience is inadequate: "The history in the Gospels is so well worn that it often slips through the head without affecting the heart" (110). Further, Stowe addresses pastoral concerns related to formalism and empty traditions. She argues that even Lenten traditions, "originating in deep spiritual influences," tend "to degenerate into a mere form" (109). Instead of literal fasting, Stowe advises "the true spiritual fasting," which she defines as turning away from "the engrossing cares and pleasures of earth" toward "things divine" (109). Such fasting involved the study of Scripture, a scene or trait or incident in Jesus' life, using "all the helps we can get to understand it fully," including parallel Gospel texts and other relevant passages in Scripture to make oneself "insensibly interested" in Jesus. She proffers that Jesus himself might draw near to those who fasted in this way as he did to the disciples on the road to Emmaus (110).

Stowe models for her readers a judicious use of scholarly tools and insights. In her discussion of Jesus' birth, she raises the thorny problem of Matthew's genealogy of Jesus and commends the solution put forward by such worthies as Lightfoot, Paulus, Spanheim, and Lange (54). In her rehearsal of prophetic passages pointing to Jesus, Stowe acknowledges the critical issue of the dating of the book of Daniel and includes a quotation from contemporary French scholar M. Lenormant regarding the position of the "German exegetical school" on the dating of Daniel and a discussion of Zoroastrian literature about the Chaldeans (45, 48). Further, in her discussion of Jesus' childhood, Stowe mentions the apocryphal Gospels and follows her husband's position on the criteria for distinguishing between true and apocryphal Gospels as outlined in his *The Origin and History of the Books of the Bible* (1868).

To the scholarly insights and debates that Stowe weaves into her book, adding to its depth and appeal as a book that feeds the soul and the intellect, Stowe adds what her British contemporary Josephine Butler called "a womanly

---

52. Harriet Beecher Stowe, *Footsteps of the Master* (St. John: Morrow, 1878), 106. Subsequent references to *Footsteps of the Master* will be provided within the text.

or mother way of reading."[53] This approach draws her to the figure of Mary, the mother of Jesus, and to what she regards as the feminine qualities of Jesus.[54] Stowe suggests that Protestants have been deprived of "a great source of comfort and edification" through their neglect of Mary, "this one Woman of women" (64). Stowe reflects on Mary's relationship with her son, whom she identified as "bone of her bone and flesh of her flesh," his life having grown out of "the union of the Divine nature with the nature of a pure woman," concluding that Jesus had more of the "pure feminine element" than any other man (70). Stowe then explores the feminine characteristics of Christ. She likens Jesus' mission to that of a mother who "when seeking a lost and helpless child, outcast in some den of misery, would pass by palaces and refuse the shelter of luxurious roofs to share the poverty of her beloved" (60). Similarly, in her discussion of Jesus' relationships with his disciples, Stowe suggests that Jesus acted more like a mother than a father. In preparing his disciples for their future work as apostles, for example, Jesus "infused" himself to them "by an embracing, tender, brooding love; ardent, self-forgetful, delicate, refined," like one of the mothers who led their children to follow in Jesus' footsteps (136). Moreover, Stowe's own experiences as a mother shaped her understanding of Jesus' relationship with individual disciples. She imagines that Jesus listened "with a grave smile" to Peter "as a mother to her eldest and more self-confident boy" and that Jesus treated John as a youngest and most tender child of the family flock, in contrast to Judas, whom Jesus loved and pitied, "the unworthy son" of the mother whose hair he whitened and whose heart he broke" (136, 140–41, 216).[55] Moreover, Stowe uses the metaphor of mother to describe contemporary believers' relationship with Jesus. She advises readers to take their burdens to Jesus and leave them with him "as entirely as the little child leaves his school troubles with his mother" (207).

Thus, enmeshed in a devotional book that shows a mature Stowe using the tools of the scholarly academy and church, there is an emphasis on Mary and the feminine side of Christ. Like his mother Mary, Christ modeled qualities that the nineteenth century identified as feminine. Stowe's depictions of Christ's motherly qualities and actions reflect her own experiences of motherhood and her idealized memories of her own mother. She uses her own experiences to help readers draw closer to Mary and her son, whom she held out to all as "their best Friend, the Shepherd that is seeking them, the generous Saviour and Giver that is longing

---

53. Josephine E. Butler, The *Lady of Shunem* (London: Marshall, 1894), 74.

54. For a detailed examination of the feminization of Christ in Stowe's fiction, see Linda Sue Miller Emery, "The Feminization of Christ: Harriet Beecher Stowe's Use of the Bible" (Ph.D. diss., Washington State University, 1992).

55. Stowe also used the metaphor of father to describe Jesus' love for his own: "then there was the love of his very own—the little church of tried, true, tested friends ... for whom his love was as strong as a father's, tender and thoughtful as a mother's" (*Footsteps of the Master*, 235).

to save them from all that they fear and to give exceedingly abundantly beyond all they can ask or think" (13).

Conclusions

Birth and marriage gave Harriet Beecher Stowe direct access to the best resources for interpreting Scripture available in nineteenth-century America. Stowe unofficially entered the male worlds of the academy and church, but through her writing, she was both participant and critic. The footprints of Stowe's personal "Rabbi," Calvin Stowe, are visible throughout her interpretive work. She shared his love for tradition and scholarship and his concern to interpret Scripture for the community of faith. Her intimate knowledge of scholarship, however, provided her with a critical eye to detect cracks in the edifice of biblical scholarship. Her critique continues to speak to those who are involved in the academic study of Scripture.

Stowe's life experiences also placed her at the heart of the distinctive women's culture of the nineteenth century. She wrestled with questions about women's place, nature, and role. Her feminine lens opened up new ways of reading and interpreting Scripture. Stowe knew the strength and power of women. She tried to redeem the women in Scripture through her writing by recovering their stories, by reinterpreting tradition, and by presenting novel readings of texts. She also created fictional characters who modeled new roles for women. Thus, she explored alternatives to male ways of doing various types of ministry (priestly, prophetic, and pastoral). Her writings empowered women.

The brilliant Stowe wed the distinctive male and female worlds together to produce entertaining, provocative, inspiring, and often unique readings of Scripture. Stowe's interpretive work is profound. She pushed boundaries of traditional interpretation; she asked new questions of the text. Yet, as *Footsteps of the Master* shows, Stowe asked her questions within the camp. Unlike her contemporary Elizabeth Cady Stanton (1815–1902), who regarded the Bible as a barrier to women's legal, social, and spiritual equality, Stowe remained a faithful reader of the Bible, which remained an authoritative and life-giving book for her and many of her readers.

Bibliography

Berkeley, Kathleen. "Catharine Beecher and Domestic Relations." Pages 1–18 in *Against the Tide: Women Reformers in American Society*. Edited by Paul A. Cimbala and Randall Miller. Westport: Praeger, 1997.

Booth, Catherine. *Female Ministry; Or, Woman's Right to Preach the Gospel*. London: Morgan & Chase, ca. 1859.

Butler, Josephine E. *The Lady of Shunem*. London: Marshall, 1894.

———. *Prophets and Prophetesses*. Newcastle-on-Tyne: Mawson, Swan & Morgan, 1898.

Caskey, Marie. *Chariot of Fire: Religion and the Beecher Family*. New Haven: Yale University Press, 1978.

Emery, Linda Sue Miller. "The Feminization of Christ: Harriet Beecher Stowe's Use of the Bible." Ph.D. diss. Washington State University, 1992.

Fields, Annie. ed. *Life and Letters of Harriet Beecher Stowe*. Boston: Houghton & Mifflin, 1889.

Gardner, Catherine Villanueva. "Heaven-Appointed Educators of Mind: Catharine Beecher and the Moral Power of Women." *Hypatia* 19/2 (2004): 1–6.

Hall, Mark David. "Catharine Beecher: America's First Female Philosopher and Theologian." *Fides et Historia* 32 (2000): 65–80.

Haynes, Carolyn A. *Divine Destiny: Gender and Race in Nineteenth-Century Protestantism*. Jackson: University of Mississippi, 1998.

Hedrick, Joan D. *Harriet Beecher Stowe: A Life*. Oxford: Oxford University Press, 1994.

———. " 'Peaceable Fruits': The Ministry of Harriet Beecher Stowe." *American Quarterly* 40 (1988): 307–32.

Kelley, Mary. *Private Woman, Public Stage: Literary Domesticity in Nineteenth-Century America*. Oxford: Oxford University Press, 1984.

Kimball, Gayle. *The Religious Ideas of Harriet Beecher Stowe: Her Gospel of Womanhood*. New York: Mellen, 1982.

Palmer, Phoebe. *The Promise of the Father*. Boston: Degen, 1859.

Rugoff, Milton Allan. *The Beechers: An American Family in the Nineteenth Century*. New York: Harper & Row, 1981.

Smith, Gail Katherine. "Reading the Word: Harriet Beecher Stowe and Interpretation." Ph.D. diss. University of Virginia, 1993.

Stowe, Calvin E. "Introductory Notice to the American Edition." In Charles J. Ellicott, *Commentary on St. Paul's Epistle to the Galatians*. Andover: Draper, 1888.

Stowe, Harriet Beecher. *Footsteps of the Master*. St. John: Morrow, 1878.

———. *The Minister's Wooing*. 1859. Repr., Boston: Osgood, 1875.

———. *Woman in Sacred History*. New York: Fords, Howard & Hulbert, 1873.

Stowe, Harriet Beecher, and John Michael Moran. *Collected Poems of Harriet Beecher Stowe*. Hartford: Transcendental Books, 1967.

Wagenknecht, Edward. *Harriet Beecher Stowe: The Known and the Unknown*. Oxford: Oxford University Press, 1965.

Westra, Helen Petter. "Confronting Antichrist: The Influence of Jonathan Edwards's Millennial Vision." Pages 114–58 in *The Stowe Debate: Rhetorical Strategies in Uncle Tom's Cabin*. Edited by Mason I. Lowance Jr., Ellen E. Westbrook, and R. C. De Prospo. Amherst: University of Massachusetts Press, 1994.

Wilson, Forrest. *Crusader in Crinoline: The Life of Harriet Beecher Stowe*. Philadelphia: Lippincott, 1941.

Florence Nightingale: A Mother to Many

Christiana de Groot

Introduction

Nightingale's Life

Florence Nightingale was much more than a nurse in the Crimean War.[1] Out of her ninety years (1820–1910), only two (1854–56) were spent in the Crimea. Yet for most of us, these years define her life. There are many possible reasons why this is the image that has endured. Certainly, nursing is an acceptable, positive vocation for women—a nurturing, serving role. Furthermore, it is a picture that was memorably captured in the poem "Santa Filomena" by Henry Wadsworth Longfellow:

> ... The wounded from the battle plain,
> In dreary hospitals of pain,
> The cheerless corridors,
> The cold and stony floors.
>
> Lo! In that house of misery
> A lady with a lamp I see
> Pass through the glimmering gloom,
> And flit from room to room.
>
> And slow, as in a dream of bliss,
> The speechless sufferer turns to kiss
> Her shadow, as it falls
> Upon the darkening walls....[2]

---

1. The title of this essay is taken from Nightingale's comment on Gen 45:8 in her Annotated Bible. It is published in Lynn McDonald, ed., *Florence Nightingale's Spiritual Journey: Biblical Annotations, Sermons and Journal Notes* (Collected Works of Florence Nightingale 2; Waterloo, Ont.: Wilfred Laurier University Press, 2001), 106.

2. The poem, inspired by Nightingale's work nursing wounded soldiers, was first published in the *Atlantic Monthly* in 1857.

In addition, Nightingale worked very hard to remain a private person upon her return from the war. She never spoke in a public setting, and few of her written works were published during her lifetime. From her modest office, she worked behind the scenes in crucial ways to create a public health-care system in England, Ireland, and India; reform the war office; establish nursing as a respectable profession for women; study the medieval mystics; write a treatise on the philosophy of religion; and revise the Authorized Version to make it accessible to school children.

Her many contributions are now more visible with the ongoing publication of her collected works. The series, edited by Lynn McDonald, will comprise sixteen volumes when it is complete. For the purpose of studying Nightingale's interpretation of Scripture, it is fortunate that her biblical and theological writings have been published first. McDonald's rationale for this order of publication is that Nightingale's faith underlay her actions, thinking, and writing. Hence, we need to understand her religious convictions before we can appreciate her writing and work at social reforms.[3]

As the foregoing indicates, Nightingale considered herself a Christian. She was a lifelong member of the Church of England and a faithful reader of Scripture. However, in contrast to some of the women interpreters presented in this volume, Nightingale is not first of all an interpreter of Scripture. In her works, there are very few places wherein she self-consciously reflects on how she is reading the text or where she engages in a discussion on how she might differ from others. This is not her focus. In the case of Nightingale, the reason for studying her work is different. She is a significant interpreter of Scripture because she played such a key role in shaping nineteenth-century England. It is the need to understand her, her times, and her living out her faith that occasions the interest in her use of Scripture. A study of her interpretation of Scripture is a piece of a larger project of understanding this woman who made such a huge impact on public life, and who did this, according to her own testimony, as a response to receiving a call to service from God.[4]

The Annotated Bible

Nightingale's Annotated Bible, made much more accessible with its recent publication, is the focus of this study on how she engaged and interpreted Scripture.

---

3. See the comments by McDonald in the introduction to *Florence Nightingale's Spiritual Journey*, 3, and "An Overview of Nightingale's Spiritual Journey" (5–13).

4. Nightingale heard a call from God to service on 7 February 1837, when she was sixteen. She refers to this call and to several others calls in various places. Her diary of 7 February 1892 lists five occasions when she heard God's call (McDonald, *Florence Nightingale's Spiritual Journey*, 516).

This Bible, the Authorized Version (KJV),[5] was given to Nightingale by her sister Parthenope and was used throughout her life.[6] The Bible invited annotation because every second page was blank, and it is these annotations as well as notes made on the sides of the pages that will be the subject of this study.[7] There are certain features of Nightingale's annotations that bear reflection before considering the individual notes. Although some of the notations are dated, most are not; hence, it is not possible to arrange them sequentially and attempt to trace a development in her thinking on various aspects of the biblical text. The ones that are dated, however, often provide a glimpse into her spiritual state, and it is intriguing to seek connections between these notations and certain events in Nightingale's life. The editor has indicated, where possible, what event might lie behind particular annotations, but it is important to realize that these are conjectures. For example, Nightingale underlines parts of Ps 18:4–6, "*The sorrows of death compassed me, and the floods of ungodly men made me afraid. The sorrows of hell compassed me* about: the snares of death prevented me. *In my distress I called upon the Lord, and cried unto my God:* he heard my voice out of his temple, and my cry came before him, even into his ears." She also writes and underlines beside it, "**This world is hell. 27 October 1862.**"[8] McDonald adds this note to Nightingale's annotation, "This is the day that Aunt Mai Smith visited her and made remarks that caused her enormous distress; the date is noted fifteen years later in her diary. Letters indicate that Nightingale was in great pain in 1862."[9] Although it is sometimes overreaching the bounds of prudent scholarship to try to make a direct connection between events and a writer's work, when a text is dated so precisely, it invites the reader to make the connection.

Another significant feature of these annotations is their private nature. Nightingale wrote them to be seen by herself alone. In reading them, we are not reading someone else's mail but rather reading someone else's diary. They give us a glimpse into Nightingale's inner life, her inner dialogue, and her dialogue with the text of Scripture. It is fascinating to note that the annotations are not only about Nightingale's response to Scripture but sometimes are her response to her own response to Scripture. In a few places, we read a series of dates after a particular notation. For example, she writes and underlines beside Ps 42, a lament psalm, "**All thy waves**

---

5. Published by Oxford University Press, 1843.

6. The earliest annotation is dated 1844 (see the frontispiece), cited in McDonald, *Florence Nightingale's Spiritual Journey*, 101, and the latest is 1875 (comment on Heb 5:8–9), 302.

7. The Bible is kept in the archives of the Florence Nightingale Museum housed at St. Thomas Hospital, London, England.

8. In the published version of the annotations, italics are used to indicate underlining, small capitals for double (or more), and bold for heavy emphasis. See McDonald, *Florence Nightingale's Spiritual Journey*, 92 .

9. Ibid., 138, for both the biblical annotation and the editor's note. Subsequent references to McDonald, *Florence Nightingale's Spiritual Journey*, will be provided within the text.

and thy billows are gone over me; **les eaux d'une violente mortification (the waters of a violent mortification). 27 October 1861, 15 October 1867, 3 January 1873, 22 February 1874**" (144).[10] Because she does not need to worry here about what others might think, she can freely express herself. Because her notes are for herself alone, the niceties that attend her letters to friends, family, and colleagues are missing here.

Because she is not writing for others, some of this is also cryptic—she has no need to explain what she already knows. For example, on the page facing Isa 6:3, "And one cried unto another, and said, Holy, holy, holy, is the Lord of hosts: the whole earth is full of his glory," Nightingale writes, "By this trisagion, or thrice holy, the rabbins understood the Sephiroth or three Persons" (170). Nightingale has moved from the seraphim in Isa 6:3 to the Sephiroth. As the editor points out, this involves a change from a masculine plural form to a feminine plural. However, it also involves the transposition of the "r" and the "ph," resulting in a new word. Nightingale is most likely referring to the Jewish mystical text known as the *Zohar*, which includes a description of ten Sephiroth that are often organized into three groups of three, with the last Sephirah, the Divine Presence, including all the previous ones.[11]

Three aspects of Nightingale's annotations will be the focus of this essay. First, Nightingale's devotional reading of Scripture will be examined. She reads the Bible first as an act of faith, and in her annotations we can see how Bible reading functions in her life as a believer. Second, she reads the Bible in a systematic way. She comes to the text with certain basic convictions about the shape of the Christian faith and engages the text intellectually, using it to build a coherent theology. Third, the annotations indicate with whom Nightingale is in conversation. She quotes writers both ancient and modern, both Christian and non-Christian, and relies heavily on German biblical scholars. Through studying her dialogue partners, one can situate her in the theological and biblical landscape of the nineteenth century. Although these different aspects of Nightingale's Scripture reading are studied separately, in her annotations they often occur together. She moves continually among academic pursuits, emotional responses, imaginative construals, and citing others in several languages. In a concluding section, this essay will characterize how hers has been a woman's reading of Scripture. This section will investigate whether we can identify insights or ways of reading as typically female or as reflecting Nightingale's particular experience as a woman.

---

10. The editor's note on this notation reads, "The first date corresponds with a particularly low period in Nightingale's life, after Sidney Herbert's death and with Clough's death expected soon; the third and fourth were periods with heavy preoccupation with her mother's care, the fourth notably soon after her father's death."

11. See the discussion in Daniel C. Matt, trans., *Introduction to Zohar: The Book of Enlightenment* (Toronto: Paulist, 1983), 20–21.

Nightingale's Devotional Reading of the Bible

When Nightingale reads Scripture devotionally, she reads it as God's Word addressed to her. She knows that these are also human words that arose out of a particular historical context, but this understanding is not at the fore as she meditates. In this way of reading, she opens up her heart and allows the words she reads to engage her emotions, her motivations, her sense of self-identity, and her vocation. There is a sort of inner dialogue between herself and God. She listens as well as responds. The richness of this dialogue testifies to the depth of meaning she finds in Scripture, as well as to her discipline of coming to the text again and again in many different moods and seasons.

The title of this essay comes from her response to the Joseph narrative. Reflecting on Gen 45:5, "Now therefore be not grieved, nor angry with yourselves, that ye sold me hither: for God did send me before you to preserve life," Nightingale writes and underlines, "BE NOT GRIEVED **NOR ANGRY WITH YOURSELVES** FOR **GOD** DID SEND ME—TO PRESERVE LIFE." Immediately following this, Nightingale responds to Gen 45:8, "*So now it was not you that sent me hither, but God: and he hath made me a father* to Pharaoh, and lord of all his house, and a ruler throughout all the land of Egypt," with these words: "So NOW **IT WAS NOT YOU** THAT SENT ME HITHER **BUT GOD**: AND HE HATH MADE ME (A MOTHER TO MANY). 30 March 1873" (106). By Nightingale's changing the text's "father to Pharaoh" to "mother to many," we can observe both her identification with and separation from Joseph. She latches onto Joseph's vocation in particular. His work was not his own but was God's work through him, and it was for the purpose of preserving life. When we contemplate Nightingale's life, we can see clear parallels. She, too, experienced a call from God for service and understood that her work in nursing, sanitation, and welfare reform was part of God's work so that life would be preserved and enhanced. This verse supports and fortifies her sense of mission (285). Nightingale also found the phrase "co-worker with God" in 1 Cor 3:9 descriptive of the relationship between her work and God's work. Both passages reveal Nightingale's high view of human agency. Humans are God's hands and feet in the world. God's work is not accomplished by miracles but through the ordinary day-to-day tasks accomplished by men and women.

As we have already seen, Scripture also functions to articulate her sense of despair—the futility of life. The book of Job and the lament psalms were especially powerful as she heard in these texts echoes of her own suffering. Often she does no more than underline the verses that were significant or write out the verse again on the blank page.[12] Sometimes she also adds a reflection that incorporated the voice of hopelessness into the larger context of the Christian

---

12. For example, across the page from Job 6 and 7, Nightingale wrote out verses taken from Job 7–17 that repeat Job's despair in response to his suffering (ibid., 130–31).

faith. For example, Nightingale underlines Job 6:11, "*What is my strength that I should hope? And what is mine end, that I should prolong my life?*" and adds these words in response, "Few people can bear to look at *life* apart from Him whose love alone makes life a blessing" (130). Nightingale's conviction that God's love is the source of blessing echoes again and again. For example, her response to Ps 118:6 is an especially moving testimony to her confidence in God's graciousness toward humanity. The text states, "The Lord is on my side; I will not fear: what can man do unto me?" and Nightingale's lengthy response concludes with these words, "Why *should* we fear, since He is so strong, so good, so faithful? The foundation of our present hope is not on anything we have been led to discover in ourselves. *It is not what* WE ARE, *but what* GOD IS, *that gives us confidence and peace.* 20 October, 1871" (161).

Despair and hope are not the only spiritual states that resonate with Nightingale. The text of Scripture also challenges her and encourages her to continue striving. In Ps 27:8, Nightingale responds to the words, "When thou saidst, Seek ye my face; my heart said unto thee, Thy face, Lord, will I seek," with this comment, "Ah! Strive to be able to say this" (141). The text occasions a yearning in her for a life lived single-heartedly before the face of God.[13] In other places, she shows regret in her realization that she has fallen short of God's commands, has been unworthy of God's love, and asks for forgiveness using a prayer of penitence. For example, in response to Ps 25:11, "For thy name's sake, O Lord, pardon mine iniquity; for it is great," Nightingale quotes a prayer that appears in several places in her writings. She pleads, "Four things, O God, I have to offer Thee which Thou hast not in all Thy treasury: My nothingness, my sad necessity, my fatal sin and earnest penitence. Receive these gifts and take the giver home."[14]

She not only reflects on her relationship with God devotionally but also uses Scripture to encourage herself to see her fellow human beings through God's eyes in their perfected state. In her reflection on 1 Cor 13:7, "Beareth all things, *believeth all things*, hopeth all things, endureth all things," she instructs herself, "Believeth that there exists in each the germ of a being destined for a beauty and perfection of its *own*; thinketh less of what they are than of what they are meant to be, of what they *will* be" (286). In a way typical of biblical faith, Nightingale sees that her view of others in the present needs to reflect their final state in the new heaven and new earth.

---

13. Another instance of Nightingale's calling herself to single-hearted devotion occurs in her response to Ps 103:1, "Bless the Lord, O my soul: and all that is within me, bless his holy name." She writes beside this verse, "When will *all* that is within me praise and sympathize with His holy name? October 1873" (ibid.,160).

14. See both Nightingale's annotation and the editor's note on this prayer in McDonald, *Florence Nightingale's Spiritual Journey*, 140. The exact source of the prayer has not been found, although in one place in Nightingale's writings it is identified as an Arabian prayer.

Nightingale's devotional engagement with the text of Scripture is very rich. She comes to the text on many different occasions and expects to hear from it the Word of God. This Word decisively shapes who she is and how she understands her task in the world and her fellow human beings. Ultimately, her beliefs support a view that is hopeful, one that sees life grounded in the love of God for all. Although she experiences much suffering due to physical pain, difficulties in her work, or the loss of loved ones, these times of despair do not have the last word. Nightingale feels at liberty forcefully to express negative emotions in response to reading Scripture and in so doing is able to find solace.

A THEOLOGICAL READING OF THE BIBLE

Nightingale's devotional reading of the Bible is seamlessly connected to her theological reading. She comes to Scripture with the conviction that it is God's Word and that the Bible is the Word of one recognizable God. There is a unity in the text that derives from its one author. This author is named in various ways, and she equates them with each other and with the divine essence. Her comment on Isa 12:2 is revealing. In response to the verse, "Behold, God is my salvation; I will trust, and not be afraid: for the Lord Jehovah is my strength and my song; he is also become my salvation," she writes, "The Lord/Jah stands simply for the divine essence, 'who *is*,' who necessarily must be. Jehovah 'who *is*, who was and who is to come'" (174). She then wonders if Jehovah and Christ are one and the same. She reads Ps 15 (16):8–11[15] in conjunction with Acts 2:25–31 and remarks, "Compare Acts 13:35 where Paul thinks this applies to Christ. Did Peter then (Acts 2) mean 'I foresaw *Jehovah* always' etc. for *Christ*? Or is 'I' Christ? My soul in hell is evidently Christ's (Acts 2:31)" (138). Nightingale then further equates *Elohim* with Christ in her annotations on Ps 45:6–7.[16] She comments, "Thy throne, O Elohim, and this is applied to Jesus Christ. Hebrews 1:8. Here the father is called Elohim, when anointing the Son. See Hebrews 1:9. In Psalm 78:56 the Son appears to be called Elohim too" (145–46). In her questions on Isa 25:7,[17] she brings these titles together and asks if they are all referring to the same being. She writes:

---

15. Psalm 15 (16): 8–11 (KJV) reads, "I have set the LORD always before me: because he is at my right hand, I shall not be moved. Therefore my heart is glad, and my glory rejoiceth: my flesh also shall rest in hope. For thou wilt not leave my soul in hell; neither wilt thou suffer thine Holy One to see corruption. Thou wilt shew me the path of life: in thy presence is fullness of joy; at thy right hand there are pleasures for evermore.

16. Psalm 45:6–7 (KJV) reads, "Thy throne, O God, is for ever and ever: the scepter of thy kingdom is a right scepter. Thou lovest righteousness, and hatest wickedness: therefore God, thy God, hath anointed thee with the oil of gladness above thy fellows."

17. Isaiah 25:7 (KJV) reads, "And he will destroy in this mountain the face of the covering cast over all people, and the veil that is spread over all nations."

Does Isaiah then believe (see in various places) Christ to have been both *Jehovah* and *Elohim* and to partake then whatever one name signifies of *power* and the other of *grace*.... He says the Adonai Jehovah shall wipe away their tears, and then acclaims, in expectation of His appearance, to this in our Elohim: this is Jehovah, we have waited for him. This was the honour the ancient church paid to their redeemer. (178)

In her interpretation, Nightingale makes several theological moves, albeit uncertainly. She concludes that the titles/names Jehovah, Elohim, Jesus, and Christ all refer to the same being. This tentative identification brings the two sections of the Christian Bible, the Old and New Testaments, together with the claim that they are testimony referring to the same deity. The whole Bible witnesses to the one God and is itself the Word of that one God.

Nightingale also notes that there is diversity in how the text presents various facets of faith, but her notion of the ongoing development of human understanding allows her to see some passages as reflecting a more primitive faith and hence not definitive for the Christian faith. For example, she responds to the prayer of Hezekiah in Isa 38:3, "And said, Remember now, O Lord, I beseech thee, how I have walked before thee in truth and with a perfect heart, and have done that which is good in thy sight," with the comment, "the prayer of an unenlightened age" (189). Later she approves of the prophet's insight shown in Isa 45:7, "I form the light and create darkness: I make peace and create evil: I the Lord do all these things." She writes here, "Isaiah seems to have been more enlightened than we are, who cannot explain the 'origin of evil'" (196–97).

The labels "unenlightened" and "enlightened" are clearly value-laden and need to be unpacked. Nightingale works with the notion that Christianity is a superior religion to Judaism and that the New Testament presents a more developed faith than does the Old Testament. She quotes Augustine approvingly in her reflections on Ps 105. Speaking of Christianity, Augustine writes, "Although formerly, by names and signs, different from those in present use. At first more obscure and afterwards more explicit. Yet it was but one and the same true religion which was declared and observed."[18]

In the Annotated Bible, there are two features of biblical faith that Nightingale sees developing from unenlightened to enlightened. First is the progression from a local to a universal religion. For example, Nightingale edits Isa 60:1 so that its ethnocentrism is eliminated. The verse reads: "Arise, shine; for thy light is come, and the glory of the Lord is risen upon thee." Nightingale has underlined the word "thee" and written "the Gentile world" beside it (209).[19] In this way she undercuts the notion that God was only the God of the Jews. A similar editing

---

18. Quote from Augustine from *Retractiones* 1.13.3 (McDonald, *Florence Nightingale's Spiritual Journey*, 160 n. 173).

19. See also the editor's comments.

occurs in Isa 51:4, "Hearken unto me, my people; and give ear unto me, O my nation." Nightingale has underlined the offending words, "my people" and "O my nation," and written beside them, "O ye peoples" and "O ye nations" (203). The new universal age is identified by Nightingale with the messianic age. She comments on Jer 3:16, a verse speaking of a future when the ark of the covenant will no longer be remembered, with these words: "In the days of the Messiah, God's worship shall not be confined to *one* place, or to *one* people" (215).

The second development in biblical religion noted by Nightingale involves the change from a ritual-based to a spiritual form of worship. She comments on the rending of the veil at the time of the Christ's death, as narrated in Matt 27:51, "Influence of Christ's death in substituting a spiritual for a ritual worship is here symbolized." (245). Concomitant with this change is her understanding that, at bottom, Christianity is a moral school. This is made clear in her response to Matt 23:8: "But be ye not called rabbi: one is your master, even Christ; and all ye are brethren." She writes, "Christianity is a moral school opened for all mankind, condition for admission, the reception of Christ as a supreme Master concerning everything connected with religion" (243).[20]

There are yet other theological themes that she sees in Scripture and that are an important part of her systematic theology. The character of God that she finds in many places in the Bible is first and foremost good and perfect. For example, she comments on Ps 31:19a, "Oh how great is thy goodness, which thou hast laid up for them that fear thee," with, "When St. Paul looks forward in the same way to the inheritance above, he calls it a weight of *glory*. The glory of God is His *goodness*" (141; see Exod 33:19). She further concludes that consistent with God's goodness is God's working for the benefit of all. She finds this claim supported in the Old Testament, for example, underlining Gen 50:20, "But as for you, ye thought evil against me; but God meant it unto good, to bring to pass, as it is this day, to save much people alive." Nightingale rewrites part of the verse and then underlines "meant it unto good." (107). She finds this theme in the New Testament as well. She underlines Matt 5:48, "Be ye therefore perfect, even as your father which is in heaven is perfect," and adds the Old Testament text Lev 19:2 (237).[21]

Because God loves all and is working to bring all to perfection, Nightingale rejects the portrayal of God as a God of wrath who punishes some with eternal

---

20. This description of Christianity coheres well with a Unitarian vision, and Nightingale did have Unitarians among her family members. Her maternal grandfather, William Smith, was a member of Parliament and sponsored the Unitarian Toleration Act in 1813. He pushed for other reform measures, including the abolition of slavery in the British possessions, which was passed in 1833. Nightingale's family influences are described in Barbara M. Dossey's biography, *Florence Nightingale: Mystic, Visionary, Healer* (Springhouse: Springhouse Corporation, 1999), 19–26. Joann G. Widerquist ("The Spirituality of Florence Nightingale," *Nursing Research* 41/1 [1992]: 49–50) also documents the heritage of dissent in Nightingale's family.

21. Lev 19:2 (KJV) reads, "Ye shall be holy: for I the Lord your God am holy."

damnation. The goodness of God requires that God work for the salvation of all, and the irresistibility of love means that eventually all will be attracted to God. To suggest otherwise is to impugn God's character or suggest that God is limited. For example, she comments on Rom 12:2, "And be not conformed to this world: *but be ye transformed by the renewing of your mind,* that ye may prove what is that good, and acceptable, and perfect, will of God," with this observation: "We shall one day be restored in body, soul and spirit to the perfect likeness of our glorified Savior, and shall we put a limit which God has not, to the degree in which even in this world the wonderful transformation shall be wrought upon us? This at least we know, that we cannot expect too much from God" (283).[22]

A subset of her belief in God's goodness is her understanding of evil. She posits that evil and suffering are used by God in the process of bringing us to perfection. They are the pedagogical tools of a good God. Nightingale's comments on the Joseph narrative have already indicated that God works through the harm inflicted by Joseph's brothers in order to bring Joseph into Egypt so that eventually he could provide for his family and the Egyptians in time of famine.[23] Furthermore, Isaiah's words emphasizing that God is the origin of all, good and evil, are considered by Nightingale to be enlightened.[24] Elsewhere she explains that through evil and suffering we are learning what we could learn in no other way. She likens our need to suffer in order to learn to a child who falls down often before she finally knows how to walk.[25]

Another theme that Nightingale developed at length elsewhere briefly surfaces in these annotations as well, namely, her disbelief in miracles.[26] This notion is based on her work in science, especially biology, which observes that nature operates in very regular and predictable ways. This disbelief in miracles is evident in her comments regarding various miracles in the New Testament. For example, Nightingale describes the vision seen by Zechariah in the temple as an intellectual

---

22. In other theological writings, such as *Suggestions for Thought,* Nightingale writes more about her understanding of God's work to bring all humanity to the state of perfection. Hell is not a place of eternal punishment but describes the present reality. This world is a place of torment, as she wrote in her comment on Ps 18:4–6. See McDonald's discussion of Nightingale's views of sin and the character of God in "Theological Views," in *Florence Nightingale's Spiritual Journey,* 14–19; and Nightingale's *Cassandra and Suggestions for Thought* (ed. M. Poovey; New York: New York University Press, 1992).

23. See her comments on Gen 45:5, 8 and 50:20 in McDonald, *Florence Nightingale's Spiritual Journey,* 106–7.

24. See her comments on Isa 45:7 in ibid., 196–97.

25. McDonald, "Theological Views," 28–30.

26. Nightingale's skepticism regarding miracles was shared by many in Victorian England. See the chapter "Biblical Criticism and the Secularist Mentality: Charles Bradlaugh and the Case against Miracles," in Timothy Larsen, *Contested Christianity: The Political and Social Contexts of Victorian Theology* (Waco, Tex.: Baylor University Press, 2004), 97–112.

apparition.[27] Furthermore, she claims that disbelieving miracles does not alter the truth of the gospel because miracles do not provide proof but function merely as signs. She comments on Acts 17:30, "In the New Testament the miracles are always adduced merely as the premises of the argument and not as the proofs. They are spoken of as 'signs' … their true meaning and intention, that intention being that of establishing in the world a new system of religious belief" (272).[28]

Of course, the most significant miracle in the New Testament is the resurrection of Jesus, and consistent with her repudiation of miracles Nightingale denies the physical resurrection.[29] In her comments on 1 Cor 15:5–8, she concludes that the vision that Paul had of the risen Lord was of the same type as the experience of the women and apostles on Easter morning. She writes, "St Paul seems to regard the vision or visions of Christ which he himself saw in the temple or on the road to Damascus as similar in character to the appearances which had been seen by the other apostles" (288).

There are other theological ideas that Nightingale sees clearly articulated in the Bible, but this survey is long enough to indicate that she comes to the text with fixed notions regarding the content of the Christian faith, her rule of faith, and sees this reflected in the biblical text. When she does not see it there consistently, she makes use of the notion of the gradual development of biblical religion or the movement from obscurity to clarity. When there are ideas there that directly contradict what she believes to be the case, she ignores them. For example, in Isaiah she applauds the prophet for his insight that God is the origin of good and evil, hence solving the problem that so plagues her contemporaries, yet we could point out that in the Song of the Vineyard, Isa 5:1–4, there is no explanation for the harvest of sour grapes. In this passage, the existence of evil makes no sense and does not fit in with the work of the owner of the vineyard. Her engagement with the text is selective and supports her convictions about the basic doctrines of the Christian faith.

Nightingale's Reading in Dialogue with Other Writers

Nightingale's annotations reveal that she was a very learned, linguistically gifted reader of Scripture. The annotations are written in several languages besides English: French, German, Italian, Latin, Greek, and some Hebrew. Her erudition is staggering. We know from other sources that she received the equivalent

---

27. See her comment on Luke 1:22 in McDonald, *Florence Nightingale's Spiritual Journey*, 253.

28. This statement is found also in her comments on Heb 2:4 (ibid., 301).

29. Elsewhere she writes of this more explicitly. For example, in a draft of a sermon written in 1871, she comments, "As to his resurrection, it is not a historical fact in the first place. But if it were, what would it prove?" (ibid., 337).

of a Cambridge education under the tutelage of her father, himself a Cambridge graduate, and that she excelled in learning. When we locate her in her conversational circle, we are struck by how large and diverse the group is. She reads both ancient and modern writers, both in the Christian tradition and in the Greek and Roman tradition. In her comments on Mark 16:1 (251), she refers to schools of Greek thought, the Epicureans, Stoics, and Peripatetics. Her reflection at the opening of John's Gospel (257) includes an approving quote from Marcus Aurelius. Paul's words on salvation are considered in dialogue with Plutarch (270). She quotes Augustine (160), St. Teresa (294), Dante (252), and Kant (250)and has knowledge of the Talmud (239–40). Her grasp of Greek was excellent: she helped Benjamin Jowett, the Regius Professor of Greek at Oxford University, prepare a new translation of Plato's *Republic*[30] and quoted from classical Greek plays in their original language.[31] Her remarkable erudition results in a very rich engagement with Scripture and the history of its interpretation.

As a literate reader, Nightingale is adept at using the tools of the study of literature. She uses Bible dictionaries and grammars and is especially fond of etymologies. She traces some that contemporary scholars would concur with and also makes some connections that are strange. An example in the former category is her discussion of the title El Shaddai. Nightingale points out that "Shaddai derived from 'Mamma'—the Breast, and signifies that we are as dependent upon God for every blessing as the infant on its mother's breast and its mother's care" (105). In our present context, Phyllis Trible has also noted this connection,[32] although, unlike Trible, Nightingale does not consider what this title might suggest about the maternal or feminine nature of God. Other word studies include the title El, which Nightingale claims means Strength/Power or Mediation/Intervention.[33] No present-day scholar would accept that El means mediation or intervention, and I have not been able to locate Nightingale's sources. Another questionable connection is her digression on Baalim in 2 Chr 34:4. She comments, "*Baalim* that is, Lord Baalbeh—city of the Lord, that is the Sun. Sun = idols" (129). Here also I have not been able to locate the sources that led her to these conclusions.

In addition to dictionaries, Nightingale also worked with a number of translations, ancient and modern. Job 19:25–27 occasioned an exploration of various

---

30. The correspondence between the two is in Lynn McDonald, ed., *Florence Nightingale on Society and Politics, Philosophy, Science, Education and Literature* (Collected Works of Florence Nightingale 5; Waterloo, Ont.: Wilfred Laurier University Press, 2003), 551–623.

31. McDonald, *Florence Nightingale's Spiritual Journey*, 239, in which she quotes from Aeschylus's *Prometheus Bound*.

32. See Phyllis Trible, *God and the Rhetoric of Sexuality* (OBT; Philadelphia: Fortress, 1978), 61, 70.

33. See the comment in her reflection on 2 Sam 22:32 (McDonald, *Florence Nightingale's Spiritual Journey*, 123).

translations, and she wrote out the literal translations found in the Vulgate; the Septuagint; one by Stork, possibly the American theologian Theophilus Stork (1814–74); one by Parkhurst, possibly Charles Henry Parkhurst (1842–1933), an American Presbyterian minister whose sermons were published; and that of biblical scholar Johann Gottfried Eichhorn.[34] Although the list of various translations is extensive, Nightingale does not follow up with any discussion of what issues intrigued her in the text, so we do not know what conclusions she drew from this exercise.

There is evidence that she knew a good deal of the current discussion in biblical scholarship. For example, in one brief comment responding to Gen 7:2, "Of every clean beast thou shalt take to thee by sevens, the male and his female: and of beasts that are not clean by two, the male and his female," Nightingale indicates that she is familiar with some form of the Documentary Hypothesis.[35] She writes, "Jehovistic because clean and unclean not known until Leviticus 11" (104). She comments on Isa 45:3, connecting it with Cyrus's taking of Babylon (196),[36]and sees traces of the age of Antiochus Epiphanes in the book of Daniel (223). In many instances we do not know on which scholar she is relying for her information regarding the historical context, but one scholar she cites often is Georg Heinrch von Ewald (1803–75).[37] Nightingale resonated with Ewald's idea that studying the history in which the biblical text was written was not a threat but rather allowed the reader to reconstruct the process of God's revelation to

---

34. See her comments and translation in ibid., 131–32. The quote from Eichhorn is from *Einleitung in das alter Testamente* 5:114–25.

35. It is possible she learned this from Johann Gottfried Eichhorn (1752–1827), although no name is mentioned here. She does refer to his work in connection with Job 19:25–27 (McDonald, *Florence Nightingale's Spiritual Journey,* 131). Eichhorn suggested that although Moses was the final author of the Pentateuch, he used documents to construct it. He spoke of a J and E source. Nightingale elsewhere refers to the giving of the law at Sinai and dates it to 1491 B.C.E. (ibid., 240.) For a brief overview of Eichhorn's work and influence, see J. W. Rogerson, "Eichhorn, Johann Gottfried," *Dictionary of Biblical Interpretation* (ed. J. H. Hayes; 2 vols.; Nashville: Abingdon, 1999), 1:324.

36. This indicates that Nightingale was convinced that Isaiah, beginning at chapter 40, is written in Babylon at the end of the Babylonian empire. Her proposal on *The School and Children's Bible* indicates that she is quite passionate about labeling the beginning of Isa 40 with a heading to indicate its new historical context. She writes, "Surely the last twenty-six chapters belong to the end of the Babylonian captivity and should be separated by a distinct division." See Lynn McDonald, ed., *Florence Nightingale's Theology: Essays, Letters and Journal Notes* (Collected Works of Florence Nightingale 3; Waterloo, Ont.: Wilfred Laurier University Press, 2002), 557.

37. Nightingale makes references to *Das Buch Job* (part 3 of *Die Dichter des alten Bundes*; Gottingen: Vandenhoeck & Ruprecht, 1854); *Life of Jesus Christ* (trans. O. Glover; Cambridge: Cambridge University Press, 1865), and *Die Propheten des alten Bundes* (Gottingen: Vandenhoeck & Ruprecht, 1867).

humanity.[38] The other author on whom she relied extensively is Johann Gottfried Herder (1744–1803).[39] She employed Herder's notions of historicity and the folly of judging an ancient, distinct culture according to modern ideas.[40] Nightingale combined historicism with the idea that through time all peoples would come to know the true, unchanging, sublime deity to whom the Bible testifies.[41] This idea was amenable to Nightingale's conviction that God is working in history for the perfection of all people and that eventually all will come to know the goodness of God.

A Gendered Reading of Scripture?

Nightingale's relationship to the nineteenth-century feminist movement is a hotly contested topic that cannot be resolved by studying her biblical annotations alone.[42] In other places Nightingale writes of the inequality of women's treatment, seeks to revise legislation that was unfair to prostitutes, and fundamentally reshapes the nursing profession to make it a respectable, paid vocation for women—all on the basis of her Christian convictions.[43] In Showalter's estimation, Nightingale's work *Cassandra* is one of the classics of English feminism, the link between Wollstonecraft and Woolf.[44]

Nightingale's reading of Scripture is noteworthy in part because of what she does not do. Nightingale never identifies with the female characters in Scripture

---

38. See J. W. Rogerson, "Ewald, Georg Heinrich von," *Dictionary of Biblical Interpretation*, 1:363–64.

39. She especially uses volume 12, on the prophets, of his *Sammtliche Werke* (33 vols.; Berlin: Weidmann, 1877–1913). See J. W. Rogerson, "Herder, Johann Gottfried," *Dictionary of Biblical Interpretation*, 1:496.

40. See the comments she quotes in regard to Ezek 22 and 23 in McDonald, *Florence Nightingale's Spiritual Journey*, 221.

41. The extensive quote from Herder cited in connection with Exod 3:16, includes, "While Jehovah was the one God, Creator of the world, He was also the God of all people, of all generations, and it only required time, unbiased thinking and the calm Spirit of God to develop this rich germ" (ibid., 108, from *Sammtliche Werke*, 12:76–77).

42. For example, those who claim that Nightingale is not a feminist point to her declining an invitation from John Stuart Mill to join a committee to work for women's suffrage. However, the correspondence reveals that Nightingale is not opposed to women's rights to vote but is rather investing her energies on women's right to economic self-sufficiency, believing that this must come first. See the correspondence in McDonald, *Florence Nightingale on Society and Politics*, 388–410.

43. McDonald ("Christian Feminism," in *Florence Nightingale's Spiritual Journey*, 68–73) describes the many facets of her work and thinking that criticized her patriarchal culture and strove for equal rights for women.

44. Elaine Showalter discusses *Cassandra* in the context of Nightingale's life and thought in "Florence Nightingale's Feminist Complaint: Women, Religion, and *Suggestions for Thought*," *Signs: Journal of Women in Culture and Society* 6 (1981): 396, 409–11.

or even comments on their actions, words, or dialogue. Perhaps this is because there is no woman in Scripture who is independent and engaged in the sort of work to which Nightingale feels herself called.[45] For example, the many women in the narratives of Genesis occasion no comment from her, but that is understandable because in the narrative they are almost completely defined by their sexuality, and their roles are almost always domestic. It is appropriate that Joseph is the only character in Scripture with whom she identifies. The work that he is called to do parallels her own work. As he was instructed to prepare for a drought by storing grain, so Nightingale worked to prevent illness through instituting health reforms and teaching proper sanitation. In addition, she believed that as God was working through Joseph's efforts to preserve life, so God was also working through her efforts. Both were co-workers with God.

Nightingale does notice certain female aspects in the text, such as her claim that Shaddai can mean breasts. Yet the significance of this feminine characteristic is not explored. We have no reflection on what it might mean if one of the names of God points to a maternal function or if the creatures who attend God's holy throne are female. Nightingale does not latch onto these in order to question or re-create the patriarchal cast of biblical religion. We could consider her fairly insensitive to issues of gender, although not completely so. She does change the self-designation of Joseph from father to mother, and she does respond to a few passages that speak more directly to women. For example, Nightingale responds to Isa 27:2–4,

> In that day sing ye unto her, A vineyard of red wine.
> I the Lord do keep it; I will water it every moment:
> lest any hurt it, I will keep it night and day.
> Fury is not in me: who would set the briers and thorns against me in battle?
> I will go through them, I would burn them together.

with the words, "I have no wall. Who will make me a fence of briers and thorns?" (180). Her response is poignant. Nightingale is responding to the feminine pronoun "her" in the first line, identifying with the vineyard, and feeling quite vulnerable and in need of a protector. Although feeling the need of protection is not unique to women, Nightingale was vulnerable as a single woman working in a man's world. For example, she faced many challenges when she arrived in the Crimea with her contingent of nurses. Dr. John Hall, Inspector General of Hospitals, initially declined their services because he saw them as meddling outsiders and Nightingale as a wealthy woman seeking adventure.[46]

---

45. For example, in *Cassandra,* an essay explicitly focusing on women, especially the roles of mother and daughter, Nightingale never uses Scripture in constructing her argument.

46. See Dossey's description of Nightingale's work in the Crimea in "Crimean War Years (1854–56)" (*Florence Nightingale,* 103–76).

Nightingale's response to another passage, Isa 39:2, is also more typical of women. In this passage Hezekiah is showing all his wealth. She connects this verse with 2 Chr 32, in which God allows exultation so that we may come to know what is in our hearts and concludes, "The trials proved that there was little else than pride and folly. God permits us to be brought into such circumstances as shall cause us to feel our prevailing propensities, and then warns us against the evils to which we are inclined.… We must expect to be called to account for the workings of our pride" (190–91). This concern with the vice of pride became more and more intense, as the editor notes, even though from all outward appearances, she certainly did not engage in any effort to promote herself. She was if anything reclusive and shunned public honor. This concern of Nightingale's that she was putting herself forward in an unbecoming way is consistent with her socialization as a woman in Victorian England.

CONCLUSION

Nightingale's interpretation of Scripture certainly merits inclusion in the history of women's interpretation, but her self-consciously female voice is quite weak in her biblical annotations. Rather than identifying herself strongly as a woman, she first of all sees herself as a human being who is a Christian. That this is her primary identification is reflected in her life's work. She worked for the advancement of the human race as a believer. She pioneered reforms for men and women, Christians and Hindus and Muslims, people of all classes, and in many parts of the world: England, Ireland, and India.

In conclusion, I want to stress what is perhaps obvious about this devout and brilliant woman's engagement with Scripture: she brings her keen mind to the text of Scripture. She reads widely in many subjects, including biblical scholarship, and considers the latest and best of academic study of the Bible without it hampering her piety. Nightingale's biblical annotations reveal that a rigorous life of the mind goes hand in hand with a deep spirituality.

BIBLIOGRAPHY

Dossey, Barbara Montgomery. *Florence Nightingale: Mystic, Visionary, Healer.* Springhouse: Springhouse Corporation, 1999.

Larsen, Timothy. *Contested Christianity: The Political and Social Contexts of Victorian Theology.* Waco, Tex.: Baylor University Press, 2004.

Matt, Daniel C., trans. *Introduction to Zohar: The Book of Enlightenment.* Toronto: Paulist, 1983.

McDonald, Lynn. "Christian Feminism." Pages 68–73 in *Florence Nightingale's Spiritual Journey: Biblical Annotations, Sermons and Journal Notes.* Edited by Lynn McDonald. Collected Works of Florence Nightingale 2. Waterloo, Ont.: Wilfred Laurier University Press, 2001.

———. "Theological Views." Pages 14–55 in *Florence Nightingale's Spiritual Journey: Biblical Annotations, Sermons and Journal Notes.* Edited by Lynn McDonald. Collected Works of Florence Nightingale 2. Waterloo, Ont.: Wilfred Laurier University Press, 2001.

———, ed. *Florence Nightingale: An Introduction to Her Life and Family.* Collected Works of Florence Nightingale 1. Waterloo, Ont.: Wilfred Laurier University Press, 2001.

———. *Florence Nightingale on Society and Politics, Philosophy, Science, Education and Literature.* Collected Works of Florence Nightingale 5. Waterloo, Ont.: Wilfred Laurier University Press, 2003.

———. *Florence Nightingale's Spiritual Journey: Biblical Annotations, Sermons and Journal Notes.* Collected Works of Florence Nightingale 2. Waterloo, Ont.: Wilfred Laurier University Press, 2001.

———. *Florence Nightingale's Theology: Essays, Letters and Journal Notes.* Collected Works of Florence Nightingale 3. Waterloo, Ont.: Wilfred Laurier University Press, 2002.

Nightingale, Florence. *Cassandra and Other Selections from Suggestions for Thought.* Edited by Mary Poovey. New York: New York University Press, 1992.

Rogerson, J. W. "Eichhorn, Johann Gottfried." Page 324 in vol. 1 of *Dictionary of Biblical Interpretation.* Edited by John H. Hayes. Nashville: Abingdon, 1999.

———. "Ewald, Georg Heinrich August." Pages 363–64 in vol. 1 of *Dictionary of Biblical Interpretation.* Edited by John H. Hayes. 2 vols. Nashville: Abingdon, 1999.

———. "Herder, Johann Gottfried." Page 496 in vol. 1 of *Dictionary of Biblical Interpretation.* Edited by John H. Hayes. 2 vols. Nashville: Abingdon, 1999.

Showalter, Elaine, "Florence Nightingale's Feminist Complaint: Women, Religion and *Suggestions for Thought." Signs: Journal of Women in Culture and Society* 6 (1981): 395–412.

Trible, Phyllis, *God and the Rhetoric of Sexuality.* OBT. Philadelphia: Fortress, 1978.

Widerquist, Joann G. "The Spirituality of Florence Nightingale." *Nursing Research* 41 (1992): 49–55.

READING BETWEEN THE LINES: JOSEPHINE BUTLER'S SOCIALLY CONSCIOUS COMMENTARY ON HAGAR

Amanda W. Benckhuysen

INTRODUCTION

Reflecting on the story of Hagar in his commentary on Genesis, Gerhard von Rad comments:

> whoever impatiently seeks a meaning in this story must first ask himself whether it is so certain that such a narrative has only one meaning. The narrative here is very spacious, so to speak, with much to be read between the lines. The narrator makes room for many thoughts and reflections and is in no hurry to prescribe one idea or opinion for the reader.[1]

Even the casual reader of this story in Gen 16 and 21 will notice that the narrator leaves many critical questions unanswered: Was Sarah's use of Hagar as a hand-maid morally problematic, or can it be justified as an acceptable social convention of the ancient Near East? What does it mean that Hagar despised her mistress, and did this behavior warrant Sarah's harsh treatment? Why did the angel of the Lord send Hagar back to an abusive situation? What does it mean that Ishmael was mocking Isaac?[2] Given his great wealth, why did Abraham give Hagar and

---

1. Gerhard von Rad, *Genesis: A Commentary* (OTL; Philadelphia: Westminster, 1972), 195.

2. The Hebrew verb *ṣaḥaq* can signify "laughter" in both a good and an evil sense. Most Bible versions, however, translate this word as "mocking," following the apostle Paul's lead in Gal 4:29, who suggested that Ishmael persecuted Isaac. John Calvin, in his commentary on Genesis, affirms this translation by noting that only a negative encounter between the two boys would provoke the indignation of Sarah (John Calvin, "Calvin's Commentaries: Genesis" [electronic ed.; Bellingham, Wash.: Logos Library System, 1998], n.p.). However, some modern translations, particularly the RSV/NRSV, have adopted the more neutral expression "to play with" in translating this verse. Von Rad, in his commentary on Genesis, argues that Sarah's jealousy could very well have been incited by the notion of Ishmael's and Isaac's playing together as equals (von Rad, *Genesis*, 232). The text itself offers few clues for translating *ṣaḥaq*, leaving the question of the relationship between Ishmael and Isaac open for the reader to reconstruct.

his son Ishmael so little provision when banishing them to the desert? Finally, why does God condone sending Hagar and Ishmael away? Genesis 16 and 21 are terse and short on details. The characters are underdeveloped. The text tells us little about the motivations, intentions, and feelings of those involved, putting the onus on the reader to make literary and theological sense of this story. In other words, what a reader brings to this text will affect how the text is read and what the text ultimately means.

This dependency of the text on the reader is especially transparent in the brilliant and unusual interpretation by Josephine Butler, who exploits the gaps in the text, interpreting this as a story about the exploitation of oppressed women. It functions for Butler as a prophetic summons that calls nineteenth-century England to reach out a compassionate hand to this neglected class. Butler's unique ability to engage the text through the lens of her own experience unlocks the power of this ancient story as the word of God for modern society. In this respect, she provides a model for readers of Scripture today of powerful and faithful interpretation of the biblical text as the living word of God. This essay will explore Butler's interpretation of this story and examine how her experience, her passions, and her theological convictions shape her reading.

Josephine Butler: Biography

In a tribute to Josephine Butler published in *The Shield* in 1907 following her death, Professor James Stuart wrote, "Mrs. Butler was one of the great people of the world. In character, in work done, in influence on others, she was among the few great people who have moulded the course of things. The world is different because she lived.... She was a great leader of men and women."[3] Butler was truly a remarkable woman. Born in 1828 to Hannah and John Grey, Butler grew up in a family that strongly supported abolition and was deeply concerned about social issues. Her family attended an Anglican church near their home, but she was also exposed to Methodism and Presbyterianism, fostering an ecumenism to which she subscribed throughout her life. Her own faith can best be characterized as liberal evangelicalism,[4] a combination of personal piety, social activism, and feminist fervor that inspired her work with the most oppressed of women. In 1852, Josephine married George Butler, who was ordained into the Church of England but worked predominantly in boys' schools. George shared Josephine's beliefs about equality between men and women and supported Josephine in her work to promote the rights of women, even to the detriment of his own career.

---

3. Published in *The Shield* (14 January 1907): 1. Quoted from Jane Jordan, *Josephine Butler* (London: Murray, 2001), 1.

4. Helen Mathers, "The Evangelical Spirituality of a Victorian Feminist: Josephine Butler, 1828–1906," *JEH* 52 (2001): 284.

Josephine and George Butler had four children; the youngest and only girl was named Eva. At age five, Eva fell off a banister and plummeted forty feet to her death. Butler never got over this great tragedy, and the death of Eva haunted her throughout her life. However, it also compelled her into the philanthropic work for which she is best known. In *Recollections of George Butler*, Butler commented on her life following Eva's death:

> I became possessed with an irresistible desire to go forth and find some pain keener than my own—to meet with people more unhappy than myself (for I knew there were thousands of such). I did not exaggerate my own trial; I only knew that my heart ached night and day, and that the only solace possible would seem to be to find other hearts which ached night and day, and with more reason than mine. I had no clear idea beyond that, no plan for helping others; my sole wish was to plunge into the heart of some human misery, and to say (as I now knew I could) to afflicted people, "I understand. I, too, have suffered."[5]

Butler is predominantly known for her work to repeal the Contagious Diseases Acts. The Acts allowed plain-clothed police to detain any woman suspected of prostitution for a mandatory internal examination and treatment of venereal disease. The treatment included a three-month period of incarceration that was extended to nine months by the passing of the third Act. The intention of the Acts was to protect the health of enlisted men for whom consorting with prostitutes was considered an acceptable and natural means of appeasing the sexual appetite. The Acts were instituted because venereal disease was a growing problem among enlisted men and had hampered the military's performance in the Crimean War. In an effort to deal with the problem, it was decided that enlisted men should routinely be examined for venereal disease, but such examinations were soon abandoned when the men protested that they were demoralizing. This resulted in the passing of the Contagious Diseases Acts that seemed unsympathetic to the notion that such examinations might also be degrading for women. The first Act was passed in 1864, followed by two others in 1866 and 1869, each expanding the number of towns to be regulated and the power afforded the police to detain and incarcerate women.

For Butler, the Acts were sexist and violated women's rights. They reinforced a double standard of morality by requiring women to submit to painful examinations with little or no evidence of prostitution, while men who engaged in sexually promiscuous behavior were free from all responsibility. Furthermore, Butler was concerned that such laws sanctioned immoral behavior and encouraged the exploitation of women as prostitutes. As the head of the Ladies National Association for the Repeal of the Contagious Diseases Acts, Butler led

---

5. Josephine Butler, *Recollections of George Butler* (London: Simpkin, Marshall, Hamilton & Kent, 1892), 182–83.

a crusade against this legislation. Her work often required her to travel far from home, giving speeches and leading protests. She was ostracized by many who considered it inappropriate for a woman to speak about such matters. Threats to her life and physical well-being resulted in her fleeing from mobs, concealing her location, and, at least once, canceling her appearance at a meeting. In 1886, her hard work paid off, and the Contagious Diseases Acts were repealed.[6]

In addition to her work with the Ladies National Association, Butler established a home for "repentant women" where they could be retrained in respectable work. She ministered to women in workhouses and brothels. She fought child prostitution and the trafficking of women for sexual exploitation. She wrote extensively on the rights of women and the need for women to have access to education, respectable work, and political influence and saw these as basic requirements to end the sexual oppression of women. Her advocacy for the rights of women, which anticipated modern feminism, was largely inspired by her Christian faith as she sought to model her life on what she understood to be the teachings and actions of Christ.

BUTLER'S HERMENEUTIC

To understand Butler's interpretation of the Hagar story, it is necessary to explore the hermeneutical and theological convictions that shaped her reading. As an evangelical, Butler had a high view of the authority of Scripture, recognizing it as the rule for faith and life. However, this did not constrain Butler to a simplistic or straightforward reading of the Bible. She recognized the humanity both of the characters reflected in the narratives of Scripture and of the authors such as the apostle Paul. Scripture was not to be read as an oracle from heaven but required interpretation and appropriation. To this end, Butler used the teachings and actions of Christ as a hermeneutical key for understanding the rest of Scripture. Thus, while Paul's writings support the subordination of women, Butler is able to dismiss his theological reflections as a culturally and gender-bound attempt to apply the principles of Jesus to specific situations.[7] Furthermore, though his writings may be theologically impressive, for Butler, they lack empathy and humanity. Commenting on Paul's interpretation of Gen 16 and 21 found in Gal 4:21–31, Butler writes, "Paul was not a father, nor was the human heart of the man stirring in him at the moment when he wrote to the Galatians."[8] This is evident in Paul's

---

6. For a helpful discussion of the Contagious Diseases Acts and Josephine Butler's opposition to them, see Lillian Lewis Shiman, *Women and Leadership in Nineteenth-Century England* (London: MacMillan, 1992), 138–50.

7. Josephine Butler, "Introduction," in *Women's Work and Woman's Culture* (ed. J. Butler; London: Macmillan, 1868), xiv–xv, lii–lvi.

8. Josephine Butler, *The Lady of Shunem* (London: Marshall, 1894), 74.

suggestion that in casting out Hagar and Ishmael, Abraham and Sarah did well. While the writings of Paul are still an important part of Scripture, for Butler they are secondary to the teaching and actions of Christ. Paul's writings need to be kept in their proper place and at times dismissed if one is to understand the will of God. This demotion and dismissal of the work of Paul has a significant impact on Butler's interpretation of Hagar.

Rather than interpreting the Bible through the lens of Paul's applications, Butler suggests it is more appropriate to look at the principles themselves, embodied in the life and teachings of Jesus. That which Butler discerns there is the theme of liberation—liberation from sin and brokenness, from disease and death, and from oppression and inequality perpetuated in modern society. The God Butler meets in the Bible is one of compassion and mercy—particularly for the outcast. In *Woman's Work and Woman's Culture*, Butler writes:

> In the Bible, I find the labourer deprived of just wages, the wronged widow, the neglected orphan, the leper driven out of society, the uninstructed from whom the key of knowledge had been withheld, the Gentile stranger oppressed by the privileged Jew, each and all in their turn tenderly mentioned in those pathetic and paternal utterances, beginning with "Thus saith the Lord." Their cry, it is said, enters into the ears of God. They are cared for by Him.[9]

More specifically, Butler argues that the life and teachings of Christ promote the equality of men and women[10] and that Jesus sought to liberate women from the oppression of human sin and cultural mores, restoring them to a position of equality. She writes,

> Search through the Gospel history, and observe his conduct in regard to women, and it will be found that the word liberation expresses, above all others, the act which changed the whole life and character and position of the women dealt with, and which ought to have changed the character of men's treatment of women from that time forward.[11]

According to Butler, God is concerned for the oppressed, and his will is for the liberation and restoration of humanity, particularly women. This is a theological nonnegotiable for Butler. Butler's God is a good God, a moral God who seeks to mitigate the unkindness of the world with his own love and compassion. For Butler, God would never condone the mistreatment of Hagar. The problem, of course, is that this is exactly what seems to be going on in this story. Why would God encourage Abraham to cast out Hagar and Ishmael? Does this not make God

---

9. Butler, "Introduction," xi.
10. Ibid., liv–lv.
11. Ibid., lix.

complicit in Abraham and Sarah's crime? Butler seems to recognize the dilemma and exploits the silences about God's motivations to offer an alternative explanation for God's actions.

Finally, Butler's understanding of eschatology is a significant influence on the way she reads this text. For Butler, the kingdom of God was inaugurated at Pentecost when Christ poured out his Spirit on the church and empowered his people to continue his work on earth.[12] We are living in the dispensation of the Spirit, "a Dispensation of Liberty, Life, Impartiality, Equality, and Justice,"[13] she writes, in which the church takes up the work of Christ until the end of time, when the "Supreme Interposition takes place which we invoke when we say from our heart, "Thy kingdom come."[14] For Butler, followers of Jesus are not simply to wait around until Jesus comes again and brings about the consummation of the new heaven and earth. They are to join in the mission of Jesus, embracing what he started and working toward instilling the values of the kingdom of God here and now: liberty, life, impartiality, equality, and justice. Yet her perspective is not triumphalistic. She has no illusions about humanity being able to achieve a perfect world. That will have to wait until Christ comes again—a day for which she longs. However, she does take seriously our ability to contribute to the kingdom of God through our work in the world now. In her introduction to *Woman's Work and Woman's Culture*, Butler concludes with these words: "Of this I am sure, that every effort which is made in sincerity and truth, every life which is spent and yielded up in the cause of suffering humanity, is hastening the advent of the Day which we long for."[15] This theological conviction not only compelled her to work with prostitutes and sexually oppressed women, but it influenced her reading of the biblical text. While Abraham and Sarah lived before Christ and thus, before the dawn of the new era, our situation is entirely different. Christ has come. He has empowered us with his Spirit. He has modeled for us the way of the kingdom. We simply have no excuse for continuing to perpetuate inequality, oppression, and injustice, for acting as if Christ's life, death, and resurrection have made no difference at all. As a result, Butler establishes Abraham and Sarah as negative models exemplifying the old order and uses this story as a prophetic wakeup call to the Christian's responsibility toward those on whom God has compassion.

BUTLER ON HAGAR

In 1894, toward the end of her life, Butler wrote about Hagar in *The Lady of Shunem*, a study of various biblical characters. For Butler, the story of Hagar and

---

12. Josephine Butler, *Prophets and Prophetesses* (London: Dyer Brothers, 1898), 6–7.

13. Ibid., 7.

14. Butler, "Introduction," lxiv.

15. Ibid., lxiv.

Sarah is a narrative about two classes of women, analogous to the class system in Victorian Britain. Butler clearly distinguished these two classes in an earlier work as

> the protected and refined ladies who are not only to *be good*, but who are, if possible, to *know* nothing except what is good and the poor outcast daughters of people whom they [men] purchase with money, and with whom they think they may consort in evil whenever it pleases them to do so, before returning to their own separated and protected homes.[16]

In *The Lady of Shunem,* Sarah is characterized as "the lawful, respected, and respectable wife," while Hagar is "of inferior rank, no wife at all, not the chosen of man through any high motive of love or soul's election, but simply made use of for a time and purpose—a supplement to what God had already bestowed on man, and claimed by him to serve his own lower interests."[17] Butler likens Hagar to the prostitutes with whom she works and whom she perceives as victims of social convention and human sin.[18] She is the typical outcast—ostracized and condemned by society.

In Butler's paradigm, Abraham represents men who frequent prostitutes to serve their own lower appetites. He is not just an acquiescent partner to Sarah's scheming, but he also participates in Hagar's oppression. While Abraham was grieved at the prospect of casting out his son in Gen 21:11, there is no mention of Hagar, the mother of his firstborn. Is he not grieved also because of her? The text is silent here, and Butler suggests that Hagar was of no concern to Abraham. She was simply a convenient pawn for Abraham and Sarah's needs. Abraham's lack of concern for Hagar is further confirmed for Butler in Gen 21:14, where Abraham sends mother and child away with the most meager of provisions. Somewhat sarcastically, Butler comments, "Abraham took some bread and a bottle of water— enough to keep the poor outcasts alive for half a day—and laid them on Hagar's shoulder, and sent her and her child away" (79). In casting Hagar and Ishmael

---

16. Josephine Butler, *Social Purity* (London: Dyer Brothers, 1882), 9–10.

17. Butler, *The Lady of Shunem*, 71. Subsequent references to *The Lady of Shunem* will be provided within the text.

18. Prostitution became a growing problem in Victorian England as the demographic discrepancy between men and women increased (by mid-century, there were up to 4 percent more women then men). Without access to education, property, meaningful employment, and political power, women were largely dependent on male relatives (husband, father, or brother) to provide for them. Should that provision fail, women had limited choices. Some sought positions as domestic help. More educated women could work as a governess. Often, however, women ended up in the dismal and despairing workhouses that institutionalized poverty. One alternative for impoverished but young and healthy women was prostitution. The ongoing demand for prostitutes and the lure of relative freedom tempted women to market the only commodity available to them—their bodies.

out, Abraham abdicated his responsibility as a father. He shamelessly left Hagar, the mother of his son, to struggle through life alone while he lived in security and comfort with his wife Sarah and their beautiful son Isaac.

If Butler is hard on Abraham, she is relentless with Sarah. Butler portrays Sarah like the virtuous women of England who, she writes, "have consented for ages that the outcast/fallen woman should exist, and continue to be an outcast" (75–76). In this case, Sarah not only gives her consent but proposes this arrangement, later blaming Abraham when things go awry. Sarah treats Hagar harshly, we read in Gen 16:6, which Butler suggests included beating her and causing her to flee in order to save her life (72–73). In demanding that Abraham cast out the bondswoman, Sarah's words reflect the attitude of virtuous women toward their fallen counterpart: "Cast her out, with her unlawful offspring. Get rid of her, keep her out of sight. Set up a barrier between these and those" (72). This barrier Butler later refers to as a great gulf, likening it to the chasm between heaven and hell described in Luke 16:26. There is no passing from one side to the other. Virtuous women want nothing to do with these fallen women. They want to keep them out of sight and mind. As such, repentance and restoration are not an option for the fallen woman. The Prodigal Son may leave home by choice with his share of his father's inheritance in hand, but the fallen woman is cast out with no resources to sustain her. The lost son returns home when he is ready to repent of his ways; for the lost daughter, there is no returning home. "All the cruelty, impurity, and avarice of earth combine to keep her hiding place unknown, to bar her return to the Father's house, to hold her down, to the end that, once fallen, she may rise no more, but may 'minister in dreadful promiscuity' to the vilest passions of the most ignoble of men" (80). Abraham and Sarah's treatment of Hagar is paradigmatic of this attitude, of this desire to maintain two classes of women that must be kept separate and apart: the virtuous wife, and the vilified concubine. For Butler, this is precisely what is wrong with society and, according to Butler's reading, what this narrative seeks to challenge and change.

In her interpretation, Butler accentuates Hagar as the victim, so she downplays Hagar (and Ishmael's) culpability in the household tension. For instance, Hagar and Ishmael were not cast out because of any wrongdoing on their part but because of Sarah's pride. To arrive at this conclusion, Butler rejects the standard translation of Gen 21:9 that Ishmael was "mocking" Isaac and argues that he was simply "playing with" the young boy (76). Sarah is bothered, then, not by what Ishmael is doing per se but by the posture Ishmael adopts with respect to Isaac, a posture of equality and familiarity that is reflected in their play. "If Ishmael had been insulting or ill-treating the child," Butler comments, "Sarah would scarcely have restrained herself so far as merely to repudiate the dreaded idea of any equality between the two boys. She would, I think, have used more denunciatory language against Ishmael" (77).

This interpretation of the Hagar story that characterizes Hagar as a victim at the hands of her cruel oppressors, Abraham and Sarah, sets Butler's reading apart from other interpretations of this story, including two of Butler's contemporaries—Sarah Trimmer[19] and Harriet Beecher Stowe.[20] Both of these women maintain a high view of Abraham as a model of faith, wisdom, and righteousness and suggest that Abraham wisely submitted to his wife's request to father a child with Hagar. Trimmer excuses Abraham's concession to polygamy by noting that he was living in a godless land without Scripture to guide him. As a result, he "acted contrary to the marriage law [that a man shall marry but one woman] by ignorance."[21] While for Butler, Abraham showed his disregard for Hagar by inadequately providing for her sojourn in the desert, Trimmer comments that by giving them only a bit of bread and water, "he [Abraham] gave a proof of his faith in God's promises, by leaving those he loved to be provided for by Providence."[22]

Like Trimmer, Stowe characterizes Abraham positively, describing him as a peace-loving and quiet man. He showed wisdom in Gen 16:6 when he decided not to interfere in the squabble between Sarah and Hagar. According to Stowe, Abraham was

> confident, as many men are, of the general ability of the female sex, by inscrutable ways and methods of their own, to find their way out of the troubles they bring themselves into. Probably he saw wrong on both sides; yet Hagar, as the dependent, who owed all the elevation on which she prided herself to the good-will of her mistress, was certainly the more in fault of the two; and so he dismisses the subject with: "Thy maid is in thy hand; do with her as pleaseth thee."[23]

Stowe, however, is not content to portray only Abraham well; she also writes sympathetically of Sarah. According to Stowe, Sarah treated Hagar with "peculiar tenderness" and was "intending to adopt and treat as her own the child of her handmaid." She describes Sarah as a "warm-hearted, generous, bountiful woman" who "in place of a grateful, devoted creature ... finds herself confronted with an imperious rival, who lays claim to her place and position." By contrast, Stowe's

---

19. For a wonderful collection of the work of nineteenth-century women interpreters of Scripture, see Marion Taylor and Heather Weir, *Let Her Speak for Herself: Nineteenth-Century Women Writing on Women in Genesis* (Waco, Tex.: Baylor University Press, 2006). Sarah Trimmer (1741–1810) was a middle-class British woman primarily known as an educationalist and author of moralizing literature for children. She wrote about Hagar in her one-volume commentary on the Bible, *A Help to the Unlearned in the Study of the Holy Scriptures* (London: Rivington, 1805).

20. Harriet Beecher Stowe (1811–96) is best known as the author of *Uncle Tom's Cabin*. She was an American abolitionist and writer of more than ten books. Stowe included a chapter about Hagar in her book on women in the Bible entitled *Women in Sacred History* (New York: Ford, 1873).

21. Trimmer, *Help to the Unlearned*, 20.

22. Ibid., 24.

23. Stowe, *Women in Sacred History*, 42. For the quotations that follow, see pages 41–45.

Hagar is a presumptuous, rebellious slave girl. Commenting on Gen 16:4, which indicates that Hagar began to despise her mistress, Stowe writes, "her ardent tropical blood boiled over in unseemly exultation." Later Stowe suggests that Hagar, "the proud, hot-hearted, ungoverned slavegirl," fled from Sarah to the wilderness "in a tumult of indignation and grief, doubtless after bitter words and hard usage from the once indulgent mistress." Although the Lord came to this "wretched creature" in kindness and grace during her first sojourn in the desert, Stowe characterizes Hagar as faithless and impatient when she finds herself in the wilderness again, forgetting "the kindly Power that once before helped her in her sorrows." Stowe goes on to apply the same positive and negative characterization to Isaac and Ishmael respectively, suggesting that Isaac's line was chosen as the people of God because his character was more adaptable to God's purposes. She describes Isaac as thoughtful, patient, and meditative, while Ishmael is wild, hot-blooded, impetuous, and untamable, embellishing the lean biblical record in an attempt to explain Ishmael's rejection.[24]

Although Butler and Stowe were both social activists and supported the abolition movement, they developed very different reconstructions of the relationship between Sarah and Hagar as mistress and slave. Stowe made a point of distancing the inhumane institution of modern slavery from that of the patriarchal period, which, she suggests, had more the character of family relations.[25] As such, Abraham and Sarah are justified in casting out Hagar who acts like an ungrateful daughter. By contrast, Butler applies her knowledge of the injustices of the British class system to her reading of this story and concludes that Abraham and Sarah are the problem. The treatment of Hagar by Abraham and Sarah must be condemned. "To abstain from condemnation of their action," Butler writes, "would be to seem to charge God with approval of heartlessness and cruelty" (73), which, as we noted above, is not an option. God is a moral and merciful God.

Butler attributes the freedom with which she openly condemns the actions of Sarah and Abraham to the exegetical decision to loose this text from the Paul's interpretation in Gal 4:

> And because the apostle made use of this incident in his passionate desire to clear away the mist of doctrinal error from the minds of his lapsed Galatians converts, and by familiar illustration to set forth the development of the purpose of God in the substitution of the covenant of Grace for the Law, shall we, therefore, speak softly of the conduct of Sarai and Abraham in this matter? I prefer to express frankly my disgust…. I am perplexed, in reading certain commentators, in noting a degree of—shall I call it complacency?—in their judgment of this story of Hagar, as if God himself had ordained each step in it, and Sarai had

---

24. Ibid., 46.
25. Ibid., 41.

done well. It may be that an exclusive dwelling on the allegorical use made by St. Paul of the facts has encouraged this complacency. (73–74)

Rejecting Paul's reading of this story, Butler adopts what she refers to as a womanly or motherly reading of this story (74), focusing her primary concern on the woman who was left to fend for herself and her child with no resources. Her characterization of Abraham, Sarah, and Hagar may have the quality of caricature. However, she succeeds in heightening and clarifying the moral dilemma in this text and by analogy, in contemporary society, such that there is no question who is in the wrong and what needs to change.

In contrast to Abraham and Sarah's mistreatment of Hagar, God is full of compassion. "It is a great relief," she writes, "to turn from the earthly actors in the drama to the over-ruling God, the ever just, and ever merciful, and full of compassion" (81). Like other interpreters, Butler recognizes that Hagar is the first woman to whom God reveals himself directly. This is, for Butler, typical of God's ways with humanity, that he would choose to reveal himself to the outcast woman rather than to Sarah the princess. Unlike Abraham and Sarah, unlike modern society, God does not turn a blind eye to the "ill-used slave" but acts with compassion and mercy, going to the darkest places of the earth where respectable people refuse to go to reach the lost and forsaken with his love. "Into the vilest prison-houses of earth (I believe) he descends alone many a time, to save those souls buried out of the sight and ken of his servants and ministers" (83).

On the first meeting in the wilderness, God exhorts Hagar to return to her mistress and bear her treatment patiently, but not before he gives her a promise of hope for the future, the birth of a son. According to Butler, Hagar was obedient to God. She returned to Sarah and served her for thirteen years in a spirit of submission (86). Sarah responds to Hagar's faithful service with the request that Abraham cast her out, and surprisingly God affirms Sarah's petition. In an effort to explain this, Butler comments,

> Sarah had acted cruelly, but God over-ruled her action for good. He bade Abraham not to oppose the advice of his imperious consort, but to act as she had decreed; for if Hagar and Ishmael had been retained in the family there never would have been peace or harmony there. God allowed the rejection of Hagar and her son, not that they should remain to the end forsaken, but that his own tender pity and grace might be extended to and manifested in them. (78)

When Abraham cast Hagar out, God took her under his own wing. He heard the weeping mother who, in misery and shame, laid her child down to die and responded with words of comfort and guidance. "The record stands here for evermore," Butler comments,

> of the undying pity and love of the Eternal Father for the myriads of those who, leaning on the stronger judgments of others, or trusting in human promises,

have been brought into misfortune and misery, whose footsteps have slipped, and who have become the despised and rejected of men. (91)

Alluding to Isa 53:5, Butler draws a clear connection between the suffering of the Son of God who bore the sin of the world and that of the fallen woman, implying that God shares in the pain of the fallen woman as much as he bears her sorrows. Throughout her exposition, Butler reveals a God who has Hagar's interests at heart, who seeks to compensate for Abraham and Sarah's misuse and ill treatment of a human life, and who, by analogy, has a heart full of compassion and love for the most destitute and hopeless of women.

Butler's embellishments, highlighting the bad behavior of Abraham and Sarah, establishing Hagar as a victim, and portraying God as one who has a heart for the poor and destitute, sets the stage for Butler's application of this text and prophetic summons to nineteenth-century England. While many of Butler's contemporaries invited the reader to identify with the "sinner" Hagar whom God meets with his love, comfort, and protection, Butler invited her readers to identify with Sarah as one who perpetuates the oppression of the outcast woman. The relationship between Sarah and Hagar serves as a negative example highlighting the need for change. While this story describes a great gulf between Sarah and Hagar, Butler claims this is part of the old era. "Christ's teaching and action inaugurated a new era," a day of liberation and equality. Unfortunately, "his professed followers have been, and still are, in a great measure, blind to the light of his new day, and unfaithful to his teaching" (75). Prostitution, child prostitution, the sex trade (all perpetuated by the inequality of the sexes) as well as a woman's lack of access to education, employment, and political influence are contrary to the gospel of Jesus Christ. However, Butler believes that this can change. "The Sarahs are beginning to repent and to stretch forth their hands to the Hagars, and to bridge over the gulf which has so long separated them," Butler writes (91). For Butler, the story of Hagar is a prophetic call to embrace the dawn of a new day and to put an end to the oppression of women. More specifically, Butler calls on virtuous women to put an end to the two classes of women that perpetuate the sexual oppression and exploitation of fallen women, encouraging the Sarahs of this world to stretch forth their hands to the Hagars, to embrace the teachings of Jesus Christ regarding women, to participate in Jesus' mission of liberation and equality for all human beings, to turn over social and religious conventions, and to fight human sin. The story of Hagar the victim of sexual oppression can be redeemed.

CONCLUSION

In *The Lady of Shunem*, Butler describes her reading of the Hagar story in this way. She writes: "I continue to regard this and every part of Abraham's history from the human side, while trying to read it truly, as under the eye of God. My reading of it may only be a motherly, a womanly reading of it, and theologically worthless" (74). Although somewhat self-deprecating, Butler indicates here that there are different ways of reading the biblical text. In many ways, Butler's observation anticipates Phyllis Trible's description of her approach to Scripture when she says, "traditional biblical scholarship has focused on authorial intentionality, but there has been a shift. And the place where I work is at the intersection of text and reader.... though that approach [discerning the intention of the author] has sometimes been helpful, that's not the only way to read a text."[26] Working at the intersection of text and reader expresses Butler's own humanly reading of Scripture well, which seems to be a product of the interaction of the text, her life experiences, and her theological framework.

What Butler's reading of the Hagar story teaches us, among other things, is that what the text means has a lot to do with who is doing the reading. Perhaps as biblical scholars we have something to learn from her—the level of detachment required for an "objective" reading of the text may actually amplify the distance between the world of the text and our world, hampering its ability to speak meaningfully to us today. Alternatively, a subjective reading that invites our experiences and convictions to play a role in interpreting the text may actually be quite fruitful and, in the case of the Hagar story, necessary in order to make sense of this story as word of God. Perhaps faithful biblical interpretation is less about objectivity and correct exegetical work and more about the fruit it bears. Does an interpretation of Scripture speak God's word to us? Does it spur us on to greater righteousness? Does it challenge us to do justice? Does it increase our love for God and for our neighbor? Although she was not a biblical scholar and did not engage in a critical reading of the biblical text, I believe that Josephine Butler's humanly reading provides us with a helpful model of interpreting Scripture as the living word of God.

BIBLIOGRAPHY

Butler, Josephine. "Introduction." Pages vii–lxiv in *Women's Work and Woman's Culture: A Series of Essays.* Edited by Josephine Butler. London: Macmillan, 1868.
———. *The Lady of Shunem.* London: Marshall, 1894.
———. *Prophets and Prophetesses: Some Thoughts for the Present Times.* London: Dyer Brothers, 1898.
———. *Recollections of George Butler.* London: Simpkin, Marshall, Hamilton & Kent, 1892.
———. *Social Purity.* London: Dyer Brothers, 1882.
Calvin, John. *Calvin's Commentaries: Genesis.* Electronic ed. Bellingham, Wash.: Logos Library System, 1998.
Jordan, Jane. *Josephine Butler.* London: Murray, 2001.
Mathers, Helen. "The Evangelical Spirituality of a Victorian Feminist: Josephine Butler, 1828–1906." *JEH* 52 (2001): 282–312.

---

26. Phyllis Trible, "Wrestling with Scripture," *BAR* 32/2 (2006): 48.

Rad, Gerhard von. *Genesis: A Commentary*. OTL. Philadelphia: Westminster, 1972.

Shiman, Lillian Lewis. *Women and Leadership in Nineteenth-Century England*. London: MacMillan, 1992.

Stowe, Harriet Beecher. *Women in Sacred History: A Series of Sketches Drawn from Scriptural, Historical and Legendary Sources*. New York: Ford, 1873.

Taylor, Marion, and Heather Weir. *Let Her Speak for Herself: Nineteenth-Century Women Writing on Women in Genesis*. Waco, Tex.: Baylor University Press, 2006.

Trible, Phyllis. "Wrestling with Scripture." *BAR* 32/2 (2006): 46–52, 76–77.

Trimmer, Sarah. *A Help to the Unlearned in the Study of the Holy Scriptures: Being an Attempt to Explain the Bible in a Familiar Way*. London: Rivington, 1805.

Elizabeth Rundle Charles:
Translating the Letter of Scripture Into Life*

Marion Ann Taylor

History remembers Elizabeth Rundle Charles (1828–96) preeminently as the author of *The Chronicles of the Schönberg-Cotta Family* (a historical novel about Martin Luther) and a number of other works of historical fiction.[1] While Charles deserves to be remembered as a novelist, she also should be recognized as a significant biblical interpreter.[2] This essay will focus on Charles's writing on Scripture. It will highlight the experiences in her life that shaped her approach to interpretation and illustrate her hermeneutic by using examples from her writings.

Early Influences

Elizabeth Rundle Charles was born in 1828 in Devon, England. She was the only child of John Rundle (1791–1864), a banker and member of Parliament, and his wife, Barbara, née Gill (d. 1889). Her parents valued education, the arts, and

---

* I am grateful for the ATS Lilly Research Expense Grant in the fall of 2004 that allowed me to acquire the works of Elizabeth Rundle Charles used in this essay.

1. S. Austin Allibone, Charles's contemporary, notes her reputation as a linguist, painter, musician, and poet, and especially as the author of *The Chronicles of the Schönberg-Cotta Family* and almost twenty-five other volumes, but he says nothing of her work as a biblical scholar (S. Austin Allibone, *A Critical Dictionary of English Literature and British and American Authors* [3 vols.; Philadelphia: Lippincott, 1908], 2:1890). Elizabeth Jay also highlights Charles's book on Luther and lists a number of her other writings but neglects to mention her writings on Scripture (Elisabeth Jay, "Charles, Elizabeth Rundle," in *The Oxford Dictionary of National Biography* [ed. H. C. G. Matthew and B. Harrison; 60 vols.; Oxford: Oxford University Press, 2004], 11:160–61).

2. Charles actually authored almost fifty volumes. Many of Charles's later books were simply designated as being written by the author of *The Chronicles of the Schönberg-Cotta Family, Early Dawn, Diary of Kitty Trevylyan*, and other successful books of historical fiction. For a complete list of her books, see Elizabeth Rundle Charles, *Our Seven Homes: Autobiographical Reminiscences* (London: Murray, 1896), 225–29.

"active" Christian faith. Charles fondly remembered her father as "liberal to the core of heart and mind, with Liberalism of faith and hope and charity, faith in God and man, hope in God and for man, love to God and man."[3] John Rundle passed on these convictions, convincing his daughter of the importance of works of charity with the poor, uneducated, and needy.

Faithful to the legacy of her father, Charles expressed interest in political and social questions[4] and was actively involved in practical and philanthropic work associated with such organizations as the North London Consumptive Hospital, the Santa Claus Society, a nursing home for children suffering from hip and spinal diseases, and the Home for the Dying.[5] These interests and experiences influenced Charles's reading of Scripture; they pushed her to explore the practical applications of the Bible. In her retelling of the biblical story of Ruth, for example, Charles holds up the Old Testament laws about widows, orphans, and strangers, suggesting they "go farther than many a charter of rights to extinguish the bitter cry of poverty and wrong."[6] Similarly, in an essay exploring women's roles in Scripture, Charles calls attention to the importance of the practical work of the women in the nascent church, describing them as "leaders in that great army of liberation, that great company of healers ever needed on all the battle-fields."[7]

Elizabeth Rundle Charles's mother also had a lasting influence on her life. Barbara Rundle "ruled" the home, which was her "kingdom … keeping all well-ordered and peaceful around her husband's busy life; having perhaps more of the gift of ruling than he had."[8] She was the template of the ideal Christian woman that Charles used in her many writings that feature women in Scripture.[9]

EDUCATION AND FORMATIVE INFLUENCES

Charles was educated at home by her parents, various governesses, and tutors. She learned classical and modern languages (Latin, Greek, French, Italian, and

---

3. Charles, *Our Seven Homes*, 8.

4. Ibid., 220. In the notes added to Charles's autobiography, Mary Davidson writes that "as a member of the Christian Social Union, her [Charles's] ideal of Christianity was full of boundless hopes for the multitudes whom she loved, and whom she always considered not as 'masses' or 'classes,' but as 'multitudes of immortal personalities.' "

5. Ibid., 219–20.

6. Elizabeth Rundle Charles, *An Old Story of Bethlehem: One Link in the Great Pedigree* (London: SPCK, 1887), 11.

7. Elizabeth Rundle Charles, *Ecce Ancilla Domini; Mary the Mother of Our Lord: Studies in the Christian Ideal of Womanhood* (London: SPCK, 1894), 167.

8. Charles, *Our Seven Homes*, 46.

9. See, e.g., *The Women of the Gospels: The Three Wakings, and Other Poems* (New York: Dodd, 1867); idem, *Sketches of the Women of Christendom* (New York: Dodd, Mead & Co., 1880); idem, *Old Story of Bethlehem*; idem, *Mary, The Handmaid of the Lord* (New York: Dodd, 1865); and idem, *Ecce Ancilla Domini*.

German) and such subjects as geography, geometry, art, and music. Charles read from the age of three and used not only her parents' extensive library but also that of her relatives.[10]

Charles began writing at a young age and received encouragement from her parents and close family friends, including the English historian James Anthony Froude (1818–94) and the poet Alfred Tennyson (1809–92).[11] As a young adult, Charles joined a women's essay-writing group where she learned to write about particular periods of history. In her later reflections on the early period of her writing, Charles recognized that "facts—men and women that had actually lived, deeds that had really been done, and words that had really been spoken and were as deeds—that is historical facts, seemed to me so sacred and beautiful beyond all, that I had intended not to write any more fiction."[12] However, her experience of writing about Martin Luther introduced her to the joys of writing historical fiction; she found she could "utter fuller truth, spiritual, moral, intellectual, write really truer history in the dramatic than in the strictly historical form."[13]

Charles's interest in history and history writing surfaced continually in her publications on Scripture. She read Scripture as history, reflected upon how history is written, and was interested in the work of historical-critical scholars. In *Te Deum Laudamus*, Charles expresses her openness to the results of historical research into the Psalms.[14] She writes: "whatever criticism (higher or lower) may discover as to the fountains from which this or that part of the river came, it is one mighty ancient river, from fountains ever fresh. Variety of authorship is indeed one of its essential characteristics."[15] Still, she suggests reading the psalms

---

10. Charles read the following books at her cousins' house: "For story books we had 'Grimm's Fairy Tales' with Cruikshanks's illustrations, and 'Robinson Crusoe,' Miss Edgeworth's 'Tales and Shades of Character,' and 'Ornaments Discovered,' and 'Pilgrim's Progress,' and a pretty wide range over the books of older people, such as various voyages and travels and Captain Marryat's novels, especially 'Midshipman Easy.'" Charles was introduced to Shakespeare by her aunt, who made the characters live when she read to children (Charles, *Our Seven Homes*, 51, 53).

11. In her autobiography, Charles recalled with gratitude Froude's "long and gentle criticism" of her early essays, stories, and poems, "so encouraging and yet so *pruning*, full of wise guidance, and also of expectation of achievement." Charles addressed her poem " 'Two Meanings of Fame,' in *Songs Old and New* 'To Lord Tennyson, after a Morning at Farringford, April 26, 1867' " (ibid., 118, 174).

12. Ibid., 175.

13. Ibid., 175–76.

14. This work features Charles's passion for history, the Christian faith, poetry, hymns, and music. She translates each hymn with a view to historical accuracy rather than literary beauty so that "the colouring of the present should not be thrown over the faith of the past" (Charles, *Te Deum Laudamus: Christian Life in Song: The Song and the Singer*, [5th ed.; London: SPCK, 1897], v).

15. Ibid., 16.

of David against the backdrop of David's "most active and eventful life."[16] Charles also read the psalms ahistorically. In her exposition of the Beatitudes, for example, she uses Ps 107 as a commentary on the comfort offered by Jesus to those who mourn (Matt 5:4). She offers a figural reading of "that great ancient Psalm of Life" that presents "this great panorama of human life, echoing to us from so far across the thousands of years," with examples of every type of human distress and sorrow and every manner of divine comfort.[17] Charles's approach to interpreting Scripture is multifaceted. She is open to the results of historical-critical studies, but she also uses a variety of more traditional approaches to open up the spiritual meaning of texts.

CHURCH AFFILIATION

Charles was raised as an Anglican but experienced the breadth of the Christian tradition. From her childhood, she was surrounded by "good and devoted Christian people, 'holy and humble of heart,'" from various denominations who convinced her of "the Divine creation of the saints on both sides of all the barriers."[18] She was personally drawn toward the Oxford Movement and the Catholic ideal of the "church indivisible" and almost converted to Roman Catholicism after a trip to France. However, a Swiss Protestant minister, César Malan, who stressed the doctrine of the atonement and upheld the unity of the "invisible church of all believers," convinced Charles to remain Anglican.[19] Charles's writings reflect her evangelical piety, her love for high-church liturgy and tradition, and her ecumenism.

Charles's understanding of the Christian faith was profound. She did not have a formal theological education, but she read widely in church history, theology, and biblical studies. She was particularly interested in the history of church music and liturgy. Charles's love for Anglican liturgy, tradition, and theology is reflected in her devotional writings on great themes and passages of Scripture, which grew out of Lenten Bible readings with personal friends from 1885 to 1891. In *By the Coming of the Holy Ghost*, for example, Charles examines the Holy Spirit in Scripture and explores the theology of the Spirit and such doctrines as the inspiration of Scripture, revelation, and the Trinity. She provides an analysis of relevant texts and considers such traditional reflections on the Spirit as the ancient advent hymn, "O Sapientia."[20]

---

16. Charles, *Our Seven Homes*, 17.

17. Elizabeth Rundle Charles, *The Beatitudes: Thoughts for All Saints' Day* (London: SPCK, 1889), 51–52.

18. Charles, *Our Seven Homes*, 87.

19. Ibid., 132–40; Jay, "Charles, Elizabeth Rundle," 160.

20. Elizabeth Rundle Charles, *By the Coming of the Holy Ghost: Thoughts For Whitsuntide* (London: SPCK, 1888), 149–60.

Marriage and Travel

In 1851, at the age of twenty-three, Elizabeth Rundle married Andrew Paton Charles, a barrister at law. They had a happy though childless marriage. When her husband died of tuberculosis in 1868, Elizabeth Charles was left without financial security. Her writing, which she regarded as a religious vocation, became her main source of income.[21] In her more senior years, Charles moved away from fiction toward writing books on Scripture and the Christian life. She was working on a revision of *Te Deum Laudamus* up until a few days before her death.

Elizabeth Charles and her husband traveled to the Holy Land,[22] Egypt, Turkey, the Greek Islands, and Italy on a trip that was partially motivated by her husband's failing health. Charles documented their travels in her popular *Wanderings over Bible Lands and Seas* (1861).[23] Their trip lasted about four months and presented a number of challenges. It predated the era of modern tourism inaugurated by Thomas Cook, who made travel to the Holy Land more accessible to the middle-class Britons beginning in 1869.[24] Charles's description of the end of one particularly harrowing day in Galilee, when a fellow traveler was lost and robbed and their bedding soaked when their mules rolled in a river, illustrates the rigor of their trip:

> We had been in the saddle for thirteen hours. The alternate baying of shepherds' dogs and howling of wolves near our tents, could not prevent us sleeping soundly that night on our bare camp beds, wrapped up in shawls. The excitement of the day, however, did not wear off immediately, and it was some time before the pictures of Galilean scenery, rocky hills, wild wooded ravines, and shady forest paths festooned with fragrant flowers, which that day's fatigues had so deeply imprinted on our minds, faded into dreams.[25]

---

21. In her reminiscences, Charles describes her vocation: "the Divine Voice speaking through the double call of dear, plain outward duty and of inward impulse—or should I rather say inspiration, since God Himself is nearer us than any of the creatures or circumstances through which He moves us; since *inbreathing* is a finer expression of His work in us than impelling" (*Our Seven Homes*, 176).

22. Like most travelers of her day, Charles uses the expression "Holy Land" to describe the geographical area known as Palestine.

23. *Wanderings over Bible Lands and Seas* was reprinted several times over a period of thirty years in Britain and the United States.

24. Timothy Larsen, "Spiritual Exploration: Thomas Cook, Victorian Tourists, and the Holy Land," in idem, *Contested Christianity: The Political and Social Context of Victorian Theology* (Waco, Tex.: Baylor University Press, 2004), 29–39.

25. Elizabeth Rundle Charles, *Wanderings over Bible Lands and Seas* (London: Nelson & Sons, 1861), 251.

Charles's reactions to the Holy Land are not unlike those of many low-church Protestants who spoke contemptuously of commercialized holy sites but found the experience of being in the land deeply moving.[26] She criticized the "petty mercenary competition" among the various churches in the Church of the Holy Sepulchre, which "taxed their ingenuity to find sacred names and events to consecrate their several territories and to secure some especial attraction for their especial votaries."[27] Instead, she advocated "a religion of life and light, not of sepulchers or relics.... Christ is not dead. He is risen" (140). Charles's incarnational theology allowed her to see beyond the commercialism of the holy sites. In contrast to superstition that "fondly treasures the dead relics of the past, some poor crumbling bone of the Body God watches over, and will raise incorruptible, some spot of dust on which holy feet have trod," Charles's theology of pilgrimage presupposed faith that "revivifies the past by a community of like with those who lived in it: 'they are not dead, but living; for all live unto him'" (140). The goal of her pilgrimage was seeing the scenes the apostles would have seen and hearing the sounds they would have heard, with the eyes and ears of faith.

Charles extended her incarnational theology to include all of creation: "Hudson's Bay, of which the apostles never heard, is as holy as the Sea of Galilee; and the streets of London which Christians tread, as sacred as the streets of Jerusalem, where our Lord was crucified" (15–16). She believes that the incarnate Jesus consecrated all of creation and that his "living presence" is everywhere (16). The importance of traveling for Charles, then, lay not in visiting particular sites because of their sanctified nature but in their association with history and with the revelation of unseen and eternal realities (17). Traveling by sea past the site of Paul's shipwreck, for example, allowed Charles to imagine what Paul had experienced as he "drifted on a broken plank through these waves, then dashing wildly in the storm, to this low, sandy, shelving beach at the head of the bay, and so escaped to this shore" (17). Her faith was strengthened as she stood on the ship and saw and felt "how his [Paul's] natural world—his body with its dangers and wants—was the same as ours, just as his heart, and the truths which warmed and fed it, were the same" (17).

Charles's experiences of travel changed how she read and interpreted Scripture. It transformed texts she had previously read as allegories into history and facts, and then, through her faith in the living Christ and the Holy Spirit, history lived again (47).

Charles's book on the Beatitudes, published almost thirty years after her trip to the Holy Land, shows the lasting impact of her travels on her reading of Scripture. With the brush of an artist, she paints a picture of Jesus preaching the

---

26. Compare travel accounts in Larsen, "Spiritual Exploration," 29–39.

27. Charles, *Wanderings over Bible Lands*, 140. Subsequent references to *Wanderings over Bible Lands* will be provided within the text.

Sermon on the Mount sitting "on that hill-side above the Sea of Galilee, its waters rippling against the shingly shore or sandy beaches, but too far below to be audible; beyond the shining expanse of the lake, the opposite rocky shore, and far above, Hermon with its slivery streak of snows."[28]

Charles's ability to describe the settings of the stories in Scripture she exposits gives her writings a unique flavor. Few nineteenth-century biblical scholars and few of the nineteenth-century women who authored books on Scripture had the opportunity to travel to the Holy Land. Fewer still were able to make the geography and history of the land live as Charles did.

TRANSLATING THE LETTER OF SCRIPTURE INTO LIFE

Charles's emphasis on the history and geography of the stories in Scripture was consonant with a shift in nineteenth-century biblical scholarship toward a historical approach.[29] However, Charles believed that the historical approach alone was inadequate. She criticized scholars who adhered strictly to the Enlightenment dictum "interpret the scripture like any other book."[30] She downplayed the importance of such questions as, "Did Deuteronomy, or Job or Daniel belong to this century or that? Were those tender fiery words written by the first Isaiah or the second, or not by Isaiah at all?"[31] Instead, Charles focused on the author of Scripture and the Holy Spirit who transforms "the husks of antiquarianism into living history";[32] so the letter of Scripture is translated into life:

> The letter of the Scriptures is good, but that it may be of its true use, the readers and writers must not be primarily "scribes," whose object is to multiply copies, or to utter repetitions of the books, but teachers whose purpose is to translate the letter into life. History is good; the Christ came not to destroy but to fulfil. But the life of history is destroyed if its continuity is destroyed, if its living seeds are kept apart in a museum of antiquarian specimens, instead of being sewn in fresh soil.[33]

---

28. Charles, *The Beatitudes*, 12.

29. John Rogerson, *Old Testament Criticism in the Nineteenth Century* (London: SPCK, 1984), 273–88. Rogerson shows, for example, how the controversial publications such as Samuel Davidson's *The Text of the Old Testament* (1859), *Essays and Reviews* (1860), Colenso's multi-volume work on the Pentateuch and Joshua (1862–79), and the ensuing debates did much to promote critical scholarship. See also W. B. Glover, *Evangelical Nonconformists and Higher Criticism in the Nineteenth Century* (London: Independent Press, 1954).

30. Benjamin Jowett, "On the Interpretation of Scripture," in *Essays and Reviews* (ed. F. H. Hedge; London: Parker & Sons, 1860), 377.

31. Charles, *By the Coming of the Holy Ghost*, 81.

32. Ibid.

33. Ibid., 80.

For Charles, the Bible was more than "a dead letter, or mere phonograph of stored-up past utterances, that dreadful mockery of a voice."[34] She believed that the voice of the living God, "a living responsive voice," speaks through Scripture.[35] Like Christina Rossetti (1830–94),[36] Charles was critical of an approach to the study of the Bible that did not recognize its spiritual nature. She emphasized the Scriptures' depths and called readers to "come again and again to draw out His meaning, for the well is deep."[37]

Integral to Charles's life-giving hermeneutic was her ongoing engagement with contemporary society. Charles was not afraid of the challenges of science. She suggests that the theory of evolution and the Genesis account of creation are compatible. She asks whether "indwelling life, continuous communication of life, countless variations and adaptations of life, from need to need, from stage to stage," are not implied in Gen 1:2, "The Spirit of God moved on the face of the waters."[38]

Charles also appropriated insights of biblical scholars into her work. In a discussion of the postresurrection narratives, for example, she addresses the issue of the authorship of John 21. She was open to the idea that biblical books may have gone through a process of editing. She contends that whether John 21 was written by John or his disciples does not change its "beauty," since "it was from St. John's heart and from his telling, if not from his pen."[39] Charles believes that the meaning of a text does not rest on the identity of a human author. Similarly, Charles refuses to be drawn into schemes of harmonizing the Gospels, a task she likens to "trying to make a perfect picture out of the fragments of an ancient mosaic of which some pieces are lost." She avers, "if we insist on joining

---

34. Elizabeth Rundle Charles, as cited in Mary Carus-Wilson, *Unseal the Book: Practical Words for Plain Readers of Holy Scripture* (London: Religious Tract Society, 1899), 154.

35. Ibid.

36. "It is, I suppose, a genuine though not a glaring breach of the Second Commandment, when instead of learning the lesson plainly set down for us in Holy Writ we protrude mental feelers in all directions above, beneath, around it, grasping, clinging to every imaginable particular except the main point. ... Take the history of the Fall. The question of mortal sin shrinks into the background while we moot such points as the primitive status of the serpent: did he stand somehow upright? did he fly? what did he originally eat? how did he articulate?" (Christina G. Rossetti, *Letter and Spirit: Notes on the Commandments* [London: SPCK, 1883], 85–86).

37. Elizabeth Rundle Charles, *By Thy Glorious Resurrection and Ascension: Easter Thoughts* (London: SPCK, 1888), 81.

38. In a footnote, Charles quotes a relevant text from the *Life of Charles Darwin*: "with respect to immortality, nothing shows me so clearly how strong and almost intuitive a belief it is as a consideration of the view now held by most physicists, namely, that the sun, with all the planets, will in time grow too cold for life.... To those who fully admit the immortality of the human soul, the destruction of our world will not appear so dreadful" (Charles, *By the Coming of the Holy Ghost*, 23–24).

39. Charles, *By Thy Glorious Resurrection*, 103.

the remaining pieces together without gaps, the pieces must be shattered, and the picture must lose its proportions and be distorted."[40] Instead, Charles listens to the distinctive voice of each Gospel. She was open to new ideas that deepened her understanding of Scripture. She refused to be boxed into traditional interpretations or approaches to interpreting Scripture. Charles believed that Scripture was the voice of God, and she used all available knowledge for the interpretive task.

Charles's linguistic expertise allowed her to study the New Testament in Greek. In her exposition of various beatitudes, she provides readers with insights into the meaning of key words, often citing the Greek text. She presents readers with various interpretive options but also presents her own views. Commenting on the meaning of "Blessed are they that mourn" (Matt 5:4), Charles writes:

> Amongst all meanings, in a sense, before all others, this Beatitude may therefore well seem to belong to those who mourn for their own sins, negligences, ignorances, transgressions, short-comings, failures; sin intertwined with our best actions, dragging us back again and again from our highest purposes, dimming and marring our truest ideals, hindering our being what we would be, doing what we would do for those we love best. Whatever other mourning for the sorrow at the root of all sorrows cannot be excluded. And it is through *this* mourning that we most naturally approach the meaning of the Beatitude on those that mourn.[41]

Charles advocates a close reading of texts, an approach she likens to drinking deeply from the well. Thus, she concludes her study of the word *comforted* (Matt 5:4): "But when we drink deep enough into this quiet word we find it indeed all we want."[42]

As a writer, Charles was aware of the relationship between literary genre and hermeneutics. On occasion she spoke candidly about the challenges of interpretation. She raised the issue of the literary genre of the story of the fall with the women in India for whom she wrote *Sketches of the Women of Christendom*. Anticipating their questions about interpretation, Charles asks if the story of the garden was "fact, or poem? parable, or history?" Her answer reveals that she understood that the literal and/or historical sense of a text did not always lead one to its truest sense:

> It is both [fact and poem, parable and history]: true, with the deepest truth, always renewed in various forms. To get at truth in all histories we must read them also as parables and poems; that is, as a sacred story which does not merely

---

40. Charles, *Ecce Ancilla Domini*, 53.
41. Charles, *The Beatitudes*, 47.
42. Ibid., 49.

gossip about the external facts, but penetrates to the divine and human meanings enfolded in these.[43]

By opening up the interpretive options of the garden story, Charles is able to apply the story to the lives of her readers, who like Eve struggled with temptation. Charles reasons that just as Eve looked at the forbidden tree and saw that "it was beautiful and seemed good," so we are all tempted by things that "seem, and probably are, beautiful and good in themselves, only not just *then* or not *for us*."[44] She argues that Eve sinned not by taking the fruit but by not trusting God, whereas Adam fell deeper into sin than Eve when he accused her of offering him the fruit.[45] Charles highlights Eve's role as the mother of all the living, suggesting that Adam and all the world would be delivered through her seed, Jesus.[46] In this way, Charles redeems Eve from the burden of guilt the history of interpretation had placed upon her for the fall.

While Charles probed the multiple levels of the garden story, she followed a narrative and historical approach to the book of Ruth. She read the book within its historical context, taking care to explain such customs as the "right and duty of the nearest kinsman of the dead husband to marry the widow, so that the name of the dead should not perish."[47] Moving toward application, she picks up on the genealogy that concludes the book, which names Ruth's son Obed as the grandfather of David (Ruth 4:17), and suggests that Bethlehem, the birthplace of Obed and Jesus, provides a further link to Jesus, son of David, and Obed.[48] Charles does not resort to a figural reading of the book of Ruth. She does not even note the significance of the meaning of the various places and characters in the book. Rather, she sets Ruth in its larger canonical context and shows how a place (Bethlehem) and a person (King David) link this story to the larger history of salvation. As a sophisticated reader of texts, Charles uses a variety of methods of interpretation. She chooses methods appropriate to the type of literature she is reading and the particular audience and the occasion for which she is writing.

Charles often used an associative approach to open up the fuller meaning of texts. She reads the Old and New Testaments as one book and connects texts from one part of Scripture with another to illumine the meaning of both texts. For example, in her exposition of Gen 1:2, Charles associates the Spirit of God in Genesis with the Bride of the book of Revelation (Rev 22:17). She moves smoothly from one text to the other to find Scripture's abiding meaning:

---

43. Charles, *Sketches of the Women*, 5.
44. Ibid., 9.
45. Ibid., 10.
46. Ibid., 13.
47. Charles, *Old Story of Bethlehem*, 28. This book was for children.
48. Ibid., 32.

"The Spirit and the Bride" still, as it were, brood over a moral chaos, not yet brought to the beauty and order of the Cosmos; still turn to a world as yet unrestored with the water of life, still say not "all is complete, the goal is reached," but, gazing upward through a new door of hope into heaven, [say] "Come, come Thou."[49]

With great passion, Charles calls her readers to a deeper relationship with God. One can imagine that in presenting her preliminary studies to her friends during Lent, her living room became her pulpit.

Charles also read the images in Scripture intertextually, exploring their full range of meaning. In her comments on the movement of the Spirit of God over the waters (Gen 1:2), for example, she likens the Spirit to a brooding mother bird and then explores the feminine images associated with God throughout Scripture.

"As a hen gathereth (Matt 23:37)." The love of the mother as well as of the father is appealed to in unveiling the love of God. "As one whom his mother comforteth (Isa 66:13)." Here it is used with reference to the material world. And how beautiful and tender the symbol is! the whole world, as it were, loved into life! the whole visible creation responding to the Personal life and love brooding over it, and waking to order, and movement, and beauty! The image is one, not of a momentary flash of creative power, but of the continuous brooding of creative life-giving love. Not as a maker, with whatever ingenuity of design, turning out a wonderful mechanism, winding it up, and letting it go; but as a mother-bird, patiently watching the first throbs of life, and quickening them into movement, is the Creation represented. Life springs from life, and is diffused through love.[50]

Charles was comforted by the female images of God used to describe the "relations of God to men [sic], watching, sheltering, seeking, recalling, welcoming."[51] Her own experiences of being mothered and of mothering those who came into her life influenced her reading of Scripture.

Charles also followed Anglican tradition of reading the Scriptures christologically. She used the lens of Jesus' life, for example, as one of the ways to illuminate the Sermon on the Mount. Commenting on "blessed are the meek" (Matt 5:5), she suggests that interpreters are not "left to Lexicons for the full and final meaning of this Beatitude. We have a Portrait, and a Voice. We have the looks and tones of Him who uttered it."[52] She then recalls incidents in Jesus' life that exemplify his gentleness or meekness. Charles also read Old Testament texts in the light of Christ. One of the several ways she understood Ps 107, for example, was in light

---

49. Charles, *By the Coming of the Holy Ghost*, 16.
50. Ibid., 22–23.
51. Ibid., 22.
52. Charles, *The Beatitudes*, 77.

of Jesus' life and ministry. While the psalmist speaks of the God of Israel as the deliverer of God's people, Charles understands the deliverer to be Jesus, the "one in Whom pity and succour were inseparable, Whose very touch was life, Who fed the hungry, healed all manner of sickness, gave sight to the blind, gave back the dead to those bereaved of them, whose days were one ceaseless course of healing, blessing, succouring, saving."[53]

Finally, Charles read Scripture typologically. She often read the stories in the Bible as the stories of us all. Thus, Eve's temptation is everyone's temptation, and Israel's history of rebellion is our history.[54] Psalm 107:23 is a "picture of human trouble as a storm, a storm encountered, not in revolt against God, not in some aimless drifting hither and thither, but, it seems, in the everyday path of duty." Charles's poem "The Widow of Nain" renders the resurrection of the widow's son from the bier first as a type of nature, which rises each spring "from her wintry bier, Throws off her grave-clothes, lives and sings," and second as a type of the final resurrection of the dead:

> And when Thy touch through earth shall thrill
> This bier whereon our race is laid,
> And, for the first time standing still,
> The long procession of the dead.
>
> At Thy "Arise!" shall wake from clay,
> Young, deathless, freed from every stain;
> When Thy "weep not!" shall wipe away
> Tears that shall never come again;
>
> When the strong chains of death are burst,
> And lips long dumb begin to speak,
> What name will each them utter first?—
> What music shall that silence break?[55]

As a poet, Charles was drawn to figurative meanings in texts. She played with words and images. Typology allowed her to make connections between the stories of Scripture and the present, between the Old Testament and the New, between life in this world and life in the future kingdom.

CONCLUSION

Elizabeth Rundle Charles was an exceptional interpreter of Scripture. She read the Bible as a historian and poet. Scripture was "fact and poem, parable and his-

---

53. Ibid., 63.
54. Ibid., 60.
55. Charles, *The Women of the Gospels*, 46–47.

tory, true, with the deepest truth, always renewed in various forms."[56] Charles was both "lay" biblical scholar and preacher. Her family, education, faith formation, marriage, and travel, together with her natural gifts of observation and writing, her knowledge of biblical scholarship, her understanding of history, literature, and hermeneutics, and her commitment to spiritual and practical applications of Scripture, shape her multivalent approach to interpretation, giving depth and sophistication to her reading of Scripture.

Charles offers modern readers a model of holding together different ways of reading texts. She read Scripture as history and used all the tools available for historical research. However, she felt that a historical approach by itself was lifeless. She believed it necessary that the Spirit breathed life into "the husks of antiquarianism," making them "living history."[57] Charles used a variety of interpretive methods to find the deeper meaning that transformed the letter of Scripture into life. In this way, she exemplifies how an interpreter can bring together the mind and the heart, history and poetry, the past and the present, this life and the next.

Charles also read the Bible as a nineteenth-century Victorian woman. In her book on women in Christendom written for women in India in 1880, Charles stresses women's call to a life of service to others epitomized by Jesus.[58] In a later work on the Christian ideal of womanhood, Charles goes further, arguing that God's ideal of womanhood is "the ideal of all humanity," for both women and men:

> The ideal of womanhood, not of poor weak crippled womanhood, but of womanhood as God made it, that is, a life that has no meaning except in relation of God and to others, has become the ideal of all humanity; a life whose essence is love, sacrificing and serving; renouncing when renunciation is the way to serve; ruling when ruling is the way to serve; rebuking when rebuking is the way to serve; silently suffering when patience is the way to serve; fearlessly fighting when resisting is the way to serve; dying when death is the way to serve.[59]

Charles celebrated the great gains for women in the nineteenth century: "all fields are indeed now open to us."[60] She argued for equality between men and women but not in their identity: "But we intend to fight together [like Deborah and Barak in Judg 4–5], man and woman, husband and wife, brother and sister, not in mean

---

56. Charles, *Sketches of the Women*, 5.

57. Ibid.

58. Charles's poem "Ministry" reflects this view of women's roles (*Sketches of the Women*, iv): "Since service is the highest lot, / And angels know no higher bliss, / Then with what good her cup is fraught / Who was created but for this."

59. Charles, *Ecce Ancilla Domini*, 163.

60. Ibid., 170.

competition, not in mad antagonism, but in co-operation, side by side, woman for ever the helpmeet over against man."[61]

While Charles was not involved in public debates about the woman question, her writings raise issues related to women's nature, role, and place. Charles's words inspired women as she preached with her pen:

> We have a glorious company to follow. Century after century they come, the women of Christianity from every section of Christendom, through every age of the Church, fulfilling the life of Christ, filling up the sufferings of Christ, healing, saving, teaching, leading up and on; refusing to recognize that any need be outcasts, to despair of rescuing from any depths, or of lifting to any heights; translating the prose of the world through Divine and human love into poetry, transfiguring the wildernesses of the world by patience and much labour into Paradises.[62]

In her notes to Charles's reminiscences, Mary Davidson wrote that Charles "profoundly influenced the religious life of many of the best and noblest leaders of women workers, in this age of women's work and influence … in many of the world's harvest fields."[63] Charles also modeled an independent lifestyle for women as she supported herself and her mother through her publications. In addition, Charles pushed vocational boundaries as she confidently published on Scripture and theology, subjects associated with the male domains of the academy and church.

Thus, Charles's own understanding of women's roles being primarily those of service and sacrifice affected how she read the stories of biblical women. Yet her sensitivities to female images and female concerns also pushed her to fresh insights. With the vision that God's ideal of womanhood is "the ideal of all humanity"—both women and men—she moved away from a traditional view that identified only women with service and sacrifice. Moreover, her extensive writings on women in Scripture and in history empowered many women to live full and useful lives of service to God and to others.

Elizabeth Rundle Charles's writings on Scripture have a timeless quality. They need to be reclaimed and celebrated as a gift she brought to her contemporaries and to those who now read her inspiring work.

Bibliography

Allibone, S. Austin. *A Critical Dictionary of English Literature and British and American Authors.* 3 vols. Philadelphia: Lippincott, 1908.

---

61. Ibid., 171.
62. Ibid., 171–72.
63. Charles, *Our Seven Homes,* 220–21.

Carus-Wilson, Mary. *Unseal the Book: Practical Words for Plain Readers of Holy Scripture.* London: Religious Tract Society, 1899.

Charles, Elizabeth Rundle. *The Beatitudes: Thoughts for All Saints' Day.* London: SPCK, 1889.

———. *By the Coming of the Holy Ghost: Thoughts For Whitsuntide.* London: SPCK, 1888.

———. *By Thy Glorious Resurrection and Ascension: Easter Thoughts.* London: SPCK, 1888.

———. *Ecce Ancilla Domini; Mary the Mother of Our Lord: Studies in the Christian Ideal of Womanhood.* London: SPCK, 1894.

———. *Mary, The Handmaid of the Lord.* New York: Dodd, 1865.

———. *An Old Story of Bethlehem: One Link in the Great Pedigree.* London: SPCK, 1887.

———. *Our Seven Homes: Autobiographical Reminiscences.* London: Murray, 1896.

———. *Sketches of the Women of Christendom.* New York: Dodd, Mead & Co., 1880.

———. *Te Deum Laudamus: Christian Life in Song: the Song and the Singer.* 5th ed. London: SPCK, 1897.

———. *The Women of the Gospels: The Three Wakings, and Other Poems,* New York: Dodd, 1867.

———. *Wanderings over Bible Lands and Seas.* London: Nelson & Sons, 1861.

Glover, W. B. *Evangelical Nonconformists and Higher Criticism in the Nineteenth Century.* London: Independent Press, 1954.

Jay, Elisabeth, "Charles, Elizabeth Rundle." Pages 160–61 in vol. 11 of *The Oxford Dictionary of National Biography.* Edited by H. C. G. Matthew and Brian Harrison. 60 vols. Oxford: Oxford University Press, 2004.

Jowett, Benjamin. "On the Interpretation of Scripture." Pages 362–480 in *Essays and Reviews.* Edited by Frederic Henry Hedge. London: Parker & Sons, 1860.

Larsen, Timothy, *Contested Christianity: The Political and Social Context of Victorian Theology:* Waco, Tex.: Baylor University Press, 2004.

Rogerson, John. *Old Testament Criticism in the Nineteenth Century.* London: SPCK, 1984.

Rossetti, Christina G. *Letter and Spirit: Notes on the Commandments.* London: SPCK, 1883.

THE PROPHETIC VOICE OF CHRISTINA ROSSETTI

Amanda W. Benckhuysen

> "What is written in the law? How readest thou?
> … This do, and thou shalt live."—St. Luke 10:26, 28

Christina Rossetti is one of the most important and well-known poets of nineteenth-century England. The youngest of four children, she was born in 1830 to Gabriele and Frances Rossetti. During her formative years, her family lived a comfortable, middle class life in London provided for by her father's work as a Dante scholar. She never married but remained devoted to her writing and her family throughout her life. In 1894, she died of cancer.

Rossetti's successful writing career began at age seventeen when she compiled and published her first volume of poetry. She continued to write poetry throughout her life, the most popular collection being *Goblin Market and Other Poems,* but in her later years she concentrated on devotional prose, including two commentaries on the Christian Scriptures: *Letter and Spirit,* a work on the Ten Commandments; and *The Face of the Deep,* a commentary on Revelation.[1] Rossetti's work is of interest not only because of her renown as a writer but because she is a nineteenth-century woman who engaged in exegetical activity on the words of Scripture. Recent scholarship has shown that writing on Scripture was an acceptable activity for women in nineteenth-century England.[2] Rossetti, however,

---

1. Rossetti refers to *Letter and Spirit: Notes on the Commandments* (London: SPCK, 1883) as "notes" on the commandments, saving the designation *devotional commentary* for her work on Revelation. It is not clear why Rossetti makes this distinction, except that the scope of *The Face of the Deep* is much greater, commenting on an entire book, in contrast to *Letter and Spirit,* which focuses on the interpretation of twenty verses (The Decalogue and Christ's summary of the law). However, because these works are similar in their intent, that is, in disclosing the meaning of the text to enrich the faith and piety of the Christian community, it is appropriate to categorize both of these pieces as devotional commentary.

2. See, e.g., the work of Patricia Demers, *Women as Interpreters of the Bible* (New York: Paulist, 1992). See also Marion Taylor, who is currently engaged in a major recovery effort of nineteenth-century women interpreters and has identified over one hundred women who wrote on the Bible.

is notable for the scope and complexity of her exegesis and her engagement with a wide readership. While most of her contemporaries wrote for women and children, Rossetti's exegetical work seems to be directed at a more learned audience including pastors, biblical scholars, and the educated population.[3] Through the very activity of engaging this audience, Rossetti implicitly challenges the limitations imposed on women by Victorian society and the more conservative wing of the Church of England.[4]

This is not to say that Rossetti was a feminist even by nineteenth-century standards.[5] She was strongly influenced by the traditional values of the Tractarian Movement[6] within the Church of England that held to the subordination of women to men. However, through her unique application of Tractarian hermeneutical principles to the study of the Christian Scriptures, Rossetti creates space for the voice of women to be heard. This essay will examine Rossetti's exegetical work on the Ten Commandments, *Letter and Spirit,* and investigate the countercultural posture she adopts as an authoritative interpreter of Scripture. Furthermore, this essay will explore how her temerity in biblical exegesis is consistent with her own traditional gender ideology.

Letter and Spirit is first of all a harmony of Jesus' summary of the law and the Decalogue, discussing how the two great commands of Jesus relate to the two tables of the law of Moses. Rossetti, however, soon moves beyond a straightforward harmony into a more complex "theological disquisition"[7] of the divine will. She is

---

3. See Diane D'Amico and David Kent, introduction to Christian Rossetti, "Notes on Genesis and Exodus," *Journal of Pre-Raphaelite Studies* 13 (2004): 54–57.

4. For further insight on the relationship between women and the church in nineteenth-century England, see Barbara Taylor, *Eve and the New Jerusalem* (New York: Pantheon, 1983), 127. See also Sean Gill, *Women and the Church of England: From the Eighteenth Century to the Present* (London: SPCK, 1994).

5. The issue of Rossetti's gender ideology has been much discussed by scholars of English literature. Some have described her as protofeminist or having feminist tendencies (see, e.g., the work of Joel Westerholm, "'I Magnify Mine Office': Christina Rossetti's Authoritative Choice in Her Devotional Prose," *The Victorian Newsletter* 84 [1993]: 11–17; and Lynda Palazzo, "The Poet and the Bible: Christina Rossetti's Feminist Hermeneutics," *The Victorian Newsletter* 92 [1997]: 6–9 on Rossetti). However, Rossetti is not easy to categorize. Her stance with respect to gender relations is unclear. She did not join outspoken feminists of her day to fight for a woman's right to vote. Furthermore, she upheld traditional ideas that a woman must submit to her husband. Yet Rossetti does push the boundaries and limitations imposed on women by conservative church members in her biblical exegesis.

6. The Tractarian or Oxford Movement was a conservative influence in the Church of England during the middle of the nineteenth century led by a group of disenchanted academics and Anglican clergymen, particularly John Henry Newman, John Keble, and Edward Pusey. Together they published ninety tracts attacking doctrinal laxity and political trends toward disestablishing the Church of England while seeking to recover the church's rich heritage and tradition.

7. Mackenzie Bell coined this description of Rossetti's *Letter and Spirit* in her biography *Christina Rossetti: A Biographical and Critical Study* (London: Burleigh, 1898), 299.

concerned to show the harmony not just between Jesus' words and the Decalogue but between humanity's duty toward God and humanity's duty toward their neighbor (the first and the second tables of the law). Each commandment is considered by itself and in relation to other commandments of the Decalogue. The result is twofold. First, Rossetti is able to treat the Decalogue as a unity within which the whole duty of humanity is embedded rather than the more common approach to the law as a series of disconnected commandments. This allows Rossetti to explore the fullest meaning of the Ten Commandments, examining the characteristics of obedience and disobedience in light of the entire testimony of Scripture. Second, this intertextual approach demonstrates not only the unity of Scripture but the unity of God's divine will and the interdependence between the two tables of the law. In other words, obedience toward God is most concretely demonstrated in our attitudes and actions toward fellow human beings. Rossetti closes her work with a harmony of 1 Cor 13 and the words and deeds of Jesus, providing the example par excellence of the moral human being.

Reading *Letter and Spirit,* one is immediately impressed by how significantly she was influenced by the theological and pietistic emphases of the Tractarians, particularly in her presuppositions about Scripture. For Rossetti, as for the Tractarians, the Bible was the authoritative revelation of God, inspired by the Holy Spirit. While this conviction was not unique to the Tractarians, Rossetti followed their more moderate understanding of the inspiration of Scripture, that the Bible is free of errors relating to piety and faith but not to all aspects of history.[8] This made her open to higher-critical concerns, as is evident in Rossetti's notes on Genesis and Exodus.[9] Commenting on the clause "I will see thy face again no more," which Moses says to Pharaoh in Exod 10:29, she notes: "Was this literally fulfilled? In 11.8, we find Moses once more speaking to Pharaoh: if the fulfilment was literal, possibly the speeches in question are not set down in order of time."[10] Here Rossetti points out that the literal meaning of these biblical words calls into question the chronological ordering of the Exodus account. Rossetti acknowledged the challenge that scientific rationalism posed to the biblical witness but was uncomfortable altering the received canon of Scripture to eliminate such problems. When possible, she attempted to harmonize empirical evidence with the biblical witness, as her reflections on Exod 20:11 exemplify:

"In six days the Lord made..., & rested the seventh day." Against the interpretation that the Days of Creation may be accounted not literal days but vast periods, it was once objected to me that the Seventh Day would then raise a special diffi-

---

8. See Peter Erb, "Edward Bouverie Pusey, 'Historical Criticism' and the Traditional Interpretation of Biblical Texts," paper presented at the Waterloo Biblical Colloquium, 30 January 2003, n. 32.

9. Ibid., 5–7.

10. D'Amico and Kent, introduction, 85.

culty (occurring, of course, within the lifetime of Man). Is it necessary, however (suppose there be any truth in the vast-periods theory) to estimate the Seventh Day according to the same standard as the preceding Six? That Seventh alone fell within the cognizance of man and might therefore be subjected to his scale: "The Sabbath was made for man, & not man for the Sabbath."[11]

In her notes on Genesis and Exodus, Rossetti engages and even rationalizes the "vast periods" theory of creation. Yet her commentary on the commandments offers none of this speculation. While it seems that Rossetti was open to higher-critical concerns, she feared that the focus on perceived "problems" in Scripture would eclipse the study of the words for the authoritative Word of God. In *Letter and Spirit*, Rossetti illustrates her own conviction that the proper interpretation of the commandments could not rest in historical methods or tools but rather in a theological reading that disclosed the divine will for nineteenth-century England.[12]

Second and closely related to this view of inspiration is Rossetti's concept of the language of Scripture. For Rossetti, the Bible was written not as a literal but rather as a poetic expression of God's Word, for only poetic language has the capacity to communicate the mysteries of the divine reality. The words themselves hold out the endless possibility of very present and mystical encounters with God.[13] In *Letter and Spirit*, Rossetti's exegetical work moves quickly beyond a discussion of the literal meaning of the commandments to a figurative one. Subsequently, it is not surprising to discover Rossetti's frequent dependence on typology, metaphor, and symbolism to disclose the meaning of the Word of God.

Interpretation then, requires first and foremost not rationalism or scholarship but a sanctified human imagination to see through biblical language to the divine realities it communicates. While this conviction validates Rossetti's own voice as an interpreter of Scripture, it obviously places her in opposition to the higher-critical methodologies common to the biblical scholarship of her day. Anticipating that some would discredit her for this unscholarly approach, she argues that the mysteries of the Christian faith are not always accessible by scholarship. One such instance is her discussion of the Trinity. She writes, "while if we ascend to contemplate the Trinity in Unity, Three Persons, One God, immediately we must confer not with flesh and blood, but walk by faith in lieu of sight."[14] Rossetti's goal in biblical interpretation was not to discover the literal meaning

---

11. Ibid., 88.

12. See Peter Erb for helpful comments on Pusey's approach to Scripture.

13. See Robert Kachur, "Repositioning the Female Christian Reader: Christina Rossetti as Tractarian Hermeneut in *The Face of the Deep*," *Victorian Poetry* 35 (1997): 196.

14. *Letter and Spirit*, 11. Subsequent references to *Letter and Spirit* will be provided within the text.

of the text but to have a revelatory encounter with God. Interpretation was conducted in faith and sought as its primary goal to further strengthen faith.

Third, Rossetti presumes the unity of Scripture; each part of the biblical witness contributes to the unified revelation of God. Harmonizing the different parts served to reveal the wholeness and coherence of the biblical witness. Rossetti masterfully draws on the most remote parts of Scripture to enrich her interpretation of each commandment. This intertextual approach, using one part of Scripture to interpret another, reveals Rossetti's interest in holding together the various biblical exhortations on the duty of humanity and stands in marked contrast to the historical-grammatical approaches common in the nineteenth century whose context of interpretation is the history of ancient Israel rather than the canon of Scripture.[15]

Finally, sacramentalism plays an important role in Rossetti's exegesis and, more particularly, in her attempt to enlarge the boundaries of women's roles within the church. Like the Tractarians, Rossetti believed that the transcendent is analogically present in the material world. Although the material world is but a shadow of the supernatural, its realities point beyond itself for those with eyes to see the divine. Rossetti comments,

> We should exercise that far higher privilege which appertains to Christians, of having "the mind of Christ;" and then the two worlds, visible and invisible, will become familiar to us even as they were to Him; and on occasion sparrow and lily will recall God's providence, seed His Word, earthly bread the Bread of Heaven, a plough the danger of drawing back; to fill a basin and take a towel will preach a sermon on self-abasement; boat, fishing-net, flock or fold of sheep, each will convey an allusion; wind, water, fire, the sun, a star, a vine, a door, a lamb, will shadow forth mysteries. (131–32)

It is noteworthy that in this example Rossetti infuses divine significance into very domestic things—baking bread, tending a garden, and serving a family—each of which "shadow forth mysteries." Furthermore, emphasis on the sacramental nature of the physical world allows Rossetti to blur the boundaries between earthly realities and divine appropriations. The result is that women preach the Word of God with ecclesiastical blessing whenever they "fill a basin and take a towel," a very domestic activity.

---

15. See, e.g., Frederic C. Cook, *The Holy Bible according to the Authorized Version with an Explanatory and Critical Commentary and a Revision of the Translation by Bishops and Other Clergy of the Anglican Church* (4 vols.; London: Murray, 1871). This commentary was designed to make biblical scholarship accessible to all educated people in order to help them understand what the original Scriptures really say and mean. Later commentaries with similar goals were increasingly influenced by historical-critical scholarship that atomized the text, challenging its inherent unity and cohesiveness. See, e.g., A. H. McNeile, *The Book of Exodus with Introduction and Notes* (WC 2; London: Methuen, 1908).

As evident from the above example, Rossetti's work is not simply the sum total of Tractarian influences. Rossetti offers her own fresh insights and nuanced interpretations of the words of Scripture. A brief comparison with the work of Isaac Williams, a preeminent Tractarian and significant influence on Rossetti, underscores the originality of her interpretive work. In 1862, Isaac Williams published a series of sermons on female characters in the Bible, the contents of which bear some resemblance to Rossetti's treatment of biblical women in *Letter and Spirit*. For instance, both Williams and Rossetti comment on the character of Eve and her transgression recorded in Gen 2–3 through the lens of Paul's comments in 1 Tim 2:14. Yet the ensuing treatment of Eve is very different. Williams heightens Eve's transgression, describing her sin as self-exaltation and pride. She indulged her own desires for power, honoring herself more than God. Williams goes on to portray Adam as a victim whose transgression is that he loved too much—loved the woman God had given him even more than God himself. Appealing to Paul's remarks in 1 Tim 2:11–12 about female silence and subjection, Williams reinforces traditional gender roles. He then rationalizes the submission of women to men as a form of God's grace, keeping in check woman's desire for influence and dominion, for they "will soon lend an ear to the serpent" and thus further evil and death in this world.[16]

By contrast, Rossetti offers a reading that is sympathetic of Eve, softening the language used to describe her sin. For Rossetti, Eve made a mistake. She was deceived. In fact, Rossetti suggests that it is Eve's intellectual gifts and kindness that made her susceptible to the serpent's deception, stating, "her very virtues may have opened the door to temptation.... she desires to instruct ignorance ... and she never suspects the serpent" (17). Like Williams, Rossetti also believes that Adam loved the creature more than the Creator, diverting his heart from God; unlike Williams, Rossetti gives the impression that Adam's was the graver sin. His was an error of the will. Adam sinned intentionally because of his love for Eve. Eve, on the other hand, was deceived and misled because of her intellectual curiosity and kindness.

By means of this sympathetic reading, Rossetti challenges Victorian ideas about the inferiority of women that are rooted in the notion that Eve caused Adam to sin. Here Eve is held equally culpable (but certainly not solely culpable) with Adam for the fall. Both sinned and fell short of the glory of God. Furthermore, Eve is portrayed as an inherently charitable and intelligent creature, deconstructing Victorian notions about women's limited intellectual power. Rossetti goes out of her way to show that Eve's sin was a "diversion of the mind," implying that this archetypal woman was a highly rational creature. Finally, whereas Williams uses this as an opportunity to reinforce traditional views, Rossetti is silent about Paul's

---

16. Isaac Williams, *Female Characters of Holy Scripture* (London: Rivington, 1862), 9.

words in 1 Tim 2:11–12 and the connection made there about Eve's sin and the subsequent submission of women.

Another worthy comparison is the treatment of Deborah. Williams feels that this story raises the pressing question about women in positions of authority. He wrestles with what this story teaches, "for," he says, "it seems to reverse the order of God, which is that the woman should be in subordination to the man."[17] He concludes that this is not normative but that God uses such instances to display more clearly his own power and authority as they work through human beings. Here again Rossetti offers a fresh reading of this narrative. She also notes that Deborah's position of authority and prominence is not the norm. However, rather than undermining her power or authority as Williams does, Rossetti validates it with the words of Jesus, "many that are first shall be last; and the last first" (57). In effect, Rossetti is suggesting that this reversal of the norm, a woman holding a position of power, the last becoming first, is fitting because it is evidence of the present and coming kingdom of God.

Finally, in her discussion of the fifth commandment, Rossetti draws equally on male and female characters of Scripture for examples of obedience. Her exposition reads almost like a tribute to the heroes of faith, highlighting some of the least-known women of Scripture and celebrating their faith and obedience. For example, Rossetti celebrates the faithfulness of Peninnah and Leah to their husbands in the face of trying circumstances (57–59). Elisabeth is described not as an exultant mother but as a prophetess of the King (46). The bravery of Jehosheba (55), the spiritual insight of the wife of Manoah (57), and the love and kindness of the little maid toward Naaman (65) each receive recognition.

Providing a biblical basis for the notion that women are the spiritual and intellectual equal of men and thereby challenging prevailing notions of women is important for Rossetti in establishing her own voice as an authoritative interpreter of Scripture.[18] It is this understanding of equality between the sexes that allows her to engage through her writing common interpretations by preachers and methodologies prevalent among biblical scholars.[19] By interacting with these discussions about Scripture, she steps beyond the boundary of a typical Victorian woman who is writing an innocuous devotional work and posits herself as a peer to other male interpreters of Scripture. By critiquing these discussions to challenge religious and intellectual trends of her day, Rossetti assumes the authority of her own interpretation.

---

17. Ibid., 96.

18. I will address this in more depth in a discussion of Rossetti's gender ideology later in this essay.

19. While she never makes explicit whose work she is responding to, she does openly engage scholarly methods of biblical interpretation and common interpretations of specific passages.

While Rossetti does not directly address the seminal work *Essays and Reviews,* which was published twenty-three years earlier and popularized the historical-critical study of the Bible, she does address the attitudes prevalent in biblical scholarship and discernible in the essays. For instance, sharing with the Tractarians a conviction about the value of tradition and the work of patristic exegetes in expositing the Christian Scriptures, Rossetti begins by addressing the hubris she finds in biblical scholarship, which rejects the prior history of interpretation as naïve and simplistic. The contemporary scholarly contention was that precritical exegesis did not grapple with the intellectual convictions of modern humanity and thus did not serve to make the Bible compelling.[20] Writing on the fifth commandment, Rossetti critiques this dismissive attitude toward precritical exegesis:

> Nor is our own day exempt from even an exceptional temptation to this sin of Distaste; for now it is common enough in some ranks for children to be better taught than their parents, and for the young to outrun the old in intellectual exercises; and those who acquire that dangerous thing, a little learning, are more likely to be puffed up by the little they know than ballasted by the much they know not; conceit spurns at reverence and submission, and the undermining of natural piety is too often followed by the repudiation of spiritual loyalty. (68)

Here Rossetti anticipates the spiritual bankruptcy of modern historical criticism, mourning the discontinuity of these intellectual movements and distaste they have for the rich faith of the past.

Second, Rossetti challenges biblical scholars for creating and highlighting problems in the words of the Christian Scriptures while losing sight of the revelation of God. Discussing the second commandment, Rossetti writes,

> It is, I suppose, a genuine though not a glaring breach of the Second Commandment, when instead of learning the lesson plainly set down for us in Holy Writ we protrude with mental feelers in all directions above, beneath, around it, grasping, clinging to every imaginable particular except the main point. ... Take the history of the Fall. The question of mortal sin shrinks into the background while we moot such points as the primitive status of the serpent: did he stand somehow upright? Did he fly? What did he originally eat? How did he articulate? ... At every turn such questions arise. What was the precise architecture of Noah's Ark? Clear up the astronomy of Joshua's miracle. Fix the botany of Jonah's gourd.

---

20. Note Jowett's comment, "No one can form any notion from what we see around us, of the power which Christianity might have, if it were at one with the conscience of man, and not at variance with his intellectual convictions. There, a world weary of the heat and dust of controversy, —of speculations about God and man, —weary, too, of the rapidity of its own motion, would return home, and find rest" (Benjamin Jowett, "On the Interpretation of Scripture," in *Essays and Reviews* [ed. F. H. Hedge; 2nd ed.; London: Parker & Sons, 1861], 414).

In the same vein we reach at last the conjecture which I have heard quoted: In which version was the Ethiopian Eunuch studying Isaiah's prophecy when Philip the Deacon met him? "By these, my son, be admonished: of making many books there is no end" (Eccl 12:12). (*Letter and Spirit*, 85–87)

One immediately notices two things about Rossetti's critique. First, Rossetti does not critique the asking of questions as if they were in themselves inappropriate. What she claims is that the answer to these questions does not get the reader any closer to the lesson of Scripture and often becomes a substitute for it. Rossetti's critique is that these intellectual pursuits hold the potential of leading to the construction of God falsely portrayed because the revelation of the Christian Scriptures goes ignored. Her attitude is best summed up in her comment, "We may make our light so shine as that men shall glorify ourselves. Or our light may be intellectual luminosity but spiritual darkness, how great darkness!" (150).

The second observation is that Rossetti includes herself among those who engage these kinds of questions and who verge on violating the second commandment. Her use of the first-person common plural pronoun *we* makes her a co-conspirator. Once again, it seems clear that Rossetti does not reject biblical scholarship out of hand. Rather, she is aware of critical tools and willing to make use of them for her own exegetical work, distinguishing between Jewish and Christian interpretations (16), employing knowledge of archaeological finds and studies on ancient Near Eastern religions (75–76), and engaging in grammatical analysis (89, 173) to explore the meaning of the biblical text. Rossetti is not anti-intellectual but rather holds to a special hermeneutic for understanding Scripture that assumes that the study of the Bible has only one goal: to disclose the Word of God.

Finally, Rossetti critiques preachers for minimizing the radical nature of the gospel, charging them with violating the first commandment. Such disobedience takes the form of "disinclination," which Rossetti describes as that which "colours and dwarfs our whole conception of duty" (27). "Who," Rossetti writes,

has not seen the incident of the Young Ruler (St. Mark 10:17–27) utilized as a check to extravagant zeal? So far, that is, as a preliminary stress laid on what it does not enjoin can make it act as a sedative. It does not, we are assured, by any means require us to sell all; differences of rank, of position, of circumstances, are Providentially ordained, and are not lightly to be set aside; our duties lie within the decorous bounds of our station. The Young Ruler, indeed, was invited to sell all in spite of his great possessions; therefore we must never suppose it impossible that that vague personage, "our neighbour," may be called upon to do so; we must not judge him in such a case, nay, we must view it not as his penalty but rather as his privilege: only we ourselves, who are bound by simple every-day duties, shall do well in all simplicity to perform them soberly, cheerfully, thankfully, not overstepping the limits of our vocation: wherefore let us give what we can afford; a pleasure or a luxury it may be well to sacrifice at the call of charity. ... Yet is a caution against "righteousness over much" the gist of our Master's lesson? His recorded comment on the incident was "How hardly shall they that have riches enter into the kingdom of God!" which He goes on to explain as they "that *trust* in riches." Is our most urgent temptation that which includes us to do too much, or that which lulls us to do too little, or to do nothing? Is it so, that the bulk of professing Christians are likely to be dazzled by the splendid error of excessive "corban," and fairly to consume themselves by zeal? Or are they not more likely so sedulously to count the cost as never to undertake building? (28–30)

Again we notice that Rossetti is not rejecting this popular interpretation because it is wrong. She critiques such an interpretation because it fails to instill and enrich the piety of the people and, thus, to disclose the Word of God.

In her candid and thoughtful critiques, Rossetti functions like a prophet, calling the people back to faith and piety. It is no accident that Rossetti chose to comment on the words of the great prophet Moses and the still greater prophet Jesus. Her voice derives its authority in alignment with theirs. The sense we get from her writing is that she has also taken up the prophetic mantle, calling the people back to God, to faith, and to obedience in opposition to contemporary false prophets around her.

This prophetic mantle is perhaps most clearly encountered in Rossetti's stinging political and cultural critique. Aligning her words with those of the Old Testament prophets Jeremiah, Amos, and Isaiah, Rossetti warns her fellow Englishmen and women of the dangers of wealth, ease, and luxury unchastened by almsgiving and self-denial. Of the words of these biblical prophets she writes, "to us of the nineteenth century, and not least to us of England, [they] speak with an awful omen." She then adds her own prophetic call to repentance. "Surely for us, as for Nebuchadnezzar of old, it is high time to 'break off our sins by righteousness, and our iniquities by showing mercy to the poor; if it may be a lengthening of our tranquility'" (107).[21]

Likewise, in her discussion on the eighth commandment, Rossetti offers a form of intercession on England's behalf for its attitudes toward wealth. "God in His mercy," she writes,

grant that we of England may penitently consider and amend our ways: for though our private and our national sins may not correspond point for point with these awful passages, yet is our spirit too much as the Jews' spirit, and our

---

21. Rossetti is here quoting from Dan 4:27. Daniel has just interpreted King Nebuchadnezzar's dream and informed him that he will be driven away from the people and forced to live with wild animals for seven years until he acknowledges that the Most High is sovereign. Daniel then counsels the king to renounce his sins and show mercy to the poor with the hope that God will have mercy on him and soften his judgment such that King Nebuchadnezzar's prosperity will continue. Through Daniel's words, Rossetti counsels the people of England to the same with the hope that God will show mercy and allow England to continue in peace and prosperity.

guilt as their guilt; and who shall say that our national honour, wealth, credit, already impaired, do not show the beginning of our chastisement, and (unless we repent) the beginning of the end? (125)

Rossetti unabashedly adopts an authoritative voice as a prophet, calling the people of England to repent of their ways. She leaves her assigned place in the domestic sphere to engage, critique, and intercede on behalf of the people of England.[22]

This posture as a prophet, standing in opposition to the dominant cultural and intellectual trends and alone disclosing the Word of God through exegetical work, is an audacious one for an untrained orthodox laywoman of nineteenth-century England. Given the strong influence of the patriarchal Tractarians on her religious convictions, this bold posture is quite surprising. Furthermore, it is evident from her biography and her other works that Rossetti herself holds to a very orthodox position regarding the role of women. How do we make sense of this apparent tension within Rossetti and her work? How do we make sense of the fact that she positions herself as an authoritative interpreter of Scripture?

I submit that the key to understanding the mystery of Rossetti's gender ideology is the concept of obedience. In her article "The Kingly Self," Betty Flowers notes Rossetti's emphasis on obedience throughout her poetry. This same emphasis on obedience to Christ is evident in *Letter and Spirit*. Rossetti writes *Letter and Spirit* first and foremost to encourage a life of obedience and submission to the law of God. For Rossetti, however, obedience is not about submitting to cultural or ecclesiastical mores that silence women but to Christ as muse "who calls forth the woman artist's kingly self and bids her sing."[23] The implication is that, although she is a woman, she is a writer who has been inspired by her own reading of Scripture and her understanding of the Word of God to speak against the cultural and religious trends that challenge the divine will of God. As a woman dedicated to her faith, she can do no other. The question remains, however, of how she reconciles her prophetic posture with her orthodox views of women's roles that are also inspired by the Word of God.

---

22. Betty Flowers ("The Kingly Self: Rossetti as Woman Artist," in *The Achievement of Christina Rossetti* [ed. D. A. Kent; Ithaca, N.Y.: Cornell University Press, 1987], 173) has noted that in her poetry Rossetti presents her role as that of a poetic messenger. Frederick S. Roden ("Two 'Sisters in Wisdom': Hildegard of Bingen, Christina Rossetti, and Feminist Theology," in *Hildegard of Bingen: A Book of Essays* [ed M. B. McInerney; New York: Garland, 1998], 227–52) argues that, comparable to the situation of medieval women mystics, the theological emphases of the Oxford Movement created an atmosphere whereby women were legitimately permitted a voice within religion under the auspices of prophecy. He suggests that Rossetti's appeal to a prophetic voice within her religion gave her authority and power that would otherwise have been denied her.

23. Flowers, "The Kingly Self," 174.

The answer is to be found in the unique biblically based gender ideology that Rossetti expresses in *Letter and Spirit*. Using the Tractarian principle of analogy, Rossetti compares the relationship of the two commandments of Jesus to that of a marriage relationship and surreptitiously offers her own comments about the relationship between men and women. The two commandments, she writes, "while of equal obligation, are nevertheless of unequal dignity; the First is the head, source, root; the Second, made after its likeness, derives from it authority and honour" (14). Here Rossetti stands closely with orthodox and traditional interpretations of Scripture. However, this is where the similarity ends; Rossetti goes on to establish the importance and equality of women with men. She writes, "to fulfil that Second [commandment] is man's only mode of making sure that he observes the First, nor can these two which God has joined together be put practically asunder" (14–15). Later, in her comments about the fifth commandment, she highlights the value of women again. By allusion to 1 Pet 3:7, she draws an analogy between woman and the second table of the law as the "weaker vessel." Here she notes, "our Lord God, merciful and gracious, has been pleased to give honour unto the weaker vessel, appending the 'first promise,' not to the First Commandment but to the Fifth" (37–38). Being the weaker vessel does not preclude God's ascribing honor. By implication, God values woman as the weaker vessel and honors her—a lesson for a culture that devalued women.

Rossetti further develops her case for equality between men and women in her comments on the tenth commandment. Here she notes:

> although "wife" follows "house" in the tenth commandment, we must first of all view her as included equally and indivisibly with her husband in that neighbour whom we must not desire to supplant. The precept is constructed explicitly for men, implicitly for women; were it not so, to covet a neighbour's *husband* would be defensible! (190)

Rossetti thus makes a subtle distinction whereby she acknowledges that the woman is the weaker vessel but upholds her inherent value. While Rossetti accepts woman's derivative and secondary status, she insists that they are also partners. Together they form a unity that God has joined together. They equally share in the partnership. Rossetti writes, "obviously she ranks with the man himself, being constituted equally with him an informing presence of a forbidden house." By emphasizing the value of women and the equality they share with men, Rossetti begins to create space for women to take their rightful place with men as interpreters of Scripture who have valuable contributions to make to the task of exegesis. Coupled with her comments about Eve as an intelligent and rational creature, Rossetti contends that women have the mental ability to offer thoughtful insights into Scripture.

For the church, however, the question is not only whether women have the ability but whether women ought to be interpreters of Scripture. Ecclesiastical tradition said no.[24] However, Rossetti challenges a reading of Scripture that denies a voice to women and offers a biblically based apologetic for her own interpretive work. Rossetti moves from a discussion about the relationship between men and women to a comparison of single and married women. The expectation for Victorian women was marriage. Because women were prohibited from owning property, they were dependent on the closest male relative for their provision—typically their father or husband.[25] Therefore, marriage was an extremely important institution for the stability of the Victorian culture and the safeguarding of the traditional roles of men and women. Frederick Roden comments on women who joined Anglican religious orders, "to reject the 'law of the father' or husband in this world in favour of the authority of a Father in heaven and [to] live in a community of non-biologically-procreative women was seen as subversive to reproductive patriarchy."[26] This same attitude characterized society's perception of all women who chose to remain single.

---

24. A theology of female subordination supported by biblical texts such as Gen 1–3; 1 Cor 14:34–35; and 1 Tim 2:11–14 and assumed by the Church of England shaped the gender ideology of Victorian England. Women were considered inferior and secondary to men, the weaker sex who existed to serve as a helpmate to men. Institutions such as marriage supported this theology, providing women with a respectable position in society under the headship of their husbands and limiting their sphere of influence and activity to the home and family. By the nineteenth century, the ideal of female virtue included such notions as submission, Christian piety, and moral sensibility. There was a growing recognition that women were well-suited for religious devotion, and they were often given sole responsibility to nurture Christian faith and obedience in the home. Teaching their children the contents of Scripture sparked a flurry of writing activity as women began to publish devotional commentaries designed primarily to train women and children in reading the Bible. This was deemed acceptable and an appropriate means of exercising responsibility in this area. However, women were not privy to the scholarly discussions about Scripture and were barred access to education that would enable them to move beyond devotional reflection. Sean Gill provides a helpful discussion in *Women and the Church of England*, 90–130. He states that for some, such as Benjamin Jowett, the issue was one of ability and practicality: "for the mass of women I doubt whether any change in the subjects of Education would do any good—a second rate mind intellectualized and crammed with information is very useless and disagreeable." (82) For others, such as Christopher Wordsworth, bishop of Lincoln, there was fear that access to education would "threaten the belief that the home was the woman's primary sphere of duty" (114) and subvert the "divinely ordained" social order (118). Still others, such as Rev. J. W. Burgon, feared that exposure to higher education would undermine the faith of women (116–17). Thus, while there was no church ruling against women interpreting Scripture, the theology of female subordination and cultural ideas about female virtue served to keep women from engaging in what was considered a male activity. For a helpful overview of the life of women in Victorian England, see Gill, *Women and the Church of England*.

25. Some women did accept positions as governesses. This was one of the few occupations available for single women.

26. Fredrick S. Roden, "The Kiss of the Soul: The Mystical Theology of Christina Rossetti's Devotional Prose," in *Women's Theology in Nineteenth-Century Britain* (ed. J. Melnyk; New York: Garland, 1998), 42.

Rossetti, however, challenges these notions of single and married women. Comparing the first and second commandments of the Decalogue to a single and married woman, Rossetti adds biblical weight to her own conviction that to remain single is to "do better." Rossetti admits that once married, a wife must serve her husband. However, she challenges the idea that marriage for women is the only viable option. Women have a choice whether or not to enter this relationship. "A wife's paramount duty is indeed to her husband, superseding all other human obligations: yet to assume this duty, free-will has first stepped in with its liability to err; in this connexion woman has to reap as she has sown, be the crop what it may" (43). Women who choose to marry are required to serve their husbands. Women who choose not to marry are free to serve the Lord. Women who marry have access to God only through their husbands. For the woman who remains single, "her Maker is her Husband, endowing her with a name better than of sons and of daughters" (91). Some women are called to marry and serve God by fulfilling their duties to husband and family. However, some women, Rossetti argues, are called to a life of contemplation, worship, and service to God. After all, Jesus praised Mary for sitting at his feet over Martha who was busy in the kitchen (28).

In this we discover Rossetti's concession, that which makes her writing authoritatively on Scripture an act of obedience. She is not called to serve a human husband; she is called to serve a heavenly one. Rossetti chooses to be the bride of Christ, to "love God with all her heart and soul and mind and strength … contemplate him and forget herself in Him" (91–92). For Rossetti, this means increasingly she will become one with God, that her voice, her mind, and her heart will be found in God's. By implication, the voice, the mind, and the heart of God are manifest in hers.

Furthermore, Rossetti writes of all Christians that "God claims our whole selves, all we are, all we have, all we may become" (15). This includes her gift as a writer. Rossetti took her writing very seriously, particularly her religious writing to which she was resolutely committed. In response to a comment Dante Gabriel once made about her religious works, Rossetti responded, "I don't think harm will accrue from my S.P.C.K. [Society for Promoting Christian Knowledge] books, even to my standing: if it did, I should still be glad to throw my grain of dust into the religious scale."[27] Writing devotional commentaries and inspirational pieces was Rossetti's way of offering her whole self to God.

Roden argues that stylizing herself as a bride of Christ was an effective means of attaining a voice within Rossetti's culture.[28] I would argue that as the bride of Christ Rossetti could do no other. As a gifted writer who spent a lifetime contem-

---

27. William Michael Rossetti, ed., *The Family Letters of Christina Georgina Rossetti: With Some Supplementary Letters and Appendices* (New York: Scribner's Sons, 1908), 92.

28. Roden, "The Kiss of the Soul," 53.

plating the revelation of God in Scripture, she could do no other than offer her gift and her insights in service for the kingdom of God. It was a natural development for Rossetti to bring together her love for and knowledge of God and his Word with her creative-writing abilities. For Rossetti, it is the very sense of dutifulness and obedience to Christ that compels her to seize an authoritative and even prophetic voice. Ignoring cultural conventions and ecclesiastical sanctions, Rossetti embraces her calling as a woman to be the bride of Christ who offers her gifts as a writer and her insight into the revelation of God in obedience and submission to her husband and master. Paradoxically, Rossetti reinforces the traditional role of married women while creating space for single women to be rightful interpreters of Scripture.

BIBLIOGRAPHY

Bell, Mackenzie. *Christina Rossetti: A Biographical and Critical Study.* London: Burleigh, 1898.

Cook, Frederic C. "Introduction to the Book of Exodus." Pages 237–49 in part 1 of vol. 1 of *The Holy Bible according to the Authorized Version with an Explanatory and Critical Commentary and a Revision of the Translation by Bishops and Other Clergy of the Anglican Church.* Edited by Frederic C. Cook. 4 vols. London: Murray, 1871.

D'Amico, Diane, and David. A. Kent. Introduction to Christina Rossetti, "Notes on Genesis and Exodus." *Journal of Pre-Raphaelite Studies* 13 (2004): 49–98.

Demers, Patricia. *Women as Interpreters of the Bible.* New York: Paulist, 1992.

Erb, Peter. "Edward Bouverie Pusey, 'Historical Criticism' and the Traditional Interpretation of Biblical Texts." Paper presented at the Waterloo Biblical Colloquium, 30 January 2003.

Flowers, Betty S. "The Kingly Self: Rossetti as Woman Artist." Pages 159–74 in *The Achievement of Christina Rossetti.* Edited by David A. Kent. Ithaca, N.Y.: Cornell University Press, 1987.

Gill, Sean. *Women and the Church of England: From the Eighteenth Century to the Present.* London: SPCK, 1994.

Jowett, Benjamin. "On the Interpretation of Scripture." Pages 362–480 in *Essays and Reviews.* Edited by Frederic Henry Hedge. 2nd ed. London: Parker & Sons, 1861.

Kachur, Robert M. "Repositioning the Female Christian Reader: Christina Rossetti as Tractarian Hermeneut in *The Face of the Deep.*" *Victorian Poetry* 35 (1997): 193–214.

Keble, John. *Sermons for the Christian Year.* Oxford: Parker, 1876.

Marsh, Jan. *Christina Rossetti: A Writer's Life.* New York: Viking Penguin, 1995.

McNeile, Alan H. *The Book of Exodus.* WC 2. London: Methuen, 1908.

Palazzo, Lynda. "The Poet and the Bible: Christina Rossetti's Feminist Hermeneutics." *The Victorian Newsletter* 92 (1997): 6–9.

Roden, Frederick S. "The Kiss of the Soul: The Mystical Theology of Christina Rossetti's Devotional Prose." Pages 37–57 in *Women's Theology in Nineteenth-Century Britain.* Edited by Julie Melnyk. New York: Garland, 1998.

———. "Sisterhood Is Powerful: Christina Rossetti's *Maude.*" Pages 63–77 in *Women of Faith in Victorian Culture: Reassessing the Angel in the House.* Edited by Anne Hogan and Andrew Bradstock. New York: St. Martin's, 1998.

————. "Two 'Sisters in Wisdom': Hildegard of Bingen, Christina Rossetti, and Feminist Theology." Pages 227–52 in *Hildegard of Bingen: A Book of Essays*. Edited by Maud Burnett McInerney. New York: Garland, 1998.

Rossetti, William Michael, ed. *The Family Letters of Christina Georgina Rossetti: With Some Supplementary Letters and Appendices*. New York: Scribner's Sons, 1908.

Rossetti, Christina. *Letter and Spirit: Notes on the Commandments*. London: SPCK, 1883.

Taylor, Barbara. *Eve and the New Jerusalem*. New York: Pantheon, 1983.

Westerholm, Joel. "'I Magnify Mine Office': Christina Rossetti's Authoritative Voice in Her Devotional Prose." *The Victorian Newsletter* 84 (1993): 11–17.

Williams, Isaac. *Female Characters of Holy Scripture*. London: Rivington, 1862.

Elizabeth Wordsworth: Nineteenth-Century Oxford Principal and Bible Interpreter*

Rebecca G. S. Idestrom

Introduction

Elizabeth Wordsworth (1840–1932) was unwittingly[1] one of the most influential pioneers of education for women at Oxford University. As founding principal of Lady Margaret Hall, a residential hall for women in Oxford, where she served thirty-one years (1878–1909), she influenced many female students over the years. In 1886, she also founded another hall for women in Oxford, St. Hugh's Hall, with money she had inherited after her father's death.[2] Although not formally trained as a theologian and Bible scholar, she had a keen interest in Bible study and theology and lectured regularly to women students on various biblical and theological topics. Daughter of Christopher Wordsworth, priest and later bishop of Lincoln, much of Elizabeth Wordsworth's biblical training came through helping her father with his multivolume commentary on the Bible. As a writer of novels, poems, plays, essays, and devotional works, she also published theological reflections on the Apostles' Creed, the Lord's Prayer, the Decalogue, and the Psalms. This chapter will explore how she approaches biblical interpretation, particularly in *The Decalogue* and *Psalms for the Christian Festivals*, works that are based on her weekly lectures to the women students under her care at Oxford.[3] This work was one of the many ways Wordsworth sought to pass on her

---

*An earlier version of this paper was read at the Canadian Society of Biblical Studies, 29 May 2006, York University, Toronto, Ontario.

1. Perhaps even a little reluctantly, as the title of her biography indicates: Georgina Battiscombe, *Reluctant Pioneer: A Life of Elizabeth Wordsworth* (London: Constable, 1978).

2. St. Hugh's Hall was for women students who could not afford the fees of Lady Margaret Hall. Elizabeth Wordsworth founded the hall in memory of her father.

3. Elizabeth Wordsworth, *The Decalogue* (London: Longmans, Green, 1893); idem, *Psalms for the Christian Festivals* (London: Longmans, Green, 1906).

own passion about teaching the Bible to the next generation of women so that they might be educated as interpreters of Scripture.

Her Life

Elizabeth Wordsworth, great-niece of the famous poet William Wordsworth,[4] was born on 22 June 1840 in Harrow, Middlesex, England, to Anglican clergyman Christopher Wordsworth and Susannah Hatley Frere. She was the oldest of seven children, having two brothers and four sisters. Her father was then headmaster of Harrow but later became canon of Westminster in 1845 and eventually bishop of Lincoln in 1869. Elizabeth Wordsworth was a very bright child who had a keen interest in and insatiable desire for learning. Although she did not receive a formal education, except for one year at a girls' boarding school in Brighton when she was seventeen (an education that she thought was very superficial and more or less fruitless),[5] she still received a fine classical education at home. She was well versed in classical Greek and Latin literature, modern languages, history, Bible and theology, music, and art. The only thing she lacked was training in mathematics and science. She was also a ferocious reader and argued that books, rather than teachers, were the best sources of education.[6]

Wordsworth learned Latin, French, Italian, German, Greek, and Hebrew, teaching herself Greek with the help of the Greek New Testament. On Sunday evenings their father would test all the children on their knowledge of the Greek New Testament after their evening meal.[7] He would also introduce them to English church history. Wordsworth recalls having to recite the names of all the bishops and their sees as part of these sessions. With the aid of her brother John's Greek grammar and dictionary and a Latin translation, she was able to read the *Iliad* and the *Odyssey* in Greek.[8] She frequently borrowed her brother's Greek, Hebrew, and Latin grammars.[9] Later she would reflect on how often girls learn

---

4. The sources for this section on her life are the following: Battiscombe, *Reluctant Pioneer*; Elizabeth Wordsworth, *Glimpses of the Past* (London: Mowbray, 1912); Nancy A. Barta-Smith, "Elizabeth Wordsworth," in *Modern British Essayists: First Series* (ed. R. Beum; Dictionary of Literary Biography 98; Detroit: Gale, 1990), 313–27; Evelyn M. Jamison, "Wordsworth, Dame Elizabeth, 1840–1932," in *The Dictionary of National Biography: 1931–1940* (ed. L. G. W. Legg; London: Oxford University Press, 1949), 921–22; Gale Reference Team, "Elizabeth Wordsworth, 1840–1932," in *Contemporary Authors Online* (Detroit: Gale, 2000).

5. Wordsworth, *Glimpses of the Past*, 38. She did appreciate the insights into "girls and their ways," which would help her later when she was principal of the hall for women.

6. Barta-Smith, "Elizabeth Wordsworth."

7. Wordsworth, *Glimpses of the Past*, 43.

8. Ibid., 43–44.

9. Battiscombe, *Reluctant Pioneer*, 23.

from their brothers' books and grammars, "picking up crumbs beneath the tables of their masculine belongings, and blushing beautifully whenever detected."[10]

Toward the end of her life, Wordsworth published a book of reflections and memories from her life entitled *Glimpses from the Past*. As she recalled her upbringing, Wordsworth wrote, "Our real 'educators' had been our parents and other relatives, especially my father, whose whole level of mind was extraordinarily high."[11] She was very close to her father, who had a tremendous influence upon her and taught her many things. Christopher Wordsworth, a devout High Anglican, was a prolific writer, having published over eighty books and several volumes of a commentary on the whole Bible. Elizabeth, along with her siblings and mother, helped her father with the commentary. She writes:

> Our home occupation, at this time, was chiefly copying out for the press the various portions of our father's Commentary, first on the New, and then on the Old Testament, and then in looking over the proof-sheets and verifying every Scripture reference. This was hard work, but we felt proud of helping him, and it taught us to know our Bibles.[12]

Although it was a family project, her role was indispensable, especially later when her father became bishop. She became his chief assistant on the commentary, a project that lasted twenty years. She also became his unofficial personal secretary when he became bishop of Lincoln.

Shortly after he became bishop, in a letter dated 3 April 1869, Wordsworth's father acknowledged the debt he owed her: "You know how much I need your help in these things now that I have no time for them myself; and I am never unthankful, my dear daughter, to Almighty God for the great blessing He has given me of your help in these important matters."[13] In the same letter, he also asked her to examine the emendations and notes that he and his wife had made on the commentary and to give her own comments and suggestions. He writes, "Let me have the benefit of them and of any remarks that may occur to you for our adoption in the proposed reprint of the Pentateuch."[14] At the conclusion of the letter, he acknowledges that the work on the commentary came as a result of a united effort, "our united labours" including Elizabeth, his wife Susannah, and Elizabeth's aunts and her sisters.[15] Although it was a group effort, one wonders

---

10. Elizabeth Wordsworth, "Colleges for Women," in *Ladies at Work: Papers on Paid Employment for Ladies* (ed. L. Jeune; London: Innes, 1893), 17.

11. Wordsworth, *Glimpses of the Past,* 40.

12. Ibid., 42–43.

13. Battiscombe, *Reluctant Pioneer,* 26; E. M. Jamison, "Appendix," in Battiscombe, *Reluctant Pioneer,* 263–64.

14. Jamison, "Appendix," 263.

15. Ibid., 264.

how much Elizabeth Wordsworth actually contributed to the writing of the commentary during these years and how much her father wrote when he was so busy. We know that she certainly gave input at her father's request. She did more than simply edit the work and was able to make suggestions on the revisions. Through this, she gained a great knowledge of the Bible. Later in her career Wordsworth would regularly lecture and teach from the Bible. Her work of editing her father's commentary and notes had given her a solid foundation for understanding Scripture. Although Christopher Wordsworth published several individual commentaries on various biblical books over a twenty-year span, the complete eight-volume commentary on the whole Bible came out in 1871.[16] This multivolume work was very popular, and several editions were published.[17] Elizabeth Wordsworth's critical role in helping with this work should not be forgotten.

In her biography of her father (co-authored with John Henry Overton, three years after her father's death), Wordsworth wrote about her father's work on the Bible and on the Old Testament in particular. This clearly demonstrates how influential her father was on her views of the Bible.[18] Her father loved the Old Testament, for example, and emphasized the unity between the Testaments—"the oneness of the Bible"—that Elizabeth Wordsworth would also emphasize later.[19]

---

16. Christopher Wordsworth began by publishing a two-volume work on the book of Revelation in 1849. Then the first commentary on the whole New Testament was published in 1856; the New Testament in Greek and the final volume of the Old Testament commentary came out in 1871. Although he published various parts separately (for example, the Epistles of Paul in 1859 and the book of Daniel in 1871), the complete eight-volume commentary on the whole Bible came out in 1871. See James Barszcz, "Christopher Wordsworth," in *British Travel Writers, 1837–1875: Victorian Period* (ed. B. Brothers and J. Gergits; Dictionary of Literary Biography 166; Detroit: Gale, 1996), 344–52.

17. Bishop Wordsworth's commentary was very popular, coming out in at least seven editions. He was continually revising certain sections and reprinting new editions. A cheaper issue of the commentary on the whole Bible came out in 1872 because of the request of many for a more affordable work. This was an eight-volume commentary: six volumes on the Old Testament and two on the New Testament. Altogether the eight volumes consisted of over four thousand pages. See Christopher Wordsworth, *The Holy Bible in the Authorized Version: With Notes and Introductions* (8 vols.; London: Rivington, 1872).

18. John Henry Overton and Elizabeth Wordsworth, *Christopher Wordsworth: Bishop of Lincoln* (London: Rivington, 1888).

19. Ibid., 414. In the preface of Christopher Wordsworth's new edition of his commentary on the Pentateuch, he emphasizes that one should not separate the Old from the New Testament. In fact, if one disparages the Old Testament, as modern-day Marcionites and Manichaeans do, treating it as "a common book" and not divine revelation, one is undermining "the foundations of the New. By separating the Law from the Gospel, and Moses from Christ, they invalidated the testimony of both" (Christopher Wordsworth, *The Five Books of Moses* [vol. 1 of *The Holy Bible in the Authorized Version*; new ed. London: Rivington, 1872], viii). In her writing on the Decalogue, Wordsworth demonstrates a positive view of the Old Testament. She does not see the God of the Old Testament as different from the God of the New Testament, and she argues

Christopher Wordsworth especially liked the book of Ezekiel. In her description of her father's love for Ezekiel, Wordsworth reveals her own views of this prophetic book as well as her admiration for her father's work.

> The grandeur of the last-named obscure and wonderful book breaks upon one like a revelation in his pages, and no mere scholar, no one who had not something of the fervour of a poet, and the devout intuition of a saint, could, we think, have entered fully into that wondrous life and prophecy, with its strangely typical symbolism, recalling Dante, alike in its vivid, homely reality, and its weird and majestic sublimity. In reading Ezekiel under Dr. Wordsworth's guidance we forget the nineteenth century and the human commentator, and are swept upward to the threshold of the ideal Temple, and onward in the flight of the mystic Cherubim.[20]

Elizabeth Wordsworth would also lecture on Ezekiel, although she never published these lectures.[21] Her father's love for this prophetic book and the Old Testament in general was certainly an inspiration to her. Wordsworth notes that her father was the happiest when he was commenting on the Old Testament.[22]

When Wordsworth's brother John moved to Oxford, she often went to visit him and his wife Esther, and, as a result, she made many friends at Oxford.[23] These connections became important because they eventually led to her being recommended for the appointment of principal of a new residential hall for women. Thus, in November 1878 Elizabeth Wordsworth accepted the invitation to become the principal of Lady Margaret Hall. Up until then, Oxford University did not accept women students, and there was no hall of residence for women.[24] Because Cambridge University had established two residential halls for women, Girton College and Newnham College, a number of people at Oxford felt that they should have the same. Even though female students could not attain a degree from the university, it was argued that "girls should be able to live and study at Oxford, enjoying the intellectual atmosphere of the place and taking advantage of such educational facilities as lectures and libraries"[25] (to learn by osmosis or by

---

for seeing unity in the Bible between the Testaments. Here the influence of her father is clearly seen (Wordsworth, *The Decalogue*, 73–74).

20. Overton and Wordsworth, *Christopher Wordsworth*, 416.

21. Battiscombe, *Reluctant Pioneer*, 161.

22. Overton and Wordsworth, *Christopher Wordsworth*, 415.

23. Elizabeth Wordsworth was particularly close to her brother John. Intellectually, they had much in common. John, who later became bishop of Salisbury, was a Latin scholar and published a critical edition of the Vulgate New Testament.

24. Only the Oxford local examinations were available to women, since 1867 (Battiscombe, *Reluctant Pioneer*, 63).

25. Ibid., 64.

breathing the atmosphere, as Wordsworth would advocate).[26] Thus, two halls for women were established: Lady Margaret Hall, supported by the Church of England; and Somerville Hall for non-Anglicans.[27] Wordsworth became principal of Lady Margaret Hall,[28] and the first nine students arrived in 1879. She remained the principal for thirty-one years. When Wordsworth retired in 1909, the hall had grown from nine students in 1879 to fifty-nine in 1909.

In the 1890s, there was much debate over the possible admission of women to the bachelor of arts (B.A.) degree. With regard to this question, Wordsworth was somewhat ambivalent. She frustrated both sides of the camp, who wanted her to take a stand. She certainly was not a feminist in the modern sense of the term, yet she did much for the education of women at Oxford. For Wordsworth, the key was that women would be given the opportunity to study and do the requirements of the degree, but whether they got a degree was not important. The degree was only a token, not the actual achievement itself.[29] She saw education not as a means to an end but as the end to be enjoyed itself; gaining the knowledge was the key.[30] When she was forced to take a stand, however, she voted in favor of

---

26. Wordsworth's philosophy of women being educated by osmosis or by simply picking it up from the environment or circles in which they were found is illustrated in her comments written in 1893: "In the old days a 'real lady' was educated by the very atmosphere she habitually breathed. She was taught by the walls of her room, the books that lay about, the people she met, etc." (Wordsworth, "Colleges for Women," 20). She also "set great store by the educational value of contact with notable people" (Battiscombe, *Reluctant Pioneer*, 79). As principal she continually wanted her female students to meet scholars and interesting people.

27. Oxford was divided between High Church Anglicans represented by Christ Church College who wanted a Church of England hall and a more liberal-minded group from Balliol College. This latter group, represented by Benjamin Jowett, head of Balliol College, "who stood for new thought and criticism," wanted a hall for dissenters from the Anglican Church. Somerville hall became known as the "undenominational" hall and was named after Mary Somerville, a woman scientist (Battiscombe, *Reluctant Pioneer*, 65, 66, 75).

28. Wordsworth was encouraged by her father to take the position. She was able to propose the name of the hall, after Lady Margaret Beaufort, mother of Henry VII, who was a patron of the arts and learning. Wordsworth described her as a gentlewoman, a scholar, and a saint, undoubtedly three qualities that she wanted her female students to emulate (Wordsworth, *Glimpses from the Past*, 144–45).

29. Battiscombe, *Reluctant Pioneer*, 138.

30. Some of her views on women being educated are seen in an essay she wrote in 1893. In promoting the importance of colleges for women, she argued that an education was not only important for unmarried women who needed to support themselves financially but also that it was "excellent training for future wives and mothers. Why should stupidity or ignorance be taken as a qualification for married life, as some people seem to think?" (Wordsworth, "Colleges for Women," 17). Even though she herself never married, she was a strong proponent of marriage. She advocated that there were three types of women who would benefit from being educated in a women's college: (1) women born scholars—women who try to learn Latin or Greek from their brothers' textbooks (which was her own experience); (2) those women who

granting degrees to women (even though the council of Lady Margaret Hall was against it). However, the motion was defeated by the Congregation, the voting members of Oxford University, in 1896. Women would have to wait another twenty-four years to get a degree from Oxford.

When degrees were finally granted to women students at Oxford in 1920, Elizabeth Wordsworth was the first of three female recipients of the honorary master of arts degree (along with Her Majesty the Queen and Mrs. T. H. Green). With the fiftieth anniversary of the founding of the Lady Margaret Hall in 1928, the University of Oxford also bestowed upon Wordsworth an honorary doctorate, the degree of doctor of civil law.[31] Her biographer Georgina Battiscombe writes:

> Though it was ironical that she, who had cared so little for degrees, should find herself thus honoured, no one had done more to deserve this recognition. She had given her life to the business of educating women.... Her wit and wisdom and, above all, the appeal of her personality, had done much to reconcile Oxford opinion to the admittance of women to university membership. No one could object to the presence of academic women if the academic woman resembled Elizabeth Wordsworth. Of all Oxford women she was the best known and the best loved, and she had earned the right to a triumph.[32]

During her thirty-one years as principal, Wordsworth gave many lectures to the women at the Hall, and every Sunday evening she lectured on the Bible and led Bible studies.[33] Many of these lectures and addresses formed the basis of her publications. In her Bible addresses, it is obvious that she had gained great Bible knowledge through helping her father with the Bible commentary. Her biographer elaborates:

> The long years which she spent helping her father with his Commentary had given Elizabeth Wordsworth an exceptional knowledge of the Bible, and this is apparent on every page of these addresses. She quotes the original Greek and Hebrew, she gives alternative readings from the Septuagint, she discusses in great detail the possible meanings of obscure words of doubtful passages, and she is learned on such matters as dating and authorship. Her approach is by no means obscurantist; she can allow that parts of the Old Testament may be myth rather than history, though personally she herself is always inclined towards belief in a basis of historical fact.[34]

---

need to secure employment; and (3) women who are around thirty years of age or older who have not had the opportunities for training. These are women who are forced to find ways to support themselves when they can no longer live at home due to their homes breaking up (ibid., 17–19).

31. Battiscombe, *Reluctant Pioneer*, 212.

32. Ibid., 199.

33. Ibid., 135.

34. Ibid., 160.

Although not as prolific as her father, Wordsworth still published twenty-seven books plus individual chapters and essays.[35] We will now turn to her interpretation of Scripture as demonstrated in her books *The Decalogue* and *Psalms for the Christian Festivals*.

THE DECALOGUE

Elizabeth Wordsworth's writing on the Decalogue, published in 1893, was based on her weekly addresses given to the women students of Lady Margaret Hall on Sunday evenings.[36] In her introduction she adopts the typical view held in the nineteenth century that the Bible reflects stages in the development of human life and society from a more primitive stage to more evolved and complex stages. She writes, "The Decalogue is as much more elaborate than the primitive command to Adam, as human life has become during the ages that have intervened" (xiii). She compares the first command "be fruitful and multiply" in Gen 1:28 with the Decalogue, which represents a higher stage of development. She argues that this is something that natural science has demonstrated in the concept of the evolution of humankind (x). Wordsworth is not discussing Darwin's concept of evolution but rather the nineteenth-century notion of progressive revelation and the progressive education of humankind.[37] Not only do humans develop physically but with time also morally and socially. She contends that "There comes a time, however, in the history of humanity, as secular no less than sacred learning teaches us, when man discovers that he has a moral as well as a physical side" (x). In the fall, humans became conscious of being individuals who can make independent choices. By the time of the giving of the Ten Commandments, they moved to a higher stage of development in becoming aware of being social beings (x–xiii). Wordsworth finds support for this gradual approach to human development in history and philosophy: "In the account of the giving of the Decalogue we find (just what history and philosophy tell us) that man has become a social being—a member of state" (xiii). With the coming of Christ, there is an even higher stage in human history when Jesus demonstrates "the lofty doctrine of self-sacrifice" (xv). She believes that modern science, philosophy, and history supports this view of the Bible. Later she also argues that this notion of progress is what precisely distinguishes the Bible from other literature. The Bible "always *has a future before it*, and sets a future before its readers" (109, emphasis original). "The Law

---

35. She published two novels under the pseudonym Grant Lloyd (Barta-Smith, "Elizabeth Wordsworth," 313–27).

36. Wordsworth, *The Decalogue*, xxiii. Subsequent references to *The Decalogue* will be provided within the main text.

37. John Rogerson, *Old Testament Criticism in the Nineteenth Century: England and Germany* (London: SPCK, 1984), 246–47.

and the Prophets are throughout *prospective*. They breathe not regret for a van-
ished past—but progress. Their 'golden age' is still to come, 'Development' is the
watchword of the Old Testament" (110, emphasis original).

Adopting this understanding of progressive development within Scripture is not unusual; what is unique is Wordsworth's application of this to the
Ten Commandments themselves. With regard to the last six commandments,
she argues that the ninth and tenth commandments represent a higher stage of
human civilization and development. She asserts that the ninth commandment,
"Thou shalt not bear false witness against thy neighbour," takes humanity to "a
stage higher up in civilization than the four which have preceded it.... The ninth
goes higher still, and looks upon man as belonging to some kind of political
organization. False witness presupposes a tribunal before which false witness
can be borne" (210). The tenth commandment, "Thou shalt not covet," moves to
an even higher level than the ninth because it focuses on the internal motivation
and desire rather than the external, outward action. "The tenth, the chief commandment in the second table ... looks exclusively at the *heart and will* of those
to whom it is addressed. We are not only not to take what belongs to our neighbour, but we are not even to desire it" (224). The fact that God sees the heart
and will will be more fully developed by Jesus in the Sermon on the Mount, but
this understanding, she argues, is already present in the tenth commandment
(224–25). Thus, Wordsworth sees different levels of development within the Ten
Commandments themselves. What is not clear is whether she applied the same
understanding to all the previous commandments. For example, did she consider the fourth commandment, to keep the Sabbath, higher than the previous
three? If she was consistent, this would logically be the case, but we will never
know for sure. She is only explicit on this point when it comes to the ninth and
tenth commandments.

Wordsworth argues that the Ten Commandments are not obsolete but that
we can still draw great principles from them.[38] They have a unique place within
the Bible as a whole, being a higher spiritual law meant for all time (50, 53, 54,
60). "The commandments are to be looked on as *principles* even more than rules.
They cover a far wider area" (61, emphasis original). Here she is following the
hermeneutical approach of finding general principles within the Bible.

Wordsworth was not afraid of science but rather saw it as an aid to theology,
supporting and enhancing our understanding of Scripture. In discussing the first
commandment, she argues that the "belief in the Unity of God is supported by
what Science teaches us about Nature" (71). Because science has shown "the radical oneness of animal life," this proves the oneness of God (72). She contends, "Is
not our theology timid just because it will not learn from Science how great and
wonderful is this God of ours?" (74). Interestingly, although she did not formally

---

38. Only the ceremonial and civil laws were obsolete.

study science in her youth, she had obviously read a lot about science by the time she wrote this.

Wordsworth used science to interpret Scripture in her analysis of the sixth and seventh commandments, "Thou shalt not murder" and "Thou shalt not commit adultery." Here she turns to science to talk about human instincts. She argues that science tells us that "self-preservation and self-reproduction are the two great instincts by which all life, from the very lowest forms, appears to be governed; and when we try to discover what man himself was in his primitive condition, we find these two instincts constantly at work" (155–56). As a result, Wordsworth argues that in the early stages of life it was quite foreign to say that to destroy life was wrong because it was a way to survive. "Thou shalt not kill" takes it to a different level. However, she admits that humans have not and perhaps never will completely emerge from the primitive stage. Nevertheless, she does see something positive with the combative instinct in that it is "training for that higher warfare against sin and Satan" (157).

In analyzing the fifth commandment, "Honor thy father and thy mother," Wordsworth's comments reflect her perspective as a woman interpreter. First, she argues that if we had authored the commandment, we would have said to love instead of to honor one's parents, because loving one's parents is instinctive, but honoring them is harder (138).[39] The reason she gives for honoring a parent even if he or she is immoral, selfish, or neglectful, is "because a father is a type of the Father of all, Almighty God" (142)[40] and the mother is a type of Christ. She writes,

> the full beauty of motherhood was never realized till the Incarnation of our Lord. No doubt this is true of fatherhood also, but perhaps in not quite so marked a degree. It was not only that by His birth from the Blessed Virgin He hallowed the office of maternity, and turned the "sorrow" of childbirth into ineffable joy; but because by giving us an example of self-sacrifice, by laying down His life for us, He has given a new beauty to that most mysterious and affecting relation between mother and child, and has made us feel that not only is fatherhood

---

39. Although she does not specifically define what she means by love and honor, she seems to understand honoring as treating one's parents respectfully. Thus, she refers to biblical examples of honoring and dishonoring and gives many practical suggestions of how one can honor one's parents, such as by rising when they enter the room, by not interrupting them when they are talking, by putting on a nice dress to cheer them up, by praying and thanking God for them, and by making use of opportunities while the parents are alive because soon they will be gone (147–52).

40. In Wordsworth's writing on the Creed, she also develops the idea that the human father is a type of God the Father. In this earlier work, however, she does not elaborate on the notion of motherhood as a type of Christ. Rather, she discusses at length Jesus' positive relations with women, setting the example to men of how women should be treated and respected. See Elizabeth Wordsworth, *Illustrations of the Creed* (London: Rivington, 1889), 43–45, 81–85.

typical of God as our Creator, but that motherhood is to be reverenced as setting forth, as no other human type can do, both the pain and the joy of our redemption. (143)

Because of the self-sacrifice of mothers for their children, and by giving birth to life through pain, motherhood has become a type of Christ. Thus, Wordsworth argues that motherhood changed after the coming of Christ and that it now is "peculiarly *Christian*" (143, emphasis original). For the rest of the chapter, she focuses more on the mother than the father and highlights the important influence mothers have on their children. She observes that the mother's name is usually given in the list of kings in Kings and Chronicles, demonstrating their important influence on their sons (146). Wordsworth also asserts that mothers are spiritually in tune and therefore the best guides to their sons' spiritual lives. "How many men have found in their mothers the truest spiritual and intellectual sympathy! To how many a man has his mother been the best interpreter of his spiritual life!" (144).

Through these statements Wordsworth reveals her view that women are inherently religious and are to be spiritual and moral examples to others, especially to their children. It also shows how highly she regards the role of motherhood, even though she herself never was a mother (although, practically, she was a mother figure to many of her female students).

In her writing Wordsworth also gives some advice specifically addressed to women, her audience. It reveals some of her views of women and their roles, shaped by upper-class Victorian ideals. She ardently believes that a woman needs to be an exemplary figure—modest and above reproach. "The well-being of a nation depends on the purity, delicacy, sweetness, and goodness of its women, especially perhaps among the more influential classes. The mere sight of a good, holy, and refined woman *is* a kind of gospel to the poor and illiterate" (28, emphasis original).

Wordsworth's views reflect the class structure of Victorian English society. "To women who are often tempted to lose themselves in petty pursuits, it may safely be said that *the* preservative is Bible-reading" (115, emphasis original). This is her advice to both men and women. In discussing the seventh commandment, she warns women against flirting, saying that it is wrong to love amusement and admiration more than the man and that it can lead to serious consequences. Wordsworth concludes that by flirting a woman is lowering herself and the ideal of womanhood (179–81). She encourages her women students to be ladies, setting the example for the lower classes and the servants, just as England is an example to America and the colonies (184). In our modern context, these words seem very patronizing, foreign, and uncomfortable to our ears, but this attitude and thinking was typical of the world in which Elizabeth Wordsworth lived, and thus we must understand her in this light.

In these examples of applying the Ten Commandments to her own context, Wordsworth clearly reads the commandments from an upper-class Victorian woman's perspective. Because her addresses were given to a group of women students who were well-off and privileged, her suggestions for application are shaped by her audience.

In her approach to interpreting the Decalogue, Wordsworth draws on archaeological discoveries, ancient history, Greek philosophers, science, nature, her father's commentary, and other dictionaries. Throughout her writing she also refers to Hebrew, Greek, Latin, the Septuagint, the church fathers, classical Greek authors, and modern authors. She assumes her audience understands Greek and does not translate the Greek when quoting from the Septuagint, the New Testament, or the *Iliad*. Her women students obviously knew Greek or were learning it while studying at Lady Margaret Hall, because she chose not to translate it for them. In her writing, she draws on a wide range of sources, making good use of her classical training.

Psalms for the Christian Festivals

Wordsworth's second work, *Psalms for the Christian Festivals,* was published in 1906 but was based on her lectures to a group of women students in 1897. In it she discusses twenty-two psalms read at Christmas, Easter, Ascension, and Pentecost according to the Anglican lectionary. In each case she explains how the psalm has become related to the Christian festival. In her introduction, she outlines her objective and her approach to interpreting the psalms. She begins by stating that she is not going to say something new about "scholarship or Biblical criticism, but to illustrate from the Church's use of the Psalter for the Christian seasons, the bearing of the Psalms on great doctrinal truths, as well as their fitness to minister to the needs of individuals, and their relation to our personal lives."[41] Although Wordsworth is aware of the historical-critical debates over the date and authorship of the psalms, she argues that the meaning and application of the psalms are universal and independent of these questions (v–vi). "As we pursue our study of the Psalms, we shall find over and over again that—whatever their origin may have been—their meaning never could have been tied down and limited to one person, or one generation, or even one set of events" (xi). The meaning of each psalm is universal and applicable to all times and all peoples:

> We should approach it with a deep spirit of reverence, using no doubt, so far as we can, the results of scholarship and historical research, but always remembering that it is not the authorship of the Psalm, nor its local and historical setting that gives it its true and lasting value, but the fact that it is the voice of God speaking to the soul, and the soul replying to God. (xiii)

---

41. Wordsworth, *Psalms for the Christian Festivals,* v. Subsequent references to *Psalms for the Christian Festivals* will cited within the main text.

Although historical-critical questions have some value, for her they are not the key to interpreting the psalms. Having said this, however, in her analysis of each psalm she begins by discussing questions related to authorship, date, and original context, being fully aware of current scholarly debates (2, 10, 36, 93, 101, 109–10, 125).[42] At the same time, she does not dwell on these questions but quickly moves on to elaborate on the meaning of the psalm.

Wordsworth finds meaning in the psalms on two levels. Scripture has a natural meaning and a spiritual meaning (74). She believes that the natural meaning is found in the real, historical events described. One must begin interpreting the psalm by looking at the original context, but the meaning of the psalm is not limited to this (10–12). In illustrating this twofold nature of Scripture, she compares the Bible to Giovanni da Bologna's statue of Mercury,

> with one foot on the earth, but just ready to soar away to heaven. That might stand for a type of the writers of Holy Scripture. One foot is firm on the earth, but there is a buoyancy, a spring, a heavenward aim which prevents their ever being satisfied with earth. They begin with this world—they *always* begin with this world—but they never end there. (11–12, emphasis original)

Thus, Ps 118 originally applied to the postexilic Jewish community under Ezra and Nehemiah, but on the spiritual level it also applies to Christ (70–71). Likewise, Ps 48 is set in the reign of Hezekiah and perhaps was authored by the prophet Isaiah, but it is also fulfilled in the church at Pentecost (109–14). With this understanding, she takes a typological approach to the psalms. For example, in Ps 19 the sun is a type of Christ (5), and in Ps 89 David becomes a type of Christ (34). She writes: "The Davidic monarchy was, as it were, the husk which, till the time of ripeness came, shrouded the kernel—the royalty, still future, of Jesus Christ" (95).[43] Although some of the psalms first applied to King David, their ultimate fulfillment is found in Jesus Christ.

Besides using this typological and christological approach to the psalms, Wordsworth is also concerned with finding application for each psalm in her own context. Although originally a marriage song probably applied to King Solomon, Ps 45 is both a type of the marriage union between Christ and the church and applicable to marriage today (10–18). Besides speaking about marriage, she also asserts that Ps 45 has something to say about "the ideal of womanhood" in her day (16). "The essentials of Christian womanhood" as seen in this psalm are: "unself-

---

42. Although well-informed on the different scholarly views, she tends to be conservative overall on the question of authorship and for the most part prefers the traditional view. However, she is willing to concede that David did not write all the psalms ascribed to him, e.g., Ps 110 (36).

43. Here she is discussing Pss 21 and 24.

ish devotion" to her husband, "exquisite perfection," giving of her very best, and so forth (17). She continues:

> Is not the lesson for us all to strive in everything to be as pure, as complete, as perfect as we can? No room for carelessness, slovenliness, half-done work, ugliness, bad taste. The ideal woman's life ought to show exquisite finish in every detail. Dress, handwriting, good manners, refined speech—none of these things should be beneath her care. (17)[44]

We see here how Wordsworth's views and application were shaped by her traditional Victorian ideals and the fact that she was addressing a group of young, impressionable women under her care. Her application is very specifically related to her context as principal of a women's college.

Other interpretive comments about women in the psalms are found in Wordsworth's discussion of Ps 68. She makes the observation that Ps 68:11 should be translated as "the women that publish the tidings are a great host," following the feminine plural in the Hebrew, contrary to the translation of the Authorized Version.[45] In this context, she argues that these verses refer to the time of Deborah and that there may be an allusion to the Song of Deborah, Judg 5:16, in Ps 68:13 (118). She also notes that women are included among the musicians in verse 25, commenting on this beautiful inclusive picture of the religious procession (120). Although a man could have made the same observations, it is perhaps because Wordsworth is a woman that she saw these things.

Before analyzing her final psalm, Ps 145, assigned for Pentecost, Wordsworth makes an interesting observation about the canonical shape of the Psalter. Studying the psalms as a whole, she sees an analogy between the canonical ordering of the psalms and that of human life and experience. She observes a movement from the theme of struggle, fleeing enemies, and seeking justice in the earlier psalms to that of deep devotion, consciousness of sin, and seeking grace and mercy in the later. Then she sees the development of a national spirit, by moving from individual psalms with the use of singular pronouns *I* or *me* to the plural *we* and *us* in communal psalms (133). Finally, she notes that the latter part of the Psalter includes more psalms of praise and thanksgiving and focuses less on hardship and struggle, thus reflecting the gratitude and quiet acceptance of life at an old age:

> As the series of a hundred and fifty Psalms draws to a close we seem to breathe a sunnier atmosphere—that serene brightness of gratitude, which we see in an honoured old age, seems to rest on the pages which close the Psalter. There is a

---

44. Her views on the ideal woman is also elaborated in her writing on women's education (Wordsworth, "Colleges for Women," 14).

45. The King James Version says, "great was the company of those who published it."

quiet after struggle, thanksgiving after release—the horizon loses itself in light, and all is joyous, calm, and hopeful. (134)

Thus, she sees parallels between the ordering of the psalms and that of human life—a movement from the struggles of youth to the maturity and acceptance that comes with life experience and age. Although her observations and conclusions are somewhat simplistic, Wordsworth tries to find an overall pattern in the canonical shaping of the Psalter as a whole that fits with her notion of development in Scripture and her own personal experience. In her own life, she approached old age without bitterness but rather with hope and gratitude.[46]

Elizabeth Wordsworth's *The Decalogue* and *Psalms for the Christian Festivals* demonstrate that her approach to biblical interpretation was shaped by a number of important factors. First of all, we see the clear influence of her father on her thinking and in her approach.[47] In her father's commentary, Christopher Wordsworth often quoted the church fathers as well as the Anglican divines and their interpretations of biblical texts. He believed that they served as important guides to interpreting the Scriptures.[48] In both her works, she, too, continually quotes the church fathers and various Anglican bishops. Following Augustine, her father firmly believed that in order to understand and interpret the Old Testament correctly, "we must begin with the New."[49] We must read the Old Testament through the lens of the New Testament. His emphasis on reading the Old Testament typologically or figuratively,[50] using the "spiritual method of exegesis,"[51] and through the lens of the New Testament is clearly seen in her approach, especially in her analysis of the psalms. Her use of typology was a very common approach in Christian interpretations of the psalms, going back to the New Testament itself and the early church fathers. Thus, it is not surprising to see her adopt this way of looking at the Old Testament. Like her father, she had a very positive view of the Old Testament as Scripture and believed in its enduring relevance. Being a classicist at heart, she also drew upon the ancient Greek authors as illustrations and made good use of her knowledge of Hebrew, Greek, and Latin. Like her father, she demonstrated a deep and wide knowledge of ancient and modern literature, history, and languages.

Although Wordsworth was generally traditional and theologically conservative in her views, she was remarkably open to new ideas and was well aware of

---

46. Battiscombe, *Reluctant Pioneer*, 200.

47. Wordsworth's admiration for her father's work is demonstrated in her references to her father's commentary on the Bible as well as his work on church history in her writings.

48. Wordsworth, *Five Books of Moses*, xxi; Overton and Wordsworth, *Christopher Wordsworth*, 407.

49. Wordsworth, *Five Books of Moses*, viii–ix.

50. Overton and Wordsworth, *Christopher Wordsworth*, 412.

51. Wordsworth, *Five Books of Moses*, xvi.

the current debates regarding historical criticism and the Bible; here we see her depart from her father. Although she did not fully embrace it, she was not afraid of the new historical-critical approach to the Bible. Her father, on the other hand, was very critical of higher criticism because it was an approach that led some to reject the inspiration and authority of Scripture and to treat the Bible as any other book. Her father labeled those who practiced such an approach as modern-day Marcionites and Manichaeans.[52] In her analysis, Wordsworth drew on the historical-critical scholarship of the following theologians and biblical scholars: S. R. Driver, Regius Professor of Hebrew at Oxford and Canon of Christ Church (1883–1914); A. F. Kirkpatrick, Regius Professor of Hebrew at Cambridge (1882–1903); and F. B. Westcott, Regius Professor of Divinity at Cambridge (1870–90).[53] She especially drew on Kirkpatrick's commentary on the psalms in the then popular *Cambridge Bible for Schools and Colleges* series as well as S. R. Driver's *An Introduction to the Literature of the Old Testament* in her own study of the psalms.[54] All of these scholars were open to the new historical-critical approach to interpreting the Bible, yet they also held to a high view of the inspiration and authority of Scripture and the belief that the Bible taught moral and spiritual truth. For them, the historical-critical approach to the Bible was compatible with Christian faith.[55] In her writing, Wordsworth clearly admires these scholars and interacts with their scholarship.[56]

In commenting on the nature of Scripture in her work on the Decalogue, Wordsworth demonstrates both her high view of Scripture and her openness to the findings of historical criticism. She rejects the verbal mechanical theory of

---

52. Ibid., vii–viii. However, Christopher Wordsworth did assert that biblical criticism was a "high and holy science" and if handled soberly and with reverence could be useful (Overton and Wordsworth, *Christopher Wordsworth*, 406–7).

53. Wordsworth, *The Psalms for the Christian Festivals*, 14, 21, 37–39, 68, 71, 102, 110, 117–19; idem, *The Decalogue*, 37; Rogerson, *Old Testament Criticism*, 273–75, 282, 285–86; C. L. Church, "Westcott, B. F., and F. J. A. Hort," in *Historical Handbook of Major Biblical Interpreters* (ed. D. K. McKim; Downers Grove, Ill.: InterVarsity Press, 1998), 389–94.

54. Although she only mentions professors Kirkpatrick and Driver by name and not their specific works, after having examined their writings, it is clear that she was using these particular works: A. F. Kirkpatrick, *Psalms XC–CL* (vol. 3 of *The Book of Psalms with Introduction and Notes*; Cambridge Bible for Schools and Colleges; Cambridge: Cambridge University Press, 1901); S. R. Driver, *An Introduction to the Literature of the Old Testament* (9th ed.; Edinburgh: T&T Clark, 1913). The first edition of Driver's *Introduction* was published in 1891.

55. Rogerson, *Old Testament Criticism*, 273–74; M. Taylor, "Driver, Samuel Rolles," in McKim, *Historical Handbook*, 302–9.

56. She writes that Professor Kirkpatrick is "a writer to whom students of the Psalms are greatly indebted" (Wordsworth, *Psalms for the Christian Festivals*, 38–39) and that S. R. Driver wrote "an interesting article on the 'Cosmology of Genesis'" (Wordsworth, *Illustrations of the Creed*, 64).

inspiration of Scripture as too extreme.[57] At the same time, she believes in the "wonderful verbal accuracy and consistency of Holy Scripture.... every word *means* something.... no paragraphs ... can be 'skipped.' "[58] Each word must be valued as fine gold, yet she recognizes that the Bible has emerged in a particular historical context and therefore will reflect its ancient cultural context. Therefore, she has no problem seeing parallel stories and similarities between the Old Testament and other ancient Near Eastern cultures. She freely admits that there are "Chaldean variants of parts of the Book of Genesis ... Levitical Law in the customs of Egypt,"[59] but these do not affect her view of Scripture as inspired. In response to difficult questions such as what the population of the earth was in the time of Cain and Abel, she responds,

> It is obvious that those early chapters of Genesis do not aim at giving an *exhaustive* account of primitive society any more than they do of giving exhaustive details of Creation. There must have been many men and women at this time on the earth whose existence we have to take for granted.[60]

She does not let these questions bother her. She is able to affirm the authority and inspiration of Scripture and at the same time raise questions of a historical-critical nature.

Wordsworth's openness to more liberal thinking is also seen in the people with whom she socialized in Oxford. Her biographer writes that Wordsworth "found the liberal thinkers of the Balliol group much better company" than the more conservative thinkers of Christ Church and Keble College.[61] She was friends with T. H. Green, the philosopher and fellow of Balliol College in Oxford,[62] and socialized with Benjamin Jowett, the master of Balliol College. Benjamin Jowett had written one of the essays in the controversial publication *Essays and Reviews* in 1860, where he advocated that the Bible should be interpreted "like any other book."[63] Her father wrote a scathing response to Jowett's essay when it first came out. Although Jowett's views were heretical to her father, Wordsworth found Jowett to be friendly, generous, and kind, not someone to be feared. She wrote,

---

57. Wordsworth, *The Decalogue*, 104.

58. Ibid., 113–14, emphasis original.

59. Ibid., 108.

60. Ibid., 158, emphasis original.

61. Battiscombe, *Reluctant Pioneer*, 104.

62. T. H. Green, fellow of Balliol College, 1860–78, represented a neo-Hegelian school of philosophy, which contributed to the popular developmental view of understanding the Old Testament in the nineteenth century, as progressing from simpler to more complex and developed thought over time (Rogerson, *Old Testament Criticism*, 280). Wordsworth quotes T. H. Green in her work on the Decalogue (Wordsworth, *The Decalogue*, 232).

63. Rogerson, *Old Testament Criticism*, 217.

"Oddly enough, I never felt afraid of him, as I believe many people did."[64] She appreciated the fact that he was friendly toward her, especially since her father had been very critical of him in print over *Essays and Reviews*.[65] We see that Wordsworth's social circles in Oxford contributed to her openness to newer thinking and ideas, which impacted her approach to biblical interpretation.

CONCLUSION

Elizabeth Wordsworth was a remarkable woman whose breadth and depth of knowledge was amazing. She was an important figure in the intellectual life of Oxford, and as principal of Lady Margaret Hall she had a very important influence on a generation of women. Although she was not a feminist in the modern sense of the word, she believed in women being educated and encouraged women to study. She set an example by her own deep desire to learn and to share that knowledge with others. Wordsworth was passionate about teaching the Bible—a passion that lasted to the very end of her life. After her retirement as principal, she lived another twenty-three years. During those retirement years, she continued to be very active in Oxford life, teaching Bible classes regularly. Her classes become known as an "Oxford institution."[66] At age eighty-eight, a friend came to visit her and found her studying the Latin Vulgate. Wordsworth told her to grab the Hebrew Lexicon and the Greek Septuagint and they would solve a translation problem that she had found in the Vulgate.[67] At this age, she was still reading the ancient languages and taking delight in her biblical and theological study. At age ninety-two she was leading a Bible study on the Hebrew poetry of Pss 107 and 45. That very night she collapsed, and two days later she died. Her mind remained sharp and clear to the very end. Elizabeth Wordsworth died 30 November 1932, teaching the Scriptures to a group of women.

BIBLIOGRAPHY

Barszcz, James. "Christopher Wordsworth." Pages 344–52 in *British Travel Writers, 1837–1875: Victorian Period*. Edited by Barbara Brothers and Julia Gergits. Dictionary of Literary Biography 166. Detroit: Gale, 1996.

Barta-Smith, Nancy A. "Elizabeth Wordsworth." Pages 313–27 in *Modern British Essayist: First Series*. Edited by Robert Beum. Dictionary of Literary Biography 98. Detroit: Gale, 1990.

---

64. Wordsworth, *Glimpses of the Past*, 166. Although she was not as close to Jowett as Florence Nightingale, Wordsworth still had a respectful friendship with him (Battiscombe, *Reluctant Pioneer*, 106).

65. Wordsworth, *Glimpses of the Past*, 165–67.

66. Ibid., 205.

67. Ibid., 216.

Battiscombe, Georgina. *Reluctant Pioneer: A Life of Elizabeth Wordsworth.* London: Constable, 1978.

Church, C. L. "Westcott, B. F., and F. J. A. Hort." Pages 389–94 in *Historical Handbook of Major Biblical Interpreters.* Edited by Donald K. McKim. Downers Grove, Ill.: InterVarsity Press, 1998.

Driver, S. R. *An Introduction to the Literature of the Old Testament.* 9th ed. Edinburgh: T&T Clark, 1913.

Gale Reference Team. "Elizabeth Wordsworth, 1840–1932." In *Contemporary Authors Online.* Detroit: Gale, 2000.

Jamison, Evelyn M. "Appendix." Pages 223–311 in Georgina Battiscombe, *Reluctant Pioneer: A Life of Elizabeth Wordsworth.* London: Constable, 1978.

———. "Wordsworth, Dame Elizabeth." Pages 921–22 in *The Dictionary of National Biography: 1931–1940.* Edited by L. G. Wickham Legg. London: Oxford University Press, 1949.

Kirkpatrick, A. F. *Psalms XC–CL.* Vol. 3 of *The Book of Psalms with Introduction and Notes.* Cambridge Bible for Schools and Colleges. Cambridge: Cambridge University Press, 1901.

Overton, John Henry, and Elizabeth Wordsworth. *Christopher Wordsworth: Bishop of Lincoln.* London: Rivington, 1888.

Rogerson, John. *Old Testament Criticism in the Nineteenth Century: England and Germany.* London: SPCK, 1984.

Taylor, M. "Driver, Samuel Rolles." Pages 302–9 in *Historical Handbook of Major Biblical Interpreters.* Edited by Donald K. McKim. Downers Grove, Ill.: InterVarsity Press, 1998.

Wordsworth, Christopher. *The Five Books of Moses.* Vol. 1 of *The Holy Bible in the Authorized Version: With Notes and Introductions.* New ed. London: Rivington, 1872.

———. *The Holy Bible in the Authorized Version: With Notes and Introductions.* The Cheaper Issue of the Bishop of Lincoln's Commentary on the Holy Bible. 8 vols. London: Rivington, 1872.

Wordsworth, Elizabeth. "Colleges for Women." Pages 14–28 in *Ladies at Work: Papers on Paid Employment for Ladies.* Edited by Lady Jeune. London: Innes, 1893.

———. *The Decalogue.* London: Longmans, Green, 1893.

———. *Glimpses of the Past.* London: Mowbray, 1912.

———. *Illustrations of the Creed.* London: Rivington, 1889.

———. *Psalms for the Christian Festivals.* London: Longmans, Green, 1906.

Annie Besant:
An Adversarial Interpreter of Scripture

Christiana de Groot

Introduction

The opening paragraph of Arthur Nethercot's two-volume biography of Annie Besant succinctly summarizes her accomplishments:

> In 1885, before she was forty, Mrs. Annie Besant was known all over the Eng-
> lish-speaking world, and by many people on the Continent, as one of the most
> remarkable women of her day. She was a Freethinker; a consorter with materi-
> alists like Charles Bradlaugh; an agitator in Radical political circles, again like
> Bradlaugh; a feminist; an early convert to Fabian Socialism, through the agency
> of Bernard Shaw; a teacher of science; an author-editor-publisher; the first
> prominent woman to dare fight openly for what is now called birth control; a
> social and educational reformer; and an orator whose power was so compelling
> and whose charm was so potent that Shaw was only one among thousands to
> extol her as the greatest woman speaker of the century.[1]

This describes only the first half of her life. She lived from 1847 to 1933, and in Nethercot's second volume he traces the second half, spent largely in India as a theosophist engaged in reform and education.[2]

This essay on Besant as an interpreter of Scripture will focus on two brief pamphlets that she wrote and published with Freethought Publishing concerning the Bible's treatment of women. The first, published in 1885, is entitled *Woman's Position according to the Bible*, and the second, published in 1890, is entitled *God's*

---

1. Arthur H. Nethercot, *The First Five Lives of Annie Besant* (Chicago: University of Chicago Press, 1960), 1. Elizabeth Cady Stanton also describes Besant as an exceptional orator in
Eighty Years and More: Reminiscences 1815–1897 (New York: Unwin, 1898), n.p. (ch. 22) [cited
14 July 2006]. Online: http://digital.library.upenn.edu/women/stanton/years/years-XXII.html.

2. Arthur H. Nethercot, *The Last Four Lives of Annie Besant* (Chicago: University of Chicago Press, 1963).

Views on Marriage. To understand these essays better, I want to situate them briefly in the context of Besant's life and the debates in Victorian England concerning marriage and divorce.

PERSONAL AND HISTORICAL CONTEXT

Annie Besant was born in London to William Wood and Emily Roche Morris. Her father had studied medicine at Trinity College, Dublin, where he met Emily, who came from an Irish family. Annie's father died when she was five years old, and her mother sent Annie off to be educated when she was nine years old. At the home of Miss Marryat she learned Latin, French, history, and geography until she was sixteen. She always had an interest in religion, and early on she was attracted to Roman Catholicism but instead joined the Oxford Movement.[3] At twenty years of age she married Rev. Frank Besant (1840–1917), a clergyman in the Anglican Church. *The Oxford Dictionary of National Biography* described him "an impecunious, parsimonious, stiff-necked young man from Portsea, whose evangelicalism was approvingly described as 'serious.'"[4] Their first child, Digby, was born in 1869, and their second child, Mabel, was born in 1870. The marriage was strained early on due in part to Besant's fear of another pregnancy and her questioning of the Christian faith after the severe illness of her young children. She began to correspond with theologians in order to better understand her beliefs, and this study eventually led her away from orthodox theologians to Charles Voysey. He denied many central doctrines of the church, such as the divinity of Christ, attacked the idea of eternal punishment as cruel, and concluded that the Bible was not the Word of God. He was eventually defrocked and came to head a "theistic" church in London.[5] He introduced Besant to Freethinker Thomas Scott and his circle. Scott encouraged her to write out her doubts and dissenting views and published them in a pamphlet in 1872 entitled *On the Deity of Jesus of Nazareth*. Although Besant was not identified as the author by name, the inscription stated, "By the wife of a beneficed clergyman."[6] Her husband was fearful that her identity as the author would become public and that this, in turn, would put his own living at risk, so he issued her an ultimatum: she was to be seen taking communion regularly at Sibsey, his parish, or she was to leave. As Besant described it, her options were hypocrisy or expulsion.[7] She chose the latter and in 1873 was awarded a deed of separation that gave her a small allowance and custody of her daughter Mabel.

---

3. Owen Chadwick, "The Oxford Movement," in *The Victorian Church* (2 vols.; London: Black, 1966), 1:167–231.

4. Anne Taylor, "Besant, Annie (1847–1933)" in *Oxford Dictionary of National Biography* (ed. H. C. G. Matthew and B. Harrison; 60 vols.; Oxford: Oxford University Press, 2004), 5:504.

5. Anne Taylor, *Annie Besant: A Biography* (Oxford: Oxford University Press, 1992), 44–52.

6. Ibid., 55–56.

7. Annie Besant, *Autobiographical Sketches* (London: Freethought Publishing, 1885), 74.

From this point on she supported herself by writing articles and speaking, and, in 1875, she was hired by Charles Bradlaugh as a writer for the Freethought newspaper, the *National Reformer*. The two set up the Freethought Publishing Company in 1877 and reissued Charles Knowlton's *The Fruits of the Spirit*, a work advocating birth control. For this, the two were charged and tried for obscenity. At a certain point in the proceedings, the court halted the proceedings and released them on their own recognizance of one hundred pounds. However, as a married women, Besant legally was not allowed to enter into her own recognizance. To save her going to prison, the court allowed Bradlaugh to pay one hundred pounds for both of them.[8] Although they were ultimately acquitted, Besant's husband used the occasion to claim that she was not fit to raise their daughter Mabel, and he gained custody.[9] Besant experienced firsthand the application of the laws regulating marriage, divorce, and custody; the right of women to their earnings; and the diminished legal rights of married women. As will be evident, Besant read the narratives and laws of the Old Testament that deal with family matters through the lens of her own efforts to secure justice.

As Besant was struggling with the personal implications of religion and the law, England as a whole was renegotiating the different spheres of church and state on several fronts: the universities, divorce and marriage laws, and the status of Jews. In all cases, the jurisdiction of the Church of England was diminished, and society became more tolerant of a diversity of religious commitments and sensitive to gender inequality. For example, the 1857 Matrimonial Causes Act/Divorces Act established secular divorce in England. It provided: (1) that a court could order maintenance payment to a divorced or estranged wife; (2) that a divorced wife could inherit or bequeath property, enter contracts, sue or be sued, and protect her earnings from a deserter; and (3) that a man could secure a divorce on the grounds of his wife's adultery. For a woman, a husband's adultery alone was insufficient grounds; she had to prove another charge such as desertion, extreme cruelty, or incest in order to secure a divorce. Then Parliament allowed Jews to take their place as members of Parliament in 1858, with the passing of the Jewish Disabilities Act. The governing body of the country was now no longer completely Anglican or Christian—England was on its way to becoming a "neutral" state.[10] This principle was applied to education when in 1871 the universities of Oxford and Cambridge, which had required that students sign the Thirty-Nine Articles of the Church of England, began admitting dissenters in 1871 after the passage of the University Tests Act. Married women were granted a measure of economic independence with the passage of the Married Women's Property Act

---

8. Taylor, *Annie Besant*, 120.

9. Besant writes poignantly of this loss in *Autobiographical Sketches*, 159–69.

10. Chadwick, "The Theory and Practice of Church and State," in *Victorian Church*, 1:476–87.

in 1870. This allowed women to keep two hundred pounds of their own earnings. This law was revisited in 1882 and expanded to allow married women to continue as the separate owners and administrators of their property after marriage.[11]

LITERARY GENRE

Besant's two essays dealing with women and the Bible are both small pamphlets written for a popular audience. The readers are assumed to be educated people concerned about public life, but they are not assumed to be academics or students of the Bible. Although Besant occasionally discusses the meaning of a word in Hebrew, she always cites the dictionary she is using and strives to make her argument accessible to the nonspecialist. It is also significant that both pamphlets are transparently tendentious and polemical. Both advocate a particular position in opposition to another, and both describe the position they are opposing in black-and-white terms. If there is any nuance or qualification in the opinions held by Besant's target, these pamphlets will not engage them.

Besant wrote these essays as an outsider protesting the positions of the establishment, which explains their polemical tone. As an outsider, she needed to raise her voice in order to be heard because she did not have any of the social clout enjoyed by members of the clergy of the Church of England. For example, her essay in response to the bishop of Manchester begins, "Every newspaper in the country some time since printed a libel on Secularism first published in the name of the Bishop of Manchester."[12] That may be an exaggeration, but it seems likely that most newspapers in the land would not have published her essay. Her response to the bishop was published by the small press, Freethought Publishing. Her flamboyant, strident writing and speaking style help her accomplish her goal of being heard as an outsider.

WOMAN'S POSITION ACCORDING TO THE BIBLE

Woman's Position according to the Bible engages the claim made by Christians that the position of women has been greatly improved where the Bible has been accepted.[13] Besant quotes an imaginary proponent of this position: "See women

---

11. Marjie Bloy, "Victorian Legislation: A Timeline," n.p. [cited 27 May 2005]. Online: http://www.victorianweb.org/history/legistl.html.

12. Annie Besant, *God's Views on Marriage* (London: Freethought Publishing, 1890), 1.

13. In Stanton's memoirs she writes that while in England in 1882 she was asked to preach and chose as her theme "What Has Christianity Done for Woman?" She summarizes the results of her historical survey in this way: "I showed clearly that to no form of religion was woman indebted for one impulse of freedom, as all alike have taught her inferiority and subjection" (*Eighty Years*, ch. 22). Stanton later published an article on this same topic. She writes, "Miss Anthony left in December, 1884, for Washington, and I went to work on an article for the *North*

among the heathen, how degraded, how hard-worked, how enslaved! say Christians. Consider her treatment among them with the liberty and respect enjoyed by women in happy Christian lands."[14] Besant begins her analysis of this claim by suggesting that the comparison is not apt. In order to compare apples to apples, she suggests that Christians not compare the life of an Australian savage with that of English aristocracy but the life of an Indian squaw with that of a married factory hand "who toils all day at the factory, and returns home at night to clean the house, wash, mend and make the children's clothes, cook the supper, etc."[15] Her description of the factory worker's life when she returns home is an example of what is now labeled the second shift.[16] Besant critiques the comparison by claiming that class needs to be taken into account when evaluating the status of women—an insight that is also of great significance to students of gender today. A patriarchal society does not result in all men having higher status than all women. There are gradations of power and privilege, with the result that upper-class women have more status than lower-class women and men. Besant concludes, for example, that the outward respect shown to a lady is shown because of her class, not her sex. She observes, "the gentleman who shows the most charming courtesy and deference to a lady, speaks with sharpness to his maid-servant when he is in a bad temper, and with insulting familiarity when in a good."[17] For Besant, as for

---

American Review, entitled, 'What has Christianity done for Women?' I took the ground that woman was not indebted to any form of religion for the liberty she now enjoys, but that, on the contrary, the religious element in her nature had always been perverted for her complete subjection. Bishop Spaulding, in the same issue of the *Review*, took the opposite ground, but I did not feel that he answered my points" (ch. 23).

14. Annie Besant, *Woman's Position according to the Bible* (London: Freethought Publishing, 1885), 1. Although the comparison is not completely parallel, research on women's abuse in Christian churches shows that the rates are very similar to those found in the population at large. See the report of the Committee to Study Physical, Emotional and Sexual Abuse, "Report 30," in *The Agenda for Synod of the Christian Reformed Church in North America* (Grand Rapids: CRC Publications, 1992).

15. Annie Besant, *Woman's Position according to the Bible*, 1. Besant's assessment is supported by Andrew August's study *Poor Women's Lives: Gender, Work and Poverty in Late-Victorian London* (London: Associated University Press, 1999). He demonstrates that lower-class women worked harder and were paid less than the men in the working world and, on top of that, had the additional responsibilities of managing a household and the risks of childbirth. They shared little in common with their middle- and upper-class sisters, except that in all cases gender ideology played a key role in restricting women and privileging men.

16. See Arlie Hochschild, *The Second Shift: Working Parents and the Revolution at Home* (New York: Viking, 1989), 21. She summarizes the results of national surveys on working couples in 1965 and 1989. In that period, the amount that fathers contributed to the household work rose from 20 to 30 percent.

17. Besant, *Woman's Position according to the Bible*, 2. Subsequent references to *Woman's Position according to the Bible* will be provided within the main text.

theorists today, gender and class are aspects of our identity that overlap and intersect and need to be taken into account together.

Besant's thesis is that the status of women is higher in those places that are civilized. Civilization rather than Christianity and the Bible's influence is the key ingredient that promotes women's emancipation. In order to demonstrate this thesis, Besant does a quick trot through the narratives and laws of the Old Testament and the teaching of Jesus and Paul in the New Testament and shows again and again that the Bible is not good news for women. She notes that there is a development within Scripture of the status of women from being "degraded in the extreme" in the early part of the Old Testament to that of a slave in the New Testament, a status that has been softened by the progress of civilization (2). The passages she considers include Gen 2–3 and its use in 1 Tim 2:11–14. She analyzes the argument that women are created second and that the priority of creation results in the priority of right by noting, "then the beasts and fishes were superior to Adam," and she adds, "but a poor argument satisfies the true Christian, when it comes from inspired lips" (3). Her argument is based on the differing order of creation found in Gen 1 and 2. In Gen 1, humanity is created last, and men and women are created together. In this account, humans are created last as the pinnacle of creation. However, in Gen 2 men and women are created separately; man is created first, and woman is created second. Interpreters, including the author of 1 Timothy, have used the order of creation to support the claim that men were created to be superior to women. Besant applies this reasoning to the account in Gen 1 to show that being second does not always mean being inferior.

Besant furthers her discussion by reflecting on Paul's words in 1 Cor 14:35 and concludes that they show contempt for women. The sentence "If they will learn anything, let them ask their husbands at home" is interpreted as scoffing women. "He clearly could not conceive why they should want to know anything, but if they are so perverse that they will learn, then let them 'ask their husbands.'" She continues by asking, "And if they have no husbands, O sapient Paul? Or if, still worse, their husbands … do not know? Many a man, I fear, tells his wife not to trouble her head about 'things a woman can't understand,' when, if he spoke the truth, he would have to answer: 'My dear, I do not know'" (3).

Besant specifically examines marriage laws and customs as related in Genesis, Exodus, Leviticus, Deuteronomy, and Judges and there finds support for her thesis that women's position improves with advancing civilization. She maps out a taxonomy of marriage in which the lowest form is marriage by capture, such that the woman is the man's property as any other spoils of war would be. Marriage by purchase gradually replaces this. "The partly civilized savage buys instead of stealing his wife" (3). In both these instances, polygamy is also part of the equation: the stronger the man, the more wives he can capture; the richer the man, the more wives he can purchase. Then polygamy is slowly replaced by monogamy with servitude, and gradually this is replaced by monogamy with equality. In this progression, justice slowly triumphs, and as it does, a society becomes more civilized. However, the progression of marriage in Scripture stops short of full justice: the Bible stops at monogamy with servitude (4). The last step, monogamy with equality, is not presented or supported in Scripture. For this reason, the Bible is not helpful for Besant's cause. Rather, those seeking equality in marriage must do battle against the teachings of the Bible.

Some examples in Scripture that support her thesis concerning the development of marriage include the relationship among Abraham, Sarah, and Hagar (Gen 16; 21); the laws dealing with the marriage between an enslaved man and woman (Exod 21:2–6); the law concerning the writ of divorce (Deut 24:1–4); and women taken as the spoils of war (Deut 21:10–14). Her description of what was involved in these legal matters shows a clever mind at work, one that understands due process and the court system very well. For example, Besant comments on the law in Deuteronomy that allows a man to write a writ of divorce—"When a man hath taken a wife, and married her and it come to pass that she find no favor in his eyes ... then let him write her a bill of divorce ... and give it in her hand and send her out of his house" (Deut 24:1, 2 [KJV])—with these words:

> There were no troublesome and lengthy proceedings, no divorce court, no judge, no jury, no evidence; the husband gave evidence before himself, summed up his own favor, delivered a verdict of guilty against his wife, pronounced a sentence of divorce, wrote it, and turned out his divorced wife. The method had the merits of cheapness and simplicity and avoided long arguments. (5)

We might expect that Besant would find a champion in Jesus, especially in his teaching concerning divorce. She notes that Jesus considers the law in Deuteronomy a concession to human weakness but also notes that Jesus and Paul both consider marriage itself to be a concession to human weakness. She cites Jesus' elevation of those who are eunuchs for the kingdom (Matt 19:10–12) and Paul's privileging of the celibate life (1 Cor 7:7–9). This teaching, she claims, is the scriptural foundation for monasteries, nunneries, and the celibacy of the clergy, adding that "the frightful sexual immorality which invariably accompanies the enforcement of an unnatural asceticism is too well known to need proof or argument here" (8).

The influence of the Bible's low view of marriage and woman is abundantly clear in the current laws in England, Besant concludes. She cites as examples:

> Thus a father can sue for damages for the seduction of his daughter while a minor, and a husband can obtain damages from the seducer of his wife; in each case the money award recognizes the damage done to the man's property. Again, a man can obtain a divorce from his unfaithful wife, but no such relief is granted to the wife whose husband has been disloyal to her, unless physical cruelty or desertion be added to the adultery. (7)

Besant noticed that a double standard existed in biblical times and as well as in Victorian England. For example, sexual relations outside of marriage put women beyond the pale of respectability, but not upper-class men. She writes, "The female prostitute is an outcast from society, and the girl, once fallen, is excluded from every home; the male profligate, however flagrant his immorality, is welcomed and caressed, and the fairest of maidens in English society lie at his feet for choice, if only wealth gilds his vileness and title covers his shame" (7).

The good news, according to Besant, is that the influence of the Bible is diminishing with the result that in England women's lives are improving. She has claimed that Paul disdained education for women and decries that in her own time the education of women has been shamefully neglected. However, she points to the admittance of women by the secular University of London, the first in England,[18] as further proof that it is not Christianity nor the Bible that promote the flourishing of women. According to Besant, it is when society frees itself from Scripture that women will truly thrive. She ends her essay with this sentence: "The chains round her by the Bible are being broken by Freethought, and soon she shall walk upright and unfettered in the sunshine, the friend, the helper, the lover, but nevermore the slave of man" (8).

God's Views on Marriage

The second pamphlet, *God's Views on Marriage*, published five years later in 1890, is at least as strident as the first and has a more focused target. Whereas in the first pamphlet the opponent was imaginary, in the second Annie Besant engages the bishop of Manchester, James Fraser (1818–85), to whom she dedicates the essay. Curiously, this pamphlet was published five years after the bishop's death. The tone of the essay gives the impression that Besant is responding immediately to remarks that were published in a newspaper, but clearly that is not the case. If there was a particular occasion in which his remarks were printed posthumously, or if they were quoted again, I have not been able to discover it. It would have been helpful to read Besant's critique of his position knowing the bishop's statements in his own words, but this essay will proceed without that information.

The bishop of Manchester is described in the *Oxford Dictionary of National Biography* as having views that were of the old high-church.[19] He was a social activist and participated in many of the movements of the day. Although he personally did not favor a high ritual, he was required to enforce the Public Worship Regulation Act, which was passed in 1874. He married late in life, in 1880, and died five years later. It is not clear from the brief biography why he would have been Besant's target. It is clear, however, that he was not in Besant's league intel-

---

18. The University of London admitted women to degree programs in 1878, graduated four women with a bachelor of arts degree in 1880, and graduated two women with a bachelor of science degree in 1881.

19. J. A. Hamilton, "Fraser, James (1818–85)," in Matthew and Harrison, *Oxford Dictionary of National Biography*, 20:847–49.

lectually. The entry notes that he was not a glowing student and not a professed theologian. He was, however, an astute administrator and was successful in arbitrating disputes between employers and employees. We might wish that Besant had engaged a theologian of more substance so that her own discussion of what the Bible says about women would be more sophisticated.

In this pamphlet, Besant's strategy is two-pronged. She disputes with Bishop Fraser on the basis of the content of his remarks, and she also engages in personal attack. For example, at the end when she has, to her satisfaction, countered his claims, she entertains the notion that he will withdraw his unfair accusations of the secularists.[20] To this thought she responds with a rhetorical question: "When was a Christian bishop fair to opponents of his creed?"[21] She concludes that this lack of integrity is due to the privilege and power inherent in his position. She writes:

> It is one of the saddest things to those who love to see goodness and truth in all men, whatever their creed may be, to watch the gradual deterioration of character which seems to be the inevitable consequence of assuming the Episcopal mitre. The social rank, the large income, the toadying of "my Lord," all these things put colored spectacles on a bishop's eyes, and he sees in those who are enemies of the Church ... the enemies of humanity at large. (16).

According to Besant, hierarchical church structure invariably leads to corruption. Truth is sacrificed in order to maintain the status and stability of the established church.

What is the issue that instigated this bitter response? Besant claims that the bishop printed a libelous attack on secularism by claiming it teaches that "a man might live tally with a woman and send her away if she became sick or otherwise unpleasant" (3). When secularists responded and asked the bishop to provide proof for his claims, he responded by saying, "it was his opinion that there would be nothing to prevent such conduct if people gave up belief in God, and in a future life wherein they would be held accountable for actions here" (3).

Not surprisingly, Annie Besant has a field day with the bishop's remarks. Before engaging the issue of what secularists teach about marriage as opposed to what the church teaches, she first ridicules his assertion that without the threat of eternal damnation Christians would not live lives characterized by love. She writes:

> It does not say much for the ennobling and civilizing effects of the religion of Christ, if, after eighteen centuries, those brought up in its midst can only be kept

---

20. Timothy Larsen describes the emergence of atheism and the founding of the National Secular Society in 1866 by Charles Bradlaugh in "Biblical Criticism and the Secularist Mentality," ch. 7 of *Contested Christianity: The Political and Social Contexts of Victorian Theology* (Waco, Tex.: Baylor University Press, 2004), 97–112.

21. Besant, *God's Views on Marriage*, 15. Subsequent references to *God's Views on Marriage* will be provided within the main text.

from filthiness of life by the "fear of hell, and the hangman's whip." Men and
women have not been taught by Christianity to love purity, but only to fear hell,
and the natural result is that a bishop of the Christian church fears a deluge of
wickedness if men loose faith in punishment after death. (3)

Having attacked the foundation of Christian morality, she goes on to engage the
issue at hand. First, she sets out the teaching of the Old Testament on marriage.
Anticipating that Christians will question the relevance of the Old Testament for
this discussion, she defends her strategy by appealing to Articles 6 and 7 of the
Thirty-Nine Articles, the creedal foundation of the Anglican Church. Article 6
lists the books of the Old and New Testament that are considered canonical by
the church, and Article 7 goes on to describe the relationship between the Old
and New Testaments. Article 7 states that the Old Testament is not contrary to
the New and that, although the ceremonial laws in the Pentateuch are not binding
on Christians, Christians are bound by the moral laws. Furthermore, the creed
declares that the God of Abraham and Moses is also the God of Jesus and Christians and that this God is eternal and unchangeable. Besant thus claims that she
is working within the tradition that the bishop upholds as she surveys the laws in
Exodus, Leviticus, and Deuteronomy and asks what this says about God and how
God wants his people to live.

Not surprisingly, Besant finds much in the laws and narratives to ridicule.
She imagines that the earliest families mentioned in Genesis must have committed incest in order to perpetuate the human race (4). She notices that even
Abraham is married to his half-sister (Gen 20:12) and that Abraham deserted
Hagar and allowed Sarah to send her into the wilderness (Gen 16). Besant notes
in a bracket, "[Abraham was no Secularist, but the friend of God]" (4), and then
asks, "Is the Bishop of Manchester so busy with the imaginary doctrines of Secularism that he has no time to launch one word of rebuke at this hoary reprobate
who "lives tally" with poor Hagar, and drives her away when he wants her no
longer, when her youth has fled?" (5–6). Her survey continues through the laws
of Exodus, focusing on the laws regarding male and female slaves given by God at
Mount Sinai. She carefully studies Exod 21:7–11, focusing on verse 7. She quotes
the KJV: "And if a man sell his daughter to be a servant, she shall not go out as the
men servants do." Quoting Bradlaugh's study that compares the translations and
dictionaries, concluding that "maidservant" is best understood as a concubine,
she concurs that the verse allows a father to sell his daughter to a master who
makes her his concubine (7). At the end of this section she remarks, "Surely Dr.
Fraser must have been reading his Bible, and have muddled up its teachings with
those of Secularism" (8).

She continues to study the laws against incest in Leviticus and concludes that
God has changed his mind about the marriages contracted in Genesis. Whereas
Abraham and Sarah should have been "cut off" from their people according to
the laws in Leviticus against incest, they were instead the founding couple of the

chosen people. The incestuous relationships between Lot and his daughters that resulted in the conception of the Moabites and the Edomites are duly noted, as well as the procedure by which a man tests whether his wife has been faithful to him (Num 5) and the laws that allow taking women as the spoils of war (Deut 31:10–14). At the conclusion of her exposé of the backwardness of Scripture Besant asks, "How would you describe this kind of conduct, commanded by your own God, Bishop of Manchester?" (10).

She surveys the historical books, noting that David, a man after God's own heart, was guilty of adultery and polygamy, and also includes the accounts in Ezra and Nehemiah when men were told by the priests to put away their wives and children (Ezra 10:3; Neh 13:23–30). Her concluding accusation after airing this dirty laundry is, "[T]his God who was thus served by breaches of marriage fidelity is the God of the Bishop of Manchester" (11).

In contrast to the regressive views of marriage presented in the Old Testament, Besant claims that secularists hold to a high view of marriage as the lifelong union of love and fidelity between two equals. She does not point to any specific article to which all secularists pledge allegiance but rather cites a conversation that Mr. Bradlaugh, founder of the secularists, had with Dr. Baylee about marriage (12). This dialogue presents marriage as a union between equals and allows for divorce and remarriage. She then goes on to advocate her own position regarding the divorce laws that were newly enacted, applauding the legislation for allowing women to hold property and also criticizing the government for allowing a double standard regarding divorce. Men were allowed to divorce their wives for unfaithfulness, while women had to prove unfaithfulness as well as physical cruelty, desertion, or incest (12–14).

BESANT'S VOICE IN THE CONTEXT OF NINETEENTH-CENTURY INTERPRETATION

Besant's two works on the Bible's teaching regarding women—specifically regarding marriage and divorce—do not advance the academic study of the Bible itself. She uncovers no new material that pertains to the historical context or to the understanding of the Hebrew or that addresses questions of authorship or readership. However, she represents a new stage in the history of interpretation. She demonstrates the result of reading Scripture while imposing nineteenth-century ideas about morality, authorship, coherence, and rationality on the text. She chronicles the inadequacies of Scripture: its internal inconsistencies; its oppressive moral dictums; and its portrait of an offensive deity. In this depiction of Scripture she is in agreement with her co-publisher Charles Bradlaugh, author of *The Bible: What It Is.*[22] In his introduction to Genesis, he states that his goal

---

22. For a fuller description of Bradlaugh in the context of Victorian religiosity, see Larsen, "Biblical Criticism and the Secularist Mentality," 97–112.

in writing this treatise is "for the purpose of demonstrating that the book is not a perfect and infallible revelation specially given from an all-wise and infinite Deity, Creator and Ruler of all worlds to his creatures on this planet alone, and that it is not an unerring guide and monitor to humankind in their constant life-struggle for happiness."[23] In the course of 434 pages, Bradlaugh documents the inconsistencies, the unacceptable morality, the primitive science, and the unworthy portrait of God present in the Pentateuch. He is familiar with the scholarship of de Wette, Eichhorn, Gesenius, and Kalisch.[24] The issue of women's treatment is part of his agenda. For example, he makes extensive comments on Exod 21:7–11. He surveys various translations and consults dictionaries, arriving at the conclusion that standard translations have obscured the meaning of the text, which is,

> That here is a law professedly from a God of truth and purity, rendering it lawful for a man to sell his own daughter, in order that she may fulfill a place in the seraglio of her purchaser. Our translations have somewhat glossed the text, partially hiding its disgusting meaning, but still enough was left to excite suspicion. Is this Book from which you let your little girls read, and from which you expect them to acquire that knowledge which shall render them happy and virtuous?[25]

As indicated, Besant quoted this section of Bradlaugh's essay in its entirety. Not only are their conclusions about individual passages similar, but their hermeneutics are also identical. Both Besant and Bradlaugh read the biblical text flatly, as a legal brief, with no consideration of literary genre or literary, historical, or canonical context. They bring the standards of coherence, logic, and morality of the nineteenth century and apply them to this ancient text and find the Bible seriously lacking.[26] By painstakingly pointing out the deficiencies of Scripture, they intend to undercut the conventional belief of their contemporaries in the Bible as the revealed Word of God and, having undermined that conviction, to create a space for the atheistic convictions advocated by secularists and Freethought.

Another possible conversation partner of Besant is Elizabeth Cady Stanton. Although her well-known work *The Woman's Bible* was published in two parts in 1895 and 1898,[27] Stanton had begun thinking about Christianity's and the

---

23. Charles Bradlaugh, *The Bible: What It Is* (London: Austin, 1870), v.

24. Ibid., 296, 253.

25. Ibid., 253.

26. For example, although Bradlaugh is aware of the scholarship on multiple authors of the Pentateuch and the possibility that parts of Exodus come from different time periods, he does not integrate this into his exegesis. In discussing the building of the tabernacle, Bradlaugh notes that Gramberg has hypothesized that the description of the tabernacle is to be dated after the construction of the temple in Jerusalem but states that he will not take this into consideration (ibid., 296).

27. Elizabeth Cady Stanton, *The Woman's Bible* (2 parts; New York: European Publishing, 1895, 1898), repr. as *The Original Feminist Attack on the Bible* (New York: Arno, 1974).

Bible's treatment of women in the early 1880s. In her memoirs, Stanton refers to a sermon she preached in England in 1882 on the topic "What Has Christianity Done for Woman?"[28] Although it cannot be proven that Besant was aware of the sermon, it is certain that Stanton was in England during part of 1882 and 1883 and that they moved in similar circles. Although I could find no documentation in Besant's biographies that she was in direct contact with Stanton or read her work, Stanton refers several times to Mrs. Besant and also to Mr. Bradlaugh in her memoir.[29] In several places the topics addressed and the thesis advocated by Besant is very similar to the work of Stanton and is written somewhat later, suggesting that Besant used and built on Stanton's ideas.

Besant's pamphlets on biblical teaching regarding women and marriage are explicitly subjective. She highlights the connections between the text and the situation of nineteenth-century Britain. She is also clearly aware of conflicting interpretations of Scripture and jumps into the fray in order to promote truth and justice as she sees it. Her exegesis of the text and engagement with others is based on the assumption that scriptural interpretation has been used to support the privileged position of men and to keep women in positions of subordination. However, she does not see the fault lying only with the interpreter of Scripture; Scripture itself is also to blame. In her analysis, the Bible itself supports patriarchy. Hence, she advocates not only reforming the interpretation of Scripture but also leaving Scripture and Christianity behind.

Nowhere in the two pamphlets was there any indication that the Bible might also contain the germs for women's emancipation. For example, Gen 1:26–27 and Gal 3:27–28 are often used to claim that the Bible in principle supports the equality of women and men, and on the basis of these principles the patriarchal narratives and laws in the Old and New Testament are read as reflecting the sinful state of humanity. By allocating a different function and status to these two types of texts, the interpreter can both work for reform and continue to claim that the Bible is God's word. However, Besant does not discriminate between texts in this way.

Another strategy used by reformists is to focus on the trajectory of biblical texts. For example, Besant notes a development in Scripture regarding marriage, from polygamous marriage by capturing wives to monogamy with wives in servi-

---

28. In chapter 22 of *Eighty Years*, Stanton summarizes her sermon: "My theme was, 'What has Christianity done for Woman?' and by the facts of history I showed clearly that to no form of religion was woman indebted for one impulse of freedom, as all alike have taught her inferiority and subjection. No lofty virtues can emanate from such a condition. Whatever heights of dignity and virtue women have individually attained can in no way be attributed to the dogmas of their religion."

29. For example, Stanton describes the controversy over the republication of Charles Knowlton's *The Fruits of the Spirit*, writing, "My sense of justice was severely tried by all I heard of the persecutions of Mrs. Besant and Mr. Bradlaugh for their publication of the right and duty of parents to limit population" (ibid.).

tude to their husbands. Besant could focus on the dynamic presented, which she describes as becoming more and more civilized. Rather, Besant concludes that the Bible stops its development at monogamy with servitude and hence is not useful for those who champion monogamy with equality for wives.

In her complete rejection of Scripture as a liberating force for women, she differs from Elizabeth Cady Stanton. Stanton understood that the Christian tradition, specifically canon law, has unremittingly oppressed women but found that Scripture itself was mixed in its value. In the introduction to the *Woman's Bible* Stanton writes, "The Bible cannot be accepted or rejected as a whole, its teachings are varied. In criticizing the peccadilloes of Sarah, Rebecca and Rachel, we would not shadow the virtues of Deborah, Huldah and Vashti. In criticizing the Mosaic Code we would not question the wisdom of the golden rule and the Fifth Commandment."[30] Although Stanton would be considered heterodox by some because she denied the plenary inspiration of Scripture, she is working within the Christian tradition in order to reform it. Besant has taken the more radical path of rejecting the Christian tradition and the authority of the Bible completely. As such, Besant can be understood as a nineteenth-century precursor to Mary Daly, who began as a reformer of the church[31] but who later abandoned that quest and instead called for an exodus from the church.[32] For Daly, as for Besant, the church and Scripture are so pervaded by patriarchy that there is nothing of value remaining if patriarchy is bracketed out. Yet both could not leave faith behind completely. Daly went on to create a new religion, and Besant eventually left the secularists and Freethought to adhere to theosophism.[33] For both of these brilliant women, the church and the Bible were experienced as overwhelmingly oppressive, and they sought liberation as women elsewhere.

BIBLIOGRAPHY

August, Andrew. *Poor Women's Lives: Gender, Work and Poverty in Late-Victorian London.* London: Associated University Press, 1999.

Besant, Annie. *Autobiographical Sketches.* London: Freethought Publishing, 1885.

———. *God's Views on Marriage.* London: Freethought Publishing, 1890.

———. *Woman's Position according to the Bible.* London: Freethought Publishing, 1885.

---

30. Stanton, *Woman's Bible*, 1:13.

31. Mary Daly's *The Church and the Second Sex* (New York: Harper & Row, 1968) is a sustained critique of the Catholic Church with the goal of reforming it. Although very critical of the Church, she yet found within it the seeds of hope and liberation.

32. Five years later, Daly's next major work, *Beyond God the Father* (Boston: Beacon, 1973), no longer worked for reform but claimed to go beyond the Church and the Christian tradition and formulated the basis for a new religion.

33. Nethercot (*First Five Lives*, 283–309) describes Besant's conversion to theosophism as the beginning of her fifth life in 1889.

Bloy, Marjie. "Victorian Legislation: A Timeline." No pages. Cited 27 May 2005. Online: http://www.victorianweb.org/history/legistl.html.

Bradlaugh, Charles. *The Bible: What It Is.* London: Austin, 1870.

Chadwick, Owen. *The Victorian Church.* 2 vols. London: Black, 1966–70.

Committee to Study Physical, Emotional and Sexual Abuse. "Report 30." In *The Agenda for Synod of the Christian Reformed Church in North America.* Grand Rapids: CRC Publications, 1992.

Daly, Mary. *Beyond God the Father.* Boston: Beacon, 1973.

———. *The Church and the Second Sex.* New York: Harper & Row, 1968.

Hamilton, J. A. "Fraser, James (1818–1885)." Pages 847–49 in vol. 20 of *Oxford Dictionary of National Biography.* Edited by Henry C. G. Matthew and Brian Harrison. 60 vols. Oxford: Oxford University Press, 2004.

Hochschild, Arlie. *The Second Shift: Working Parents and the Revolution at Home.* New York: Viking, 1989.

Larsen, Timothy. *Contested Christianity: The Political and Social Contexts of Victorian Theology.* Waco, Tex.: Baylor University Press, 2004.

Nethercot, Arthur H. *The First Five Lives of Annie Besant.* Chicago: University of Chicago Press, 1960.

———. *The Last Four Lives of Annie Besant.* Chicago: University of Chicago Press, 1964.

Stanton, Elizabeth Cady, *Eighty Years and More: Reminiscences 1815–1897.* New York: Unwin, 1898. Online: http://digital.library.upenn.edu/women/stanton/years/years.html.

———. *The Woman's Bible.* 2 parts. New York: European Publishing. 1895, 1898. Repr. as *The Original Feminist Attack on the Bible.* New York: Arno, 1974.

Taylor, Anne. *Annie Besant: A Biography.* Oxford: Oxford University Press, 1992.

———. "Besant, Annie (1847–1933)." Pages 504–7 in vol. 5 of *Oxford Dictionary of National Biography.* Edited by Henry C. G. Matthew and Brian Harrison. 60 vols. Oxford: Oxford University Press, 2004.

Etty Woosnam:
A Woman of Wisdom and Conviction

Donna Kerfoot

In nineteenth-century Victorian England, religious education for girls and young women took place in the home, which was considered a safe haven in a hostile world. One of the most important subjects stressed by educators of the day was the topic of domestic economy, as evidenced by ladies' magazines published during the mid-1800s.[1] These magazines taught women what was deemed to be the proper function of their sphere by society. They presented the home as the center of a woman's life. A woman was instructed to manage the household so well that "the family would love home and feel happy there."[2] Religion was often appealed to as a way to encourage women to fulfill their circumscribed roles in the home, church, and society. Both male and female writers and educators advocated separate spheres for men and women. One such writer was Etty Woosnam, who wrote two books entitled *Women of the Bible: Old Testament* and *Women of the Bible: New Testament*[3] for the edification and instruction of young women in a Bible class situated in Weston-super-Mare, Somerset, England.[4] These books, published in 1881 and 1885, are important examples of the contributions women made as religious educators, particularly in the study and interpretation of Scrip-

---

1. Some examples of magazines endorsing a domestic approach to women's education were *The Ladies' Pearl; Arthur's Home Magazine; The Lily;* and *The Sibyl,* as cited in Eleanor Wolf Thompson, *Education for Ladies, 1830–1860: Ideas on Education in Magazines for Women* (New York: King's Crown, 1947), 48.

2. Sarah J. Hale, "Domestic Economy," Godey's Lady's Book 20/1 (1840): 42.

3. Etty Woosnam, *The Women of the Bible: Old Testament* (London: Partridge, 1881); idem, *The Women of the Bible: New Testament* (London: Partridge, 1885).

4. Woosnam's books contained "thoughts which were collected for Sunday Bible readings with a few intelligent girls of the upper class, on a subject of their own choosing, and are the first twelve of a series of lessons which are being given." Her purpose for writing them is that "other young women reading them, may be led to study that Sacred Book which alone can make wise unto salvation; and by that study to learn more of Jesus Christ, whom to know is Life Eternal" (*Women of the Bible: Old Testament*, 5).

ture. To better understand the particular contribution of Etty Woosnam, this essay will recover biographical information concerning her and explore her work as a teacher of the Bible. This study will enrich our understanding of the author, her religious convictions, and her approach to the interpretation of Scripture and suggest what twenty-first-century readers might gain from her writing when considered in the context of the life of women in Victorian England during the late nineteenth century.

A Biographical Sketch of Etty Woosnam

Soon after the marriage of James Bowen Woosnam to Agnes Bell, the Woosnams traveled to India and took up residence in Fort Ahmednuggur, India, where their first two children were born: Elizabeth in 1842 and Esther (nicknamed Etty) in 1849. Altogether James and Agnes had six daughters and two sons, who were all born in India.[5] The family lived in northwest India for approximately sixteen years and moved among the British-occupied towns of Ahmednuggur, Poona, and Bombay.[6]

Education in India was accessible to all the Woosnam children, including the girls. The first girls' school had been started by American missionaries in Bombay in 1824, and by 1829 the school enrolled four hundred pupils. The same mission started two girls' schools in Ahmednuggur in 1831.[7] The Scottish Missionary Society also opened a girls' school in Bombay, and the students who attended these schools came from Christian families, were orphans, or were from poor low castes in India. It is probable that Etty Woosnam attended one of these schools for girls while her family lived in India. The Woosnam family returned to England in 1860, most likely due to the dissolution of the East India Company by the British crown in 1858. Etty Woosnam would have been twelve years old at the time of their move to England. The family settled in Weston-super-Mare, where they employed household servants, an indication that they were members of the more affluent class of society.[8]

---

5. Nela Soldatov-Jones, "Bell Genealogical Extracts," n.p. [cited 14 June 2006]. Online: http://www.recyclegen.com/archives/montg_coll/abc/bell.htm.

6. The British occupation of these three places took place during the second Mahratta War (1803–5), when Arthur Wellesley (Duke of Wellington) led a force against Poona to reinstall the Baji Rao who made an alliance with the British. Wellesley also marched upon and laid siege to Fort Ahmednuggur in 1803 and secured this position for the British (Cathy Day, "2nd Mahratta War: 1803–1805," n.p. [cited 14 June 2006]. Online: http://members.ozemail.com.au/~clday/maratha.htm).

7. M. D. David, *John Wilson and His Institutions* (Bombay: n.p., 1975), 89.

8. By the late nineteenth century, the "middle classes expanded rapidly in number, as a result of the industrialization." For those families who could afford to hire servants, there were a growing number of books and magazines, such as Isabella Beeton's *Book of Household Man-*

In Woosnam's second publication, *Women of the Bible: New Testament,* the name of "Mrs. Theobalds" is recorded on the title page. In 1882, Etty Woosnam married John R. Theobalds, a retired surgeon-general on the medical staff in Madras, India, in the district of Axbridge, Somerset, England.[9] A genealogical extract also states that about a year after their marriage Esther died suddenly. The record does not state the cause of death, only noting that she died "childless."

The preface to Etty Woosnam's second book, *The Women of the Bible: New Testament,* dated November 1884, states that "her sorrowing husband" kindly consented to the publication of her last book so that "she being dead may yet speak, not only to those who enjoyed her loving teaching while on earth, but also to any others into whose hands this little volume may fall."[10] The final remaining genealogical record relating to Woosnam's death is the birth notice of a niece named Esther Ann Woosnam in March 1883 in Merthyr Tydfil of Breconshire. It is likely that one of her brothers, Bowen or Charles Woosnam, named this child in honor of Etty and her legacy of faith.

THE RELIGIOUS CONVICTIONS OF WOOSNAM

Woosnam's writings suggest that she was a typical moderate Calvinist from the Low Evangelical party of the Anglican Church.[11] She emphasized participation in the sacraments, the authority of Scripture, and the use of reason in the interpretation of Scripture. She had a high view of the importance of personal faith, piety, and good works. Woosnam was aware of the political and religious tensions existing between various movements and parties of the Church of England in addition to the divisive debates[12] taking place between Anglicans, Roman Catholics, and

---

agement, published in 1861 to instruct women on the handling of servants. See Joan Perkin, *Victorian Women* (London: Murray, 1993), 87.

9. According to the Hart's Army List, John Robert Theobalds was promoted to Surgeon Major on 20 December 1848 and served with the twenty-first Native Infantry for twenty years until he retired on 20 December 1868. John Theobalds was fifty-nine years old and Esther Woosnam was thirty-three when they married (Nela Soldatov-Jones, "Theobald Genealogical Extracts," n.p. [cited 6 June 2006]. Online: http://www.recyclegen.com/archives/montg_coll/tuv/theobald.htm).

10. Woosnam, *Women of the Bible: New Testament,* 3.

11. The term *evangelical* is defined by David Bebbington as exhibiting four characteristics in Britain: "conversionism, the belief that lives need to be changed; activism, the expression of the gospel in effort; biblicism, a particular regard for the Bible; and what may be called crucicentrism, a stress on the sacrifice of Christ on the cross" (David W. Bebbington, *Evangelicalism in Modern Britain: A History from the 1730s to the 1980s* [London: Unwin Hyman, 1989], 2–3).

12. During the Oxford Movement (1830–48), there were divisive debates between the evangelicals and Tractarians over the presence of Christ in the Lord's Supper and the tendency in Tractarian worship to move toward what most Reformers considered the dreaded "popery." John Henry Newman (1801–90) became an effective leader of the Tractarians through his writ-

the Nonconformists.[13] This ecclesiastical context was reflected in the illustrations she used in her books. For example, she raises the issue of denominational differences when she writes: "one man is brought up with a horror of High Churchism; and perhaps led to the foot of the Cross by a High Church friend. Another has a strong dislike to Methodism, and it may be that he learns the love of God and the way of salvation in a Methodist chapel."[14] The underlying lesson in Woosnam's use of examples drawn from contemporary church life was to emphasize to the reader the importance of a personal faith in the gospel of Christ over and above denominational loyalties. However, in her chapter entitled "Miriam," Woosnam also warned her readers about *emotional religion*, "a sort very common in our day," and encouraged them to persevere in a Christlike life rather than be caught up in the eloquence of "the rhetorical powers" of an emotional preacher.[15] This caution was probably in reference to the more charismatic expressions of faith found in the Baptist, Pentecostal, and Wesleyan Methodist denominations in England during the nineteenth century. Woosnam had a more rational approach to religion and tended to emphasize serious prayer and meditation as a way of reflecting upon the moral lessons of the Bible.

Although Woosnam was drawn to a rational faith, she also voiced her antagonism toward the intellectual vices of the "intolerant, dogmatical, self-asserting warmth and so called 'earnestness' of many noisy professors."[16] This is not to say that Woosnam was anti-intellectual, for her expositions on characters in the Bible reveal the breadth of her reading. For example, in the chapter "Lot's Wife: Worldly-Mindedness," Woosnam mentioned Sir Isaac Newton and his scientific discoveries of "calculus and the theory of universal gravitation." She also used the phrase "telescope of faith" to teach her readers how to overcome their "spiritual shortsightedness," a condition many people experienced with the "advancing age" of science. Her solution to their "constitutional myopy" was to

---

ings and sermons, "especially in his inspiration of the series of *Tracts for the Times* (1833–1841)" (Josef L. Altholz, "High Church," in *Victorian Britain: An Encyclopedia* [ed. S. Mitchell; New York: Garland, 1988], 361).

13. The Church of England was the established church during the early nineteenth century until its status changed as a result of Protestant dissenters and Roman Catholics being admitted to Parliament with the institution of the Roman Catholic Relief Act in 1829. The Oxford Movement also contributed to changes in Anglicanism with the inclusion of Anglo-Catholicism by the mid-1800s, which became instrumental in shaping the doctrine of the church and sacraments for more than a century and a half. Overall, by the end of the nineteenth century, a predominant modernist worldview became more commonplace in England's religiously pluralistic society, resulting in a growing indifference toward Christianity in general (Josef L. Altholz, "Church of England," in Mitchell, *Victorian Britain*, 154).

14. Woosnam, *Women of the Bible: New Testament*, 12.

15. Woosnam, *Women of the Bible: Old Testament*, 79.

16. Ibid.

acknowledge God as the "Great Oculist" and to ask him to "open our eyes" in order to receive sight.[17]

Woosnam had no particular interest in historical-critical approaches to the study of the Bible, although her work reflected the value she placed on reading the biblical stories in their historical contexts. For example, Woosnam observed that "the Old Testament chapters make us realize how life-like and natural these characters are with whom in days gone by [God] spoke and dealt, and whose experiences have been laid bare for our learning and profit."[18] Woosnam also used historical resources such as *The Epistle of Ignatius to the Romans*, quoting Ignatius's declaration that "it is better for me to die for Jesus Christ than to reign over the ends of the earth," made prior to his martyrdom by wild beasts in the Roman amphitheater.[19] She also taught her readers using historical stories, such as Napoleon's retreat from Moscow, showing how the rear guard of the army perished in the snow because they lagged behind, and used this story as an analogy to Lot's wife when she looked back "from behind him" and turned into a pillar of salt.[20] Woosnam then proffered a typological reading of the story of Lot's wife as an example of how the satanic enemy attacks stragglers who lack religious commitment, causing them to fall into sin. This was meant to be a lesson to the worldly minded Christian to flee from the temptations of fleshly lusts and to pursue holiness in a Christlike life.[21]

Woosnam taught the importance of women's roles in the Bible as a way of sharing her faith and instructing young women how properly to interpret Scripture. This in turn would benefit them in their conduct as single women, wives, and mothers. The task at hand was to encourage women to "read the Bible … read history … and read human nature" in order for them properly to understand the application of God's word to their lives.[22] Her applications are perhaps more interesting than her actual biblical teaching because they reveal her values and give us a window into her experience in the 1870s and early 1880s in Britain.

WOOSNAM'S HERMENEUTICAL APPROACH

Woosnam's hermeneutic does not reflect a scholarly exegetical analysis of Scripture nor a proficient use of the ancient languages of Hebrew and Greek. She does draw on a variety of resources, including the writings of biblical scholars, poets, theologians, and politicians. Her main resources appear to be Kitto's *Cyclopedia*

---

17. Ibid., 79.
18. Ibid., 57–58.
19. Ibid., 44.
20. Ibid., 48.
21. Ibid.
22. Ibid., 88.

of *Biblical Literature*[23] and Brown's *Dictionary of the Holy Bible*,[24] in addition to citing well-known politicians and theologians, such as Dr. Joseph Cook, Dr. Frederic William Farrar, and Dr. Horace Bushnell. Woosnam used a quote from Canon Farrar's *Seekers after God*, for instance, in which he speaks of Eve's "innocence of ignorance [as] a poor thing," explaining that she was only innocent until she faced temptation and failed in obedience to God's command not to eat from the tree of knowledge.[25] Woosnam believed that Eve was innocent as long as she was "untried" by the temptation of sin, contrary to the popular views of biblical commentators who "speak of Eve before the disobedience, as in a state of innocence."[26] She used a quotation from an old proverb of the Talmud to buttress her point: "When the thief has no opportunity for stealing, he considers himself an honest man."[27] Woosnam argued that innocence is a nonexistent state of being for humans, and the only solution to the problem of sin is to put on the white robe of Christ's righteousness in order to please God.[28] The negation of innocence was understood by Woosnam in opposition to a romantic philosophical view in society, which viewed children as innocent of wrongdoing.[29] Woosnam used the example of a child to prove her point, stating that

> we speak of children's innocence because they are quite unable to understand or carry out much that is wrong, their liberty is comparatively so very small. But yet they soon show their sinfulness. Before they can speak clearly they try on

---

23. John Kitto (1804–54), a deaf scholar and poet, produced works such as *The Pictorial Bible*; *Pictorial History of Palestine*; *The Lost Senses*; *Deafness and Blindness* and more. He founded the *Journal of Sacred Literature*. One of his books, called *Cyclopedia of Biblical Literature*, was published in London in 1845. See John Eadie, *Life of John Kitto, D.D., F.S.A.* (Edinburgh: Oliphant, Anderson, & Ferrier, 1886), 3.

24. The *Dictionary of the Holy Bible* was written by John Brown (1722–87). According to comments in the introduction, it contains a historical account of biblical characters, a geographical account of the places, a literal, critical, and systematical description of other objects, whether natural, artificial, civil, religious, or military: "It serves as an informative resource concerning the Antiquities of the Hebrew nation and church of God; forming a sacred commentary; a body of scripture history chronology, and divinity; and serving as a Concordance to the Bible" (John Brown, *The Dictionary of the Holy Bible* [Glasgow: Khull, Blackie, 1821]).

25. Woosnam, *Women of the Bible: Old Testament*, 13, quoting Rev. Frederic William Farrar, late Dean of Canterbury, *Seekers after God* (London: MacMillan, 1873).

26. Woosnam, *Women of the Bible: Old Testament*, 13.

27. Ibid.

28. Ibid.

29. According to Elisabeth Jay, "the phrase, 'Child of innocence,' serves as a reminder of a fundamental conflict between Evangelical dogma and Romantic philosophy." The idea of a human pilgrimage from the "innocence" of childhood to the "experience" of adult life, as portrayed in Romantic poetry such as Woodsworth's *Ode: Intimations of Immortality from Recollections of Early Childhood*, was totally incompatible with the evangelical's vision of children (Elisabeth Jay, *The Religion of the Heart* [Oxford: Clarendon, 1979], 55).

their little artifices, their petty deceits. "As soon as they be born they go astray" in willfulness, disobedience, and lying.[30]

Woosnam's biblical interpretation of the fall reflects the Reformed view, which postulates that just as Adam's sin entered into the world leading all people to becoming sinners, so Christ's obedience leads to righteousness (Rom 5:12–21).

Woosnam's method of interpretation was to retell the biblical narrative, reflecting on what the female characters of Scripture may have experienced during the events of the story. Although Woosnam was averse to the philosophical views of the Romantic movement, she embellished the text with sentimental language that upheld the value of the family as a social unity, an idea similar to that of Evangelical Romanticism.[31] For example, in her chapter entitled "Ruth: Dutiful Daughters and God's Provision for Them," Woosnam wrote about the extreme anguish Ruth and Orpah felt in their decision about whether to leave their home in Moab to accompany their mother-in-law Naomi to the foreign country of Israel after the deaths of her husband and two sons.[32] Woosnam paints a woeful picture of Orpah "regretfully clasping the hand of the kind and motherly Naomi while looking back to her native vales, like the 'Multitudes, multitudes in the valley of decision.'"[33] In contrast to Orpah's reluctance to leave her homeland, Ruth was regarded as a truly dutiful daughter-in-law who faithfully followed Naomi into a new culture. Woosnam quickly made a transition at this point in the story and challenged young people as to whether their decisions in life have been faithful responses to Christ. A poem written by the progressive poet James Russell Lowell (1819–91) is inserted into the story as Woosnam challenged youth to remain loyal to Christ:

> Once to every man and nation
> Comes the moment to decide,
> In the strife of Truth with Falsehood,
> For the good or evil side;
> Then it is the brave man chooses
> While the coward stands aside,
> Doubting in his abject spirit,
> Till his Lord is crucified.[34]

---

30. Woosnam, *Women of the Bible: Old Testament,* 14.

31. Evangelical Romanticism promoted religious teachings to uphold an ideal of family life that was contrary to the Romantic philosophical view of the "family unit as a natural organism which could serve to protect the weak," although authors from both viewpoints used sentimental language in their writing (Jay, *Religion of the Heart,* 147).

32. Woosnam, *Women of the Bible: Old Testament,* 109.

33. Ibid., 111.

34. Ibid.

This poem was only one of many used by Woosnam to capture the attention of her readers and to emphasize the moral truth of her lesson. Her use of the male pronoun without comment suggests that Woosnam had no difficulty in assimilating the meaning of the poem in a positive manner for herself and her readers. She also quoted from other contemporary poets, such as Frederick William Faber (1833–63) and the American poet William Cullen Bryant (1794–1878).

In addition, Woosnam used more traditional interpretive methods such as typology. For example, in her lesson on Ruth, she read the text through the lens of the prophet Joel (Joel 3:14) and interpreted Orpah as a type of lost soul in Hades while Ruth is considered a type of faithful follower of Christ.[35] Other uses of typology include Hagar, the slave of Abraham's wife Sarah, described by Woosnam as a type of "penitent sinner" who ran away from her mistress into the wilderness only to be told by an angel of the Lord to "return to her mistress and submit herself under her hands" (Gen 16:6–10). Woosnam intended that Hagar's life teach the reader "how tenderly God has compassion on them that are ignorant and out of the way."[36] Moreover, she encouraged young women to submit to the authorities and accept the circumstances "ordained" for them despite their dismal outlook on life. Woosnam's treatment of Hagar was shared by many of her contemporaries, who either sought to reinforce the class distinctions in society by upholding Abraham and Sarah's privilege in contrast to Hagar's servanthood or instead neglected the role of this "poor dishonoured, outcast slave" altogether.[37]

Typology was also employed by Woosnam in her story of Rahab, a prostitute who hid two Israelite spies from their enemies in Jericho (Josh 2). In return for her hospitality and protection, Rahab was told to tie a scarlet cord in her window as a promise that she and her family would be spared from certain death by the Israelites when the city was invaded by the tribes of Israel. Woosnam followed a traditional typological reading of the scarlet line (cf. Clement of Alexandria) as a "forcible type of the redeeming blood of Christ," pointing to the atonement of Christ.[38] Woosnam also portrayed Rahab as the first Canaanite to confess faith in Israel's covenant with God, thus identifying her as a precursor of true conversion found in the salvation plan of God in Christ.[39] Woosnam's reading of the Rahab story was typical of many Victorians who read the Old

---

35. A type may be defined as a symbol of something future and distant or an example prepared and evidently designed by God to prefigure that future thing. See George Landow, *Victorian Types, Victorian Shadows: Biblical Typology in Victorian Literature, Art and Thought* (London: Routledge & Kegan Paul, 1980), 22–23.

36. Woosnam, *Women of the Bible: Old Testament*, 35.

37. Compare nineteenth-century women's writings on Hagar in Marion Ann Taylor and Heather E. Weir's *Let Her Speak for Herself: Nineteenth-Century Women Writing on Women in Genesis* (Waco, Tex.: Baylor University Press, 2006), 185–254.

38. Woosnam, *Women of the Bible: Old Testament*, 87.

39. Ibid.

Testament in light of the New Testament and looked for various ways of linking the two Testaments together.[40]

Woosnam's readings of the stories of women in the Bible were often enriched by her use of a mixture of allusions and illustrations from poetry, nature studies, classical books, and historical and political literature. The richness of Woosnam's allusions is seen in her chapter on the Queen of Sheba,[41] which shows how she was influenced by debates about science, evolution, and faith.[42] In this lesson Woosnam developed the idea of Solomon's wisdom and associated it with her personal knowledge and experience of the world as well as what she had learned from notable science. She examined the natural evolution of animals in God's creation, such as, "the polar bear" in the Artic, "the grouse and woodcock of the moors" in England, and "the beautiful little birds that nest on the tips of long branches" in the Indian jungles.[43] She suggested that the study of animals demonstrated how God had adapted every creature with a natural ability to blend into its environmental background in order to protect it from danger. Woosnam spiritualized this lesson from nature and suggested that Christians, like animals, had been created to develop and use their talents, natural or acquired, in order to serve God in their natural habitat. Woosnam's use of the language of evolutionary biology taught students to balance "true secular knowledge" with the study of Scripture. The two sources of truth would prove beneficial to her readers in their overall view of the world.[44]

Woosnam also included historical and geographical information to enrich her retelling of the stories of the Bible and to emphasize the stories' accuracy. For example, in the chapter entitled "The Woman of Samaria," Woosnam suggested that the well where Jesus and the woman from Samaria met was "90 feet deep" and was "clearly indicated to Palestinian travelers."[45] She also gave a brief historical account of the veracity of the well's geographical location, making reference to a war on Jerusalem by the Romans under Vespasian, which took place thirty years after the death of Jesus, during which the Samaritans were encamped on Mount Gerizim and Cerealis, the Roman general, occupied the valley at its foot, where Sychar and its well were located.[46] By providing important historical and geographical information, Woosnam made the biblical text come alive for her readers. In her application of this story, Woosnam focused on the theme of worship, comparing the religious practice and tradition of Samaritan worship with

40. Landow, *Victorian Types, Victorian Shadows*, 15.

41. There are three papers based on Old Testament subjects included by the publisher as the final chapters of *Women of the Bible: New Testament*.

42. Woosnam, *Women of the Bible: New Testament*, 97.

43. Ibid., 104.

44. Ibid.

45. Ibid., 8.

46. Ibid.

that of the Israelites in Jerusalem, and then drew the reader's attention to Christ as the "Living Water," the one who quenches the spiritual thirst of people, and the only "temple where men [sic] ought to worship."[47]

As these examples illustrate, Woosnam was a well-educated woman whose desire was to teach her young students about the Christian life and to provide them with further education as a means of improving their knowledge of the secular world in relation to the spiritual realm spoken of in the Bible. She moved away from her reflections on a biblical story to a personal application for her readers' spiritual lives. In many lessons, particularly in her lesson on the woman of Samaria, Woosnam preached the good news to her readers using a homiletic style of writing to deepen their spiritual faith in Christ. She encouraged young women to become witnesses to the gospel of Christ just as the Samaritan woman was an "apostle" to the Samaritans, "for she was a brave witness of the Lord who had found her and saved her."[48]

LESSONS OF VICTORIAN FEMININITY IN THE BIBLE

Woosnam chose female biblical characters in the Bible to study because they provided her students and readers with role models to follow. She intended to catechize girls, and the stories of women allowed her to raise spiritual and practical issues related to the lives of young women that would prepare them for marriage and motherhood. Woosnam focused many of her lessons on the theme of a woman's influence. For example, in her study of Eve she described Eve not only as the "mother of all living" but also as "the mother of all death."[49] She argued that, because of Eve's disobedience to God by eating from the tree of knowledge, all of humanity must now suffer the consequences of God's judgment. Woosnam's interpretation followed the traditional notion of Eve as the one who was responsible for bringing sin into the world. However, she also mentioned the fact that Adam was also responsible for imitating Eve's action, rather than acting to resist her offer to eat from the tree of knowledge.[50] In this way Woosnam recognized Eve's influence but also softened the tradition and implied joint responsibility for her act of sin in relationship to her partner Adam.

Woosnam explored the idea of Eve's power and influence further and applied the temptation story to Christian marriage, especially women's roles in the marital decision-making process. In Woosnam's opinion, Adam's decision to give in to the desires of Eve in the garden of Eden supported a remark she once heard that "the more a woman loves you, the more she will hinder you from right purposes,

---

47. Ibid., 17.
48. Ibid.
49. Woosnam, *Women of the Bible: Old Testament*, 7.
50. Ibid., 8.

and strew flowers on the road that leads to hell."[51] Woosnam thought that, unless women exercised care in how they used their gift of "wife-power" and "mother-power, they could destroy relationships."[52] Woosnam then reads the garden of Eden narrative as a cautionary tale that raises the question of how power and influence operate in relationships between husbands and wives and between parents and children. Rather than dwelling upon the traditional view of Eve as the temptress in Scripture, Woosnam focused on Eve's influence and by implication all women's influence in family relationships. Then she shifted the focus away from Eve as the mother of death to the position women held in the family for good.[53] Woosnam's pedagogical aims pushed her to explore the dynamics in the relationship between Eve and Adam and enabled her to teach young women to use their power and influence in the home wisely.

Woosnam's views on the power of women in the home reflect the ideology of the cult of domesticity. The cult of domesticity encouraged the erection of boundaries between the nuclear family and the world outside it and elevated the role of women in the private sphere. While men pursued activities in the economic and political order of society, women accepted second-class citizenship in the separate domestic sphere under the protection of the husband.[54] As a result, the family unit became isolated from the larger community except through formal ties such as the church, public organizations, and schools. Thus, segregation between genders in middle-class families made it difficult for women to participate in public life. This segment of society had a great deal of impact on English public life during the Victorian era.[55]

As an evangelical, Woosnam supported the ideal of women as mothers in the domestic sphere but also challenged women to think about public-policy issues and their roles in comparison to female reformers who were advocating for change in society. For example, Woosnam raised the issue of women's rights and the question of whether women should seek more direct power by obtaining the right to vote. Although Woosnam stressed the importance of women's influence, she was not willing to support women's suffrage. In a lesson to her young

---

51. Ibid., 9.

52. Ibid., 11.

53. As Taylor and Weir's anthology of nineteenth-century women writers on the subject of Eve shows, Woosnam was not the only female interpreter who tended to shift her focus from a traditional reading of Scripture to view the text in a more positive manner. See also the collections of nineteenth-century women's writings on Eve in Taylor and Weir, *Let Her Speak for Herself*, 21–105. See also page 6.

54. Lillian Lewis Shiman, *Women and Leadership in Nineteenth-Century England* (New York: St. Martin's, 1992), 35.

55. Queen Victoria supported the values extolled by the urban, middle classes—a lifestyle that came to be known as *Victorian* in future references to the mid-nineteenth century (ibid., 60).

students, Woosnam argued that women held political power even if they did not vote. To make her point, she rehearsed a story about a man who admitted that his wife would be involved in deciding whom to vote for. Then to garner further support for her argument, Woosnam invoked the authority of the opinions of John Stuart Mill (1806–73) and Benjamin Disraeli (1804–81).[56] Woosnam's comments were that "wife-power and mother-power are often quite as great forces in the more educated classes up to the very highest—as was shown by the infatuation of Mr. John Stuart Mill for his wife."[57] This statement is followed by a reference to the wife of the "late Lord Beaconsfield … when he dedicated one of his books to her as 'The severest of Critics and the best of Wives.' "[58] Thus Woosnam acknowledged a woman's power but thought her power should be exercised in the private sphere. At the end of Woosnam's story about voting, the wife ultimately decided "whether more coal and blankets are to be had out of one party or the other."[59] It was the wife's influence that prevailed as the "guiding star" in the couple's final decision. Thus, Woosnam held that women indirectly had a voice in politics and did not support the suffragist movement.[60]

In Woosnam's lessons from women in the New Testament, she placed special emphasis on the importance of women's work in spreading the gospel and on their roles as servants. In her chapter entitled "Lydia: Good Listeners," for example, Woosnam described the conversion of a young woman, the purple seller, who sat and listened to the apostles Luke and Silas at a riverside meeting in Philippi (Acts 16) and in response to their proclamation of the gospel became a follower of Christ.[61] Woosnam stated that Lydia was one of the first converts in the church of Philippi and was most probably the "foundress" of the church of Thyatira in her native city.[62] Woosnam viewed the character of Lydia as an ideal role model for readers. She stated that Lydia was a positive influence "mostly on those of her own sex" in the early church, a conclusion drawn from the fact that there were many other women who "laboured with Paul in the Gospel (Phil. 4:3)."[63] Woosnam also mentioned a great number of female names in the early church referred

---

56. Woosnam used the names of Mill and Disraeli to support her argument for a husband's respect for his wife but did not align herself with the political issues they promoted, such as when J. S. Mill presented a women's suffrage petition to Parliament in 1867.

57. Woosnam, *Women of the Bible: Old Testament,* 11.

58. Ibid.

59. Ibid.

60. Woosnam reflected a concern held by many people in the Victorian era that a married woman was part of a family group represented by the male householder and that giving the wife a vote could introduce discord into the family circle, especially if husband and wife voted for different political parties (Shiman, *Women and Leadership in Nineteenth-Century England,* 194).

61. Woosnam, *Women of the Bible: New Testament,* 65.

62. Ibid., 68.

63. Ibid.

to by the apostle Paul as "those women which laboured with me in the Gospel."[64] She believed that these servants of God provided a religious model of femininity for contemporary women to follow. Woosnam argued that women should open their hearts to Christ and make their service profitable both in public and private worship: they were to pray, to listen to the word preached from the pulpit, and to go to church regularly. Woosnam considered these activities of spiritual formation an important part of the Christian life and claimed that they were prerequisite to women using their natural abilities in service to others in society and the church. In this way, Woosnam was instrumental in encouraging women to move outside of their domestic sphere by giving them experience in the public sphere, which ostensibly belonged to men.

Woosnam also emphasized the importance of New Testament models of servanthood. She taught that women as servants in the church were to "minister to ordained ministers, provide for their bodily necessities, furnish the poor and those engaged in missionary travels" in a way that pleased God.[65] In a chapter entitled "The Servants of the Early Church," Woosnam used the example of Lydia and the women who labored with Paul in the work of the early church as a further means of encouraging women in this role. Woosnam believed that women could accomplish servanthood by supporting those in full-time ministry, praying, giving financially, visiting the sick, giving to the poor, and offering comfort to the desolate and discouraged. The specific example of Phoebe's ability to organize was used by Woosnam to encourage women in their work as charitable organizers on behalf of the poor in society.[66]

Woosnam also discussed issues related to household duties. She anticipated that young girls would continue to follow cultural expectations and use their natural abilities in occupations such as nursing, business, teaching, organizing the household, managing servants, and even using gifts of art and music.[67] It was

---

64. Woosnam questions whether the name *Junia* in Rom 16 is male or female and footnotes a reference from "Kitto's Cyclopedia" to Chrysostom and Theophylact, who "say this was a woman's name," but Woosnam's remark is that this assumption is still being debated by scholars (ibid., 77).

65. Ibid.

66. Evangelicals performed works of charity both as a moral obligation and as a means of bringing other people to Christ. They believed that by regenerating society they could stamp out sins that led people into situations of despair such as drunkenness and crime. Victorian humanitarian evangelicals abolished "the slave trade, ended flogging in the army and navy, got rid of public hanging, strove to convert criminal justice from 'punishment' to 'reform', established schools, cleared slums, built decent housing for workers, abolished blood sports and protected animals from cruelty, worked steadily toward raising the age at which children could work full-time, founded refuges and orphanages, built schools for the mentally and physically disabled, and rethought the treatment of insanity" (Sally Mitchell, *Daily Life in Victorian England* [Westport, Conn.: Greenwood, 1996], 252).

67. Woosnam, *Women of the Bible: New Testament*, 38.

quite common for young women in upper-middle-class homes to learn how "to participate in the social and charitable occupations with which adult women at this social level were involved."[68] Woosnam suggested that women fulfill their duties to their husbands, families, and society just as Priscilla was always found with Aquila—helping him in his teaching, tent making, and traveling.[69] Woosnam taught women the importance of their acts of service in the church and as philanthropists in society, although she was careful to support a traditional biblical view of submission to male leadership both in the church and the family.

CONCLUSIONS

Woosnam's studies for adolescent girls depict the lives of female characters in the Bible as role models for young women in Victorian society. In her work Woosnam challenged young women to pursue an independent study of Scripture and to think through what they learned about the spiritual and practical realms of their Christian life. She openly confronted young women with the dilemmas they encountered in their homes, in society, and in the church. Woosnam shared her personal convictions as she worked through her interpretation of the Bible. She tended toward a more traditional reading of Scripture that demonstrated a strong evangelical faith in her writing. Woosnam's reasonable appeal to the study of science is a reflection of the atmosphere of her day in that she apprehended the text historically, blended science and faith, used traditional approaches such as typology, and read the canon as a whole relating the Old Testament to the New Testament.

The wisdom and convictions of Etty Woosnam can benefit readers in the twenty-first century who are willing to take time to read her work and to listen to her perception of the world she lived in. Her work is a study in contextual hermeneutics in that she teaches us to be better readers of the text and more sensitive to how the issues we bring to the text shape the message we see in the text. Woosnam is an example of a woman who wrestled with the issues of her day such as the right to vote, ethical concerns, and the role of women in the church and society. Although she was not progressive in her thinking, she does model a woman who is thinking through the cutting-edge issues of her day.

Woosnam took her responsibility as a teacher seriously and became a mentor to other women who learned from her knowledge of the Bible. She was an intelligent teacher who used knowledge from secondary sources to aid young women in learning more about the world they lived in. Not only did she teach her students, but she preached from a pulpit of her own making in the use of her written

---

68. Deborah Gorham, *The Victorian Girl and the Feminine Ideal* (Bloomington: Indiana University Press, 1982), 27.

69. Woosnam, *Women of the Bible: New Testament*, 81.

homilies at a time when most women were barred from using their oratory skills in the church. Woosnam's work provides a fascinating study of how a nineteenth-century woman used her Bible to teach spiritual, ethical, moral, and social values to young women. In all these ways, Woosnam was an inspiration to younger women in Victorian Britain as they pressed forward into new ways of living out their hopes and aspirations.

BIBLIOGRAPHY

Altholz, Josef L. "Church of England." Pages 154–57 in *Victorian Britain: An Encyclopedia.* Edited by Sally Mitchell. New York: Garland, 1988.

————. "High Church." Pages 361–62 in *Victorian Britain: An Encyclopedia.* Edited by Sally Mitchell. New York: Garland, 1988.

Bebbington, David. *Evangelicalism in Modern Britain: A History from the 1730s to the 1980s.* London: Unwin Hyman, 1989.

Brown, John. *The Dictionary of the Holy Bible.* Glasgow: Khull, Blackie, 1821.

David, M. D. *John Wilson and His Institutions.* Bombay: n.p., 1975.

Day, Cathy. "2nd Mahratta War: 1803–1805." No Pages. Cited 14 June 2006. Online: http://members.ozemail.com.au/~clday/maratha.htm.

Eadie, John. *Life of John Kitto, D.D., F.S.A.* Edinburgh: Oliphant, Anderson, & Ferrier, 1886.

Farrar, Frederic William. *Seekers after God.* Sunday Library for Household Reading 3. New York: Macmillan, 1873.

Gorham, Deborah. *The Victorian Girl and the Feminine Ideal.* Bloomington: Indiana University Press, 1982.

Hale, Sarah J. "Domestic Economy." *Godey's Lady's Book* 20/1 (1840): 42–45.

Jay, Elisabeth. *The Religion of the Heart: Anglican Evangelicalism and the Nineteenth Century Novel.* Oxford: Clarendon, 1979.

Landow, George. *Victorian Types, Victorian Shadows: Biblical Typology in Victorian Literature, Art and Thought.* London: Routledge & Kegan Paul, 1980.

Mitchell, Sally. *Daily Life in Victorian England.* Westport, Conn.: Greenwood, 1996.

Perkin, Joan. *Victorian Women.* London: Murray, 1993.

Shiman, Lillian Lewis. *Women and Leadership in Nineteenth-Century England.* New York: St. Martin's, 1992.

Soldatov-Jones, Nela 2004. "Bell Genealogical Extracts." No pages. Cited 14 June 2006. Online: http://www.recyclegen.com/archives/montg_coll/abc/bell.htm.

————. "Theobald Genealogical Extracts." No pages. Cited 14 June 2006. Online: http://www.recyclegen.com/archives/montg_coll/tuv/theobald.htm.

Taylor, Marion, and Heather Weir, eds. *Let Her Speak for Herself: Nineteenth-Century Women Writing on Women in Genesis.* Waco, Tex.: Baylor University Press, 2006.

Thompson, Eleanor Wolf. *Education for Ladies, 1830–1860: Ideas on Education in Magazines for Women.* New York: King's Crown, 1947.

Vickery, Amanda, ed. *Women, Privilege, and Power: British Politics, 1750 to Present.* Stanford, Calif.: Stanford University Press, 2001.

Woosnam, Etty. *The Women of the Bible: New Testament.* London: Partridge, 1885.

————. *The Women of the Bible: Old Testament.* London: Partridge, 1881.

Contributors

Amanda W. Benckhuysen is a Ph.D. candidate in Old Testament Studies at Wycliffe College in Toronto. Her research interests are in the areas of Old Testament narrative, history of interpretation, and hermeneutics.

Elizabeth M. Davis is a member of the Congregation of the Sisters of Mercy of Newfoundland and Labrador, Canada. She is a doctoral student in Scripture at Regis College, Toronto School of Theology, University of Toronto, and a part-time faculty member at St. Augustine's Seminary, Toronto School of Theology, where she teaches introduction to the Old Testament to masters' students and deacons. She is a member of the Mercy International Research Commission sited in Dublin, Ireland.

Christiana de Groot is a Professor in the Religion Department at Calvin College, Grand Rapids, Michigan. She has written in the area of feminist hermeneutics and is currently working to recover the contributions of women interpreters. Recent publications include, "Genesis," in the *IVP Women's Bible Commentary* (2002), and "Was Rosa Parks Proud?" in *Perspectives: A Journal of Reformed Thought* (2006).

Rebecca G. S. Idestrom is Associate Professor of Old Testament at Tyndale Seminary in Toronto, Ontario, Canada. Her *From Biblical Theology to Biblical Criticism: Old Testament Scholarship at Uppsala University, 1866–1922* (2000) reflects her interest in the history of biblical interpretation. Besides this monograph, she has published a number of articles. Her teaching and scholarship demonstrate her interest in prophetic literature, women in the Bible, Old Testament theology, Jewish interpretation of Scripture, and Old Testament interpretation.

Donna J. Kerfoot is a Th.D. candidate at Trinity College, Toronto, Ontario, Canada, and serves as adjunct faculty member at Emmanuel Bible College, Kitchener, Ontario, Canada. Her other publications include "The Baptist Family" in The Encyclopedia of Protestantism (2003).

Bernon P. Lee is Assistant Professor of Old Testament in the Department of Religious Studies at Grace College, Winona Lake, Indiana. Currently his research centers upon the contribution of law to the interpretation of narrative in Leviticus and Numbers.

Marion Ann Taylor is Professor of Old Testament at Wycliffe College in Toronto. She has always been interested in the history of the interpretation of the Bible: her Yale Ph.D. thesis was on the study of Old Testament in the Old Princeton School. Since 2000 she has focused her research on recovering forgotten women interpreters of the Bible. *Let Her Speak for Herself: Nineteenth-Century Women Writing on Women in Genesis* (2006), which she co-edited with Heather Weir, features the writings of fifty women writing on women in Genesis. She is currently preparing a biographical dictionary of women interpreters of Scripture.

Heather E. Weir is studying at Wycliffe College in the Toronto School of Theology, where she is currently writing her doctoral dissertation on "Teaching the Bible with Sarah Trimmer." Her research interests include the use of narrative in teaching and women interpreters of the Bible. She is the co-editor of *Let Her Speak for Herself: Nineteenth-Century Women Writing on Women in Genesis* (2006).

The Reverend Dr. **Lissa M. Wray Beal** is the Associate Professor of Old Testament at Providence Theological Seminary in Otterburne, Manitoba, Canada. Her research interests include kingship within the Psalms and the Deuteronomistic works and narrative and canonical interpretive approaches. Her publications include "Evaluating Jehu: Narrative Control of Approval and Disapproval in 2 Kings 9 and 10," in *From Babel to Babylon* (2006), *The Deuteronomist's Prophet* (forthcoming), "History of Interpretation of the Psalms" in *Dictionary of the Old Testament: Wisdom, Poetry and Writings* (forthcoming). She is currently preparing a commentary on 1 and 2 Kings for Apollos Old Testament Commentaries.

Index of Ancient Sources

Hebrew Bible/Old Testament

OTHER PREMODERN AUTHORS AND WORKS

Index of Modern Authors

Printed in the United States
98537LV00007B/242/A

9 781589 832206